Misfit Sisters

Misfit Sisters

Screen Horror as Female Rites of Passage

Sue Short

First published 2006 by
PALGRAVE MACMILLAN
Houndmills, Basingstoke, Hampshire RG21 6XS and
175 Fifth Avenue, New York, N.Y. 10010
Companies and representatives throughout the world

PALGRAVE MACMILLAN is the global academic imprint of the Palgrave Macmillan division of St. Martin's Press, LLC and of Palgrave Macmillan Ltd. Macmillan® is a registered trademark in the United States, United Kingdom and other countries. Palgrave is a registered trademark in the European Union and other countries.

ISBN-13: 978-0-230-00020-9 hardback
ISBN-10: 0-230-00020-7 hardback

This book is printed on paper suitable for recycling and made from fully managed and sustained forest sources.

A catalogue record for this book is available from the British Library.

Library of Congress Cataloging-in-Publication Data
Short, Sue, 1968–
   Misfit sisters:screen horror as female rites of passage/Sue Short.
      p.   cm.
   Includes bibliographical references and index.
   ISBN 0-230-00020-7 (cloth)
   1. Horror films—History and criticism.   2. Women in motion pictures.
   I. Title.
   PN1995.9.H6S532006
   791.43′6164—dc22

                                                              2006049418

10   9   8   7   6   5   4   3   2   1
15   14   13   12   11   10   09   08   07   06

Printed and bound in Great Britain by
Antony Rowe Ltd, Chippenham and Eastbourne

For Carrie and Nancy, Ginger and Brigitte, Faith and Dahlia, and all my misfit sisters out there.

The daughter is too bold
to be anything but
a cuckoo in the nest.
Good girls sit home
and sew in the dark.
They don't go seeking fire
in the witch's woods.

– 'Bone Mother',
Holly Black

Contents

Preface   viii

Introduction   1

1 Telling Tales: Fairy Tales and Female Rites of Passage
   Narratives   22

2 Sex and the Final Girl: Surviving the Slasher   45

3 Maternal Monsters and Motherly Mentors: Failed Initiations
   in *Carrie* and *Carrie II*   68

4 Misfit Sisters: Female Kinship and Rivalry in *The Craft* and
   Ginger Snaps   88

5 Fighting Demons: Buffy, Faith, Willow, and the Forces of
   Good and Evil   111

6 Demeter's Daughters: Wronged Girls and the Mother
   Avenger   132

Conclusion   153

Notes   173
Bibliography   187
Filmography   191
Index   193

Preface

> The wolf, I knew, would lead me deep into the woods,
> away from home, to a dark tangled thorny place
> lit by the eyes of owls.

– 'Little Red-Cap', Carol Ann Duffy

To argue, as this book does, that horror shares many concerns with fairy tales is not as strange a suggestion as some might think, for although we tend to associate them with cosy bedtime stories, fairy tales frequently contain the stuff of nightmares. Indeed, once upon a time, they often started out as scare stories that were intended to chill and thrill their audiences by inviting them to empathise with various imperilled protagonists. While the fear factor often became diluted as stories were 'gentrified' it can still be seen amid the tales we know today, and many tropes have since found new expression within horror cinema: including the fear of being abandoned and made vulnerable, threatened by inhuman monsters, or otherwise placed in mortal danger in a world that is somehow askew. Fairy tale resonances are to be found in a number of horror films, despite contemporary surburban settings like Elm Street and Woodsboro, and some narratives have even led us back into the woods again. *The Blair Witch Project* (1999) places its three leads in 'Hansel and Gretel' territory of being lost in strange woods, at the mercy of an evil witch they have rashly consigned to myth. Conversely, *The Village* (2004) dresses up its version of 'Red Riding Hood' in a yellow cloak, gives her a romantic mission to save her love, rather than familial duty, and reveals the monster she battles to be man-made. These examples indicate how horror has revised familiar templates, exposing the path the genre has followed, like stones in moonlight, and thereby showing where certain motifs have come from.

Horror's kinship with fairy tales is demonstrated through several shared elements, including an emphasis on fear – used to add drama, emotionally involve the audience, and express particular anxieties; a mutual interest in the pleasure of fantasy – often involving the transgression of existing laws and boundaries; and what many critics perceive to be the social function of both forms: their invocation of particular initiation rites – with plots highlighting the necessity of separation

from friends and family (and comforting familiarity) prior to maturation. It is the last factor this study examines more closely, asking how
female protagonists, in particular, are forced to prove themselves in
horror; evaluating what risks they take, what roles they play, and what
such stories tell us about changing gender roles and expectations. As
we shall see, fear and fantasy also feature prominently in what is to
come, primarily in the threats facing (and sometimes emanating from)
female protagonists, and in both the anxieties and the desires that are
voiced.

Although the characters assessed are not all teenagers their stories are
equated with coming-of-age tales because they are all asked to grow up
over the course of their narrative journey, requiring a necessary loss
of innocence and the assumption of particular responsibilities. Transformation is a key theme, yet unlike the 'Cinderella' fantasy of finding
fulfilment through romance it is just such myths that horror elects
to question. Conventional models of mature womanhood are accordingly tested in the many thwarted initiations presented, with protagonists who do not make the grade often proving to be the most interesting. Female power may be decisively reigned in at times, in keeping
with so many tales we have heard over the years, yet ample room is
also given to question the intended function of such a denouement.
Fairy tales have often associated female initiation with dangers that
take explicitly female form, such as wicked stepmothers, cannibalistic
witches, and vengeful fairies, all of whom must be avoided and overcome. Horror has similarly censured attendant flaws such as vanity,
jealousy, selfishness, and rage, as many of the texts evaluated here attest,
yet it has also pushed at the boundaries surrounding female transgression, often championing protagonists who dare to disobey – an aspect
that was also to be found in the earliest forms of certain fairy tales. In
one of the earliest known versions of 'Red Riding Hood', for example,
the protagonist may fail to mind her mother when she ventures out
into the forest, yet she also escapes the wolf single-handedly, by using
her wits, and thus learns a valuable lesson in survival. As Cristina
Bacchilega puts it: 'Straying from the path is necessary to acquire
knowledge.'[1]

Although they do not all manage to survive, it is through breaking
with convention, in various ways, and straying from the path usually
given to female characters that the protagonists assessed in this study
each distinguish themselves. Some gain supernatural powers, often with
the onset of puberty, some are armed with no more than the quick-
minded cunning and bravery exhibited by Red Riding Hood's oral

ancestor, all assume narrative agency and learn valuable lessons in self-reliance. In fact, male saviour figures are thin on the ground in these revised coming-of-age tales, just as they were centuries ago, with no benign woodsman or handsome prince arriving to intervene in our heroine's fate. The story of 'Red Riding Hood' is revised in many of the narratives horror has presented about females in peril, and serves as the cover image of this book for a number of reasons. Because the main character of this story has undergone such an interesting literary transformation, from a formerly active protagonist to a largely passive one, it illustrates the ways in which narratives alter over time, articulating differing expectations about appropriate 'female' behaviour and thus revealing the extent to which gender roles are themselves open to interpretation and revision – a development horror's variations can be seen to perpetuate. The story has often served as a synonym for puberty, with the colour of her cloak and her journey through the woods indicating the transition from innocent child to knowing woman, yet if this is a cautionary tale it does not necessarily censure female curiosity and independence as much as champion these qualities as necessary survival skills in a dangerous world. In fact, Red Riding Hood is one of the few remnants of wilful clever and resourceful females that once populated the stories that were told to young girls, stories that were offered as rites of passage tales as they themselves approached womanhood and were given such figures to identify with. As Catherine Orenstein reminds us: 'Red Riding Hood's empowered sisters have been found all over the globe . . . which ought to make us question our so-called timeless and universal stories about women, and our very notion of a heroine.'[2] Contemporary horror has seen fit to revise these neglected sisters, placing them centre-stage once again, and this book is intended to evaluate why this is so.

My maternal grandmother was named Piroska – Hungarian for Red Riding Hood – which I find a truly inspiring name to give a daughter – invoking as it does the ability to make necessary journeys through dangerous territory, into adulthood and beyond. Both my grandmothers had intensely difficult lives, with each having to raise children alone, long before the term 'single mother' was ever used, as many did before them. Heroic females may be experiencing a revival of interest in popular culture, yet their legacy reaches back in time to the countless women who contributed to the stories we share, both in the tales they told and the experiences which informed these narratives, offering real-life examples of courage and tenacity. This book was written with these women in mind, and the female characters they helped to create, figures who show us that we can make it through the woods.

My thanks go to Melanie Blair and Jill Lake at Palgrave for approving this project and for all their help with it; to Tanya Krzywinska for kindly reading and commenting on it; and to Julian Keogh – for keeping the wolf from the door.

Introduction

> You must renounce this power. You must give it up. You must
> never use it.
>   – Margaret White to her daughter, *Carrie*

> Somewhere every culture has an imaginary zone for what it
> excludes, and it is that zone we must try to remember today.
>   – Catherine Clement, *The Newly Born Woman*[1]

A young woman starts her first period in the school shower and
mistakenly thinks she is bleeding to death – her mother having kept
her ignorant of female biology in the equally ignorant belief that she
can keep her as a 'sinless' child forever. Taunted by the other schoolgirls
around her, slapped and shouted at by her gym teacher to 'grow up',
she focuses her anger and frustration on making a light bulb explode
overhead, causing everyone to hush . . .

The opening to *Carrie* (1976) is as familiar as its famous shock ending,
highlighting as it does the moment when its downtrodden protagonist
first discovers a burgeoning power within her, and slowly starts to stand
up for herself. Although her telekinetic abilities render her seemingly
invincible, Carrie (Sissy Spacek) ultimately opts to die alongside the
mother who has, like the school bitch who engineers her humiliation at
the prom, shown her little other than hatred – eliminating herself from a
world in which she seemingly has no place. This tragic tale has lived on,
however, in the various misfits that have populated the horror genre,
each of whom provide equally compelling insights into the horrors of
adolescence, and the specific nightmare of growing up female. It is in
evaluating *Carrie*'s legacy that forms the basis of this book.

The narratives explored are not all scare stories about 'monstrous'
females with powers they are ill-equipped to use – many can even be seen

1

to celebrate young women who prove themselves extraordinary in various ways – yet while an unrivalled degree of freedom is shown to be afforded by the genre in exploring issues of gender, sexuality, and female empowerment, there are also clear limits in the extent to which such freedoms are permitted, a fact that makes them all the more interesting. *Ginger Snaps* (2000), released a quarter of a century after *Carrie*, reprises much the same theme in charting a female outsider's coming-of-age, yet its protagonist is keen to avoid the limitations that conventional femininity offers and chooses to stand out from the crowd, rather than seeking to fit in. In seeming fulfilment of this wish Ginger (Katherine Isabelle) is bitten by a werewolf the very same night that she begins menstruating, undergoing a metamorphosis that endangers everyone around her, and which eventually ends in her death, much like her predecessor. Far from signalling their initiation into womanhood, puberty is shown, like the power each figure acquires, to be a curse neither woman is able to survive. What has led to horror's focus on female outsiders and the traumas they experience? What purpose does the supernatural serve in such narratives? To what extent are horror's misfit sisters allowed their transgressions? And what forms of identification are made possible via such texts?

Misfit Sisters sets out to explore new territory concerning female representation in horror, arguing that the genre has taken a direction which demands that many assumptions that have been made about its presumed function and intended audience now require rethinking. For example, the most prominent examinations of gender in horror cinema, Barbara Creed's *The Monstrous Feminine* (1993) and Carol Clover's *Men, Women and Chainsaws* (1992), each assume that the genre's main audience is male and utilise psychoanalytic principles to argue that its representation of women either reiterates male fears surrounding sexual difference, or anxiety about female power in general. Among the aims governing this book is a reappraisal of these claims about horror's audience, particularly in light of the prominence, and growing level of sympathy, given to female figures in contemporary horror – a phenomenon, it is argued, which suggests that female audiences are being explicitly targeted by film makers. The extent to which these developments reflect feminism's influence on horror deserves some consideration, especially in terms of the complex response given to the powerful women portrayed, and *Misfit Sisters* asks what significance these characters, and their experiences, might hold for a female audience – a group whose existence and motivations have been so severely neglected that Isabel Cristina Pinedo describes this as a 'structuring absence of horror film criticism'.[2]

It is time to revise prevailing assumptions. Recent research conducted by Brigid Cherry contests the idea, raised by Linda Williams, that women cringe from horror films because they have been socialised to do so, providing valuable insight instead into why they have been drawn to the genre.[3] The factors of appeal noted in her research include a strong female lead, high production values, a romantic/erotic element, subtlety rather than explicit violence, and a fascination and sympathy with monsters.[4] Cherry further argues that female fans actively negotiate meaning by tending to 'elide those narrative aspects of the films which conform to patriarchal repression' – employing what she terms as 'feminine interpretive strategies' in selecting what they want from texts.[5]

Misfit Sisters questions what range of meanings, and possible pleasures, the narratives chosen for analysis might have to offer a female audience. As Pinedo has argued, 'the pleasure women derive from watching horror films deserves to be explored',[6] and this is particularly so given the number of female characters taking the lead in contemporary horror. Not only adolescents, but an increasing number of older females are placed in scenarios which force them to demonstrate extraordinary capacities within themselves, providing an unparalleled degree of agency. That they each acquire elements of 'monstrosity' in breaking with convention, and are frequently ostracised in their communities, is considered to be one of their most alluring features, and it is suggested that, in the trials they face, and the levels of courage and determination shown, our sympathy and admiration are evoked. Certain characters may be demonised as 'dangerous' in some way yet the punishment this yields, far from being approved by viewers, may, as Cherry's research indicates, be 'elided' instead, along with any other elements that are obviously designed to fit a patriarchal agenda, rather than a feminist one. The very fact that women take precedence in the texts evaluated, together with the many admirable qualities these figures are imbued with, suggests that they are made with a female audience in mind – but they also go some way to avoid alienating male viewers entirely. Indeed, any discernible radicalism is clearly tempered, as we shall see, revealing a number of interesting contradictions in terms of how female identity, presumed abilities, and appropriate conduct are considered and, at times, questioned today. The ideological conflicts within such texts are not easily resolved, but they provide a fascinating opportunity to explore the prominence given to females in a genre many have viewed as misogynist, to evaluate the increasing tendency to sympathetically adopt a female protagonist's outlook, and to assess the possibilities that result when we see the world, for some time at least, from her perspective.

The texts discussed, *Carrie* aside, have all been released in the last few years. Many have drawn upon this landmark film in various ways, particularly in relating the problems experienced by a troubled female outsider in attempting to cope with puberty, locating a latent power within themselves as they do so. The material selected has, on the whole, received very little critical discussion, and includes *Carrie*'s sequel, *Carrie II: The Rage* (1999), the *Scream* trilogy (1996, 1997, 2000), *The Craft* (1996), *Ginger Snaps* and *Ginger Snaps: Unleashed* (2000, 2004), and the TV series *Buffy: The Vampire Slayer* (1997–2003). Those chosen for analysis have one main factor in common: they are all narratives of female maturation that have recently emerged in horror. In largely dealing with adolescents who face mortal threats, overcome unhappy family situations, embark upon problematic relationships, and grow up, in some way, over their narrative journey they can, it is contended, be likened to a female rite of passage. The narrative focus is placed upon young women having to face and fight specific threats, battling to survive as they approach adulthood. That they do not all manage to do so is as notable as the contrasting images provided in terms of acceptable 'feminine' behaviour. While all the characters discussed are considered to be transgressive in some way, some are more so than others, as their varying fates reveal. They may each push at certain boundaries yet those who survive invariably corroborate the idea that approved womanhood is signalled by a demonstration of moral responsibility, while their counterparts prove that female power, without such attendant ethical affiliations, is unacceptable.

The female rite of passage is considered to be a crucial sub-text within certain examples of contemporary horror, and *Misfit Sisters* duly asks what roles are made available to women and what myths are drawn upon in presenting a female coming-of-age narrative. Parables of female maturation have been severely neglected in popular culture and surrounding criticism, so an analysis of horror's recent interest in this theme, and the influences it draws upon, is considered to be both worthwhile and necessary. Indeed, while the male journey from adolescence to adulthood is relatively commonplace, the female passage towards maturity has been virtually ignored.

This tendency is ably exemplified by George Lucas's *Star Wars* saga, which openly draws, as many have observed, on Joseph Campbell's analysis of mythological archetypes, *The Hero With a Thousand Faces* (1949). The hero of *Star Wars* (1977) is Luke Skywalker (Mark Hamill), and the original trilogy traces his path from simple farmhand in his native Tatouine to a man equipped with the self-knowledge, assertiveness, and integrity that will qualify him to battle the forces of evil and earn his place as a true hero. Discovering that his father is the villainous Darth Vader (David Prowse) in *The Empire Strikes Back* (1980) warns Luke about what he might become, while additionally explaining the source of his latent power – termed in *Star Wars'* mythology as 'the Force'. However, as we learn in the third part of the (initial) trilogy, *The Return of the Jedi* (1983), Luke has a twin sister, Princess Leia (Carrie Fisher). This discovery seems intended to complete the family saga conceived by Lucas, yet begs a question that is never resolved, namely why Leia has no equivalent claim to Luke's destiny, given that she shares the same parentage? She shows no propensity towards using the 'Force' and even seems to diminish in her assertiveness as the trilogy develops. Indeed, by the last instalment, Leia is reduced to the role of a helpless female waiting to be saved – the very cliché the first film seemed to confront in her acerbic humour and authoritative manner. The simple explanation for this is that the *Star Wars* trilogy is not Leia's story, but Luke's. She merely exists in order to equip the hero with a reason for being heroic, and does not presume to question why she lacks his power. Her position is nevertheless instructive because it puts female rites of passage into perspective, demonstrating the degree to which mainstream culture has tended to focus on male rites and initiations at the exclusion of women.

The journey undertaken by males in learning how to deal with their emotions and behave 'appropriately' is a standard trope. It is not simply Luke Skywalker's fight against the 'dark side' of human (presumably masculine) nature, but a thousand such narratives that deal with a similar theme. From the young protagonists who lose their innocence in journeying to view a dead body in *Stand By Me* (1986) to the imma-ture yuppie salesman who finally gets his familial priorities right in *Rain Man* (1988), Hollywood has provided countless examples of how to be a man. By comparison, stories about a female path to adulthood have been all too thin on the ground.[7] This has typically been attributed to a continued privileging of patriarchal concerns in contemporary film and television, with male experiences and relationships taking priority. Laura Mulvey famously outlined the options at stake for the female audi-ence in the mid-1970s, arguing that, given the paucity of strong female characters on screen, female viewers were forced to identify either with problematically weak female characters, or with the male characters that tend to dominate most fiction.[8] The options, in her terms, are either masochism or transvestism, and it is worth considering the extent to which this limited choice is as true today. Within one specific genre *Misfit Sisters* intends to argue that such a dilemma has been confounded, for in contemporary horror female characters frequently take centre stage. Furthermore, unlike Leia's narrative disenfranchisement, it is their capacity to wield power, and to avoid being corrupted by it, that forms the main narrative quest.

Within mythic terms female rites of passage are traditionally marked by losing one's virginity, getting betrothed, or giving birth, yet horror has shown that numerous perils surround these events. Protagonists frequently find that a love interest lets them down, while marriage, far from being viewed as the culmination of female aspirations, is treated with great scepticism. The genre has recently provided a number of older female characters who learn that finding a husband does not amount to keeping him, and their consequent status as a single mother significantly coincides with the ways in which they are narratively interrogated. Accordingly, in addition to the adolescents that make up the main body of this analysis, who are variously tested, as we shall see, according to their ability to balance a necessary degree of courage and compassion, attention is also given to films in which more mature characters are featured, including *Wes Craven's New Nightmare* (1994), *Halloween H20: 20 Years Later* (1998), *What Lies Beneath* (2000), *The Gift* (2000), *The Ring* (2002), *The Ring Two* (2005), and *Dark Water* (2005).

Each narrative involves the supernatural in terms of the power these women acquire, the enemy being fought, or the assistance they receive in defending both themselves and their families. Some have to fight off superhuman killers in order to protect their children, some are forced to realise that an object of romantic interest is not what he seems. All have their abilities as mothers questioned, even as they are ultimately championed, interestingly confirming that even the most culturally approved role for women is rife with potential problems, and that marriage and motherhood do not necessarily lead to living 'happily ever after'. Indeed, *Misfit Sisters* sets out with the contention that contemporary horror can best be understood as a means of revisiting, and at times refuting, many of the assumptions contained in fairy tales.

The premise taken in this analysis is that fairy tales are an integral influence upon horror, particularly teen horror, and that the narratives evaluated here are best understood as updated fairy tales, sharing a mutual interest in both imaginatively exploring, and often subverting, what is deemed to be culturally permissible. Elizabeth Wanning Harries refers to fairy tales as 'a narrative world where the supernatural is commonplace, where the rules of our ordinary world do not apply, where wishes come true'.[9] All these factors might equally be applied to horror also, except that, far from aiming to reassure its audience, horror aims to unsettle us, even as it draws upon many of the same motifs. Harries suggests that the revisions that have been made to traditional fairy tales work to 'pry the old stories open, revealing their inadequacies and their silences'.[10] The narratives assessed in *Misfit Sisters* also return to familiar territory, reusing a number of the same archetypes and tropes, yet in a manner that invites us to question existing assumptions. Fairy tale elements can be found in all the texts we will look at, which invoke a similar need to grow up and put away 'childish things', to prove oneself and recognise the societal expectations that surround women – even as certain characters, on occasion, refuse to do so.

Clover identifies a mutual concern in both fairy tales and horror as the 'engagement of repressed fears and desires and its reenactment of the residual conflict surrounding those feelings'.[11] Put simply, she claims that they embody subconscious anxieties and aspirations. The argument that horror functions as a means of expressing repressed fears and fantasies is very established in critical theory. Robin Wood's articulation of 'the return of the repressed' gives a Freudian idea subversive weight, arguing that the genre allows those who are culturally marginalised a means of representation, particularly in its treatment of 'monsters'. As Wood contends: 'The conditions under which a dream becomes a nightmare are that the repressed wish is, from the point of view of consciousness, so terrible that it must be repudiated as loathsome, and that it is so strong and powerful as to constitute a serious threat.'[12] This form of 'abjection', to use Kristeva's term, has often been used to undermine women by amplifying the presumed threat they evoke. However, if we perceive horror as an imaginary zone for what is culturally excluded, reiterating the epigraph given at the beginning of this chapter, then the genre's abjection of women may be utilised more progressively than either Kristeva or Creed have acknowledged. In allowing certain wishes to be expressed, horror offers female audiences the pleasure of seeing another female both acting up and stating a sense of discontentment that many might identify with. Even where such characters are punished, simply through voicing deeply felt wishes attention is given to specific hopes and fears, to the obstacles that are faced, and to the attendant factors that transform a supposed dream into a living nightmare.

Some critics have argued that fairy tales and horror both set out to preserve social limits rather than question them. James Twitchell, for example, regards horror's main purpose as being essentially conservative, socialising the adolescents he perceives as the main audience of such films into culturally approved roles. As he argues: 'Like fairy tales that prepare the child for the anxieties of separation, modern horror myths prepare the teenager for the anxieties of reproduction. They are fantastic, ludicrous, crude, and important distortions of real life situations, not in the service of repression, but of instruction.'[13] Twitchell claims that horror gives audiences a reason for retaining, rather than overcoming, their repressions, arguing that it functions in 'laying down the rules of socialization and extrapolating a hidden code of sexual behaviour'.[14] This involves warning against taboos such as incest, and provoking unease about sexual activity in general. Far from enabling us to question and confront existing cultural norms, as Wood has argued, Twitchell claims that the genre works to conserve them.

While a certain cautionary element is clear, I would argue that horror's preoccupation is not with sex alone, nor even with sexual difference, but a host of concerns that reflect the period in which films are produced, the diverse interests of their makers, and the various meanings people have cared to read into the resulting texts. While Clover has argued that 'horror movies look like nothing so much as folk tales – a set of fixed tale types that generate an endless stream of what are in effect variants, sequels, remakes and rip-offs', she also describes the genre as 'frustratingly protean'.[15] In fact, like the folk or fairy tales that they frequently reference, horror films have always responded to changing cultural conditions, the degree of flexibility permitted by censors, the differing interests of those who produce them, and the presumed tastes of their audience. Like fairy tales, horror has undergone a process of refinement, especially as it has attracted scholarly interest, yet it remains on the fringes of acceptability – a position which grants it particular significance. As is perhaps fitting for a genre that Clover describes as operating within a 'low-mythic universe',[16] horror may be credited with its ability to communicate potentially unsettling ideas in an accessible manner. However, it is precisely its ability to disturb, its perceived crudity, and the frequently fantastical situations presented (as much as its popularity) that have also caused it to be derided. Fairy tales have had a similar fate for similar reasons, yet have also been reclaimed by theorists as important cultural documents reflecting changing concerns, as is highlighted in the transition they underwent from their origins as oral folk tales.

As numerous folklorists have argued, folk tales first developed in pre-literate societies and were spread by word of mouth, later becoming transformed, in printed variations during the 19th century, into the fairy tales we know today – a process of adaptation that had major ramifications for the ideological meanings of such stories, particularly in their treatment of gender. Heroines became divested of former qualities such as courage, intelligence, curiosity, and cunning in favour of traits such as passivity, tolerance, and fortitude, while a marked cautionary tone regarding sexual relations was replaced with romance. A chief contention of this study is that contemporary horror reinstates some of the cautionary elements that were first set out in the early folk tale, including concerns voiced about male violence and the brutalities of life, while additionally championing female characteristics that typically escaped inclusion in the stories selected for print. The genre can thus be seen to invert the revisions that folk tales underwent, providing a forum for repressed material to resurface and offering a chance to review familiar motifs in a new light.

Although Twitchell perceives many fairy tale archetypes operating in horror – including the 'damsel in distress, the beast, the wicked stepmother, the wise guardian'[17] – he fails to address how many of these are deliberately subverted in the genre. For example, damsels in distress typically save themselves from peril rather than wait for a prince (of which there is a significant absence in horror); the beast is often a male figure close to them – who is usually eliminated rather than redeemed as a romantic interest; wicked stepmothers have been balanced by a growing number of maternal heroes; and there is virtually no equivalent of a wise guardian. Indeed, if fairy tales were designed to help children psychologically separate themselves from their parents (as some scholars contend), then contemporary horror also stresses the need for independence – and all authority figures are suspect. Police and teachers are generally either sadistic or ineffectual and adolescents express a keen awareness of parental disappointments. The main protagonist of *Christine* (1983), which is very much a male version of *Carrie*, puts his Oedipal suspicions clearly: 'They don't want me to grow up 'cause then they'd have to face getting old. Did it ever occur to you that part of being a parent is trying to kill your kids?' An equally cynical protagonist in *Cherry Falls* (2000), an execrable attempt to catch some of *Scream*'s satirical glory, states the situation with comparable bitterness: 'You lose your spiritual virginity when you realise that your parents are even bigger frauds than your friends are.'

Nevertheless, while such sentiments neatly chime with Bruno Bettelheim's suggestion that the fairy tale fosters personality development through such motifs as 'resistance against parents and fear of growing up',[18] it is a mistake to conceive of either form quite so innocently. Sibylle Birkhauser-Oeri may argue that 'a fairy tale is an unconscious product of the subconscious, just like a dream',[19] but this does not acknowledge the social processes involved in their construction, their later revisions, or their various interpretations. A similar problem underscores the psychological attempt to claim horror cinema as a product of the subconscious, assuming as it does that a similar set of universal and unchanging fears and desires are unthinkingly reflected back to us through these films. Teen horror may touch upon common experiences associated with adolescence, including the sense of estrangement often felt between teenagers and their parents, yet in inaugurating the commencement of adulthood, and the mixed feelings surrounding this stage, we should be aware of the differing warnings that have been issued over the years, and particularly the impact gender has played in coming-of-age tales.

Fairy tales may have been intended to provide a child audience with moral instruction in the 19th century, but they originally had a different purpose. Noting that the oral folk tale was initially devised to entertain adults and children engaged in repetitive chores, Maria Tatar points to their early association with horror in citing scenes of dismembered bodies and gruesome deaths, arguing that 'those living in the premodern era probably had a higher tolerance for descriptions of brutal behaviour and violent deaths owing to the hardships to which they were exposed on a daily basis'.[20] Infanticide, child abandonment, public executions, and death through famine or disease were, according to her research, common experiences influencing the stories circulated, rather than symbolic exaggerations of unconscious drives. Marina Warner also affirms the relevance of material conditions in which these stories first developed, yet stresses that the gender of those who primarily told tales is equally important to note, arguing that storytelling provided a rare opportunity for women to 'share their experiences in narrative'.[21] What are commonly referred to as 'old wives tales', she argues, warned younger women of the tribulations associated with growing up, of having to deal with predatory men and female rivalries – both in their own family situations and those they might marry into. Warner points out that women's stories have always been subject to the context (and constraints) of their times, articulating how later aristocratic female writers in the 18th century wrote tales that 'teach the limits of a growing girl's hopes', even as they aimed 'to reveal possibilities, to map out a different way and a new perception of love, marriage, women's skills, thus advocating a means of escaping imposed limits and proscribed destiny'.[22] Although fairy tales have undergone successive mutations in which their intent 'to help, to teach, to warn' has often had to disguise itself, Warner maintains that the fairy tale's power remains in its ability to 'speak of the unspeakable'.[23]

This brings us back to Wood's contention that horror provides a cultural space for the return of the repressed, reflecting a similar preoccupation with testing boundaries. By forcing female characters to take action against specific threats, and equipping them with the capability and assertiveness to do so, these texts can similarly be seen to 'speak of the unspeakable', often challenging particular conventions surrounding female expectations. Marriage, where it occurs, proves to be unhappy or short-lived, and the fact that characters are forced towards independence can be seen to reflect a changing social climate, one that has heralded a greater testimony to female agency than was previously deemed possible. Yet even as these narratives champion specific qualities in women they also censure perceived flaws, and if they impart a certain feminist cynicism in promoting the need for self-sufficiency they also reflect a level of distrust towards females that seemingly short-circuits any feminist potential. The anxieties (and desires) that are made manifest in horror are considered to be an important articulation of pressing concerns and conflicts regarding female identity and aspiration, and, it is argued, we can use such narratives to re-evaluate such concerns in a genre that delights in casting fairy tale characters in new roles, questioning many of our assumptions and expectations accordingly.

A number of parallels exist in the scholarship surrounding horror and fairy tales: both have been claimed as reactionary in their intentions yet radical in their possibilities; each has been subjected to psychoanalytic scrutiny and said to offer a means of articulating subconscious fears and desires – with the underlying assumption that these are 'primal' and universal; while cultural theorists have stressed the way in which they reflect changing social conditions and expectations. The ideological value of a text is always subject to interpretation, and often constrained, and horror is no different in this respect to any other narrative form, but in the examples evaluated within this study it is claimed that a rare opportunity is provided to question and challenge existing norms. While psychoanalytic ideas are touched upon, this is accompanied by a wariness expressed towards the universalising tendencies often found in this approach, arguing that socio-cultural changes need to be borne in mind in acknowledging that subconscious desires and anxieties are themselves liable to alter over time, and within differing circumstances, as is especially evident when it comes to gender roles and expectations.

The main concern of this research is an exploration of contemporary horror's intersection with fairy tales, with a particular interest in narratives involving the female initiation to adulthood, and the obstacles presented therein. The approach adopted centres on closely evaluating characterisation and thematic developments within texts as a means of tracing affinities between them and highlighting key trends. Common experiences are noted in the narrative journey undertaken by female protagonists in horror, including parental disappointments, conflicts with peers, and sexual anxieties. Many characters encounter similar threats to those formerly outlined in fairy tales, such as female rivalry, maternal malice, and untrustworthy men. Mothers are frequently vilified, while fathers fade into the background, yet far from providing a means of deliverance from troubles at home, liberation is not found through romance, as in the conventional fairy tale ending, but in the ability to see beyond simplistic myths. Indeed, the love interests that feature in the texts assessed are often found to be severely wanting, if not downright dangerous.

Sexuality is a particular area of concern in the slasher, in which a cautionary tone regarding relations with men is all too evident, yet although attention is paid to this sub-genre – and the important development of the surviving female – dubbed by Clover as the 'Final Girl', an equivalent aim is to investigate less overtly heroic representations offered by the genre – including those caste in a more negative, if not explicitly villainous, role. Theorists have either tended to focus exclusively on horror's representations of dangerous women, with Creed claiming that male anxieties about a threatening female sexuality are at issue,[24] or have viewed seemingly progressive examples with equivalent scrutiny, with Clover reading the heroic Final Girl as no more than a 'feint' designed for male pleasure.[25] It is time to move the debate on from this intellectual impasse, to ask what images have been produced, in what context they have developed, and what they might mean to women.

All the protagonists featured in the pages to come are seen as 'misfits' because they do not fit the conventional mould of socially approved femininity, and can be seen to question it instead. The misfit ranges from obvious examples such as Carrie White, who is ridiculed throughout her community and despised at home; the *Scream* trilogy's Sidney Prescott (Neve Campbell), who is set apart from her peers not only in terms of her relative 'virtue' but the seriousness with which she views life in the wake of her mother's murder; self-exiles portrayed in *The Craft* and *Ginger Snaps*, who glory in their outcast status and the supernatural powers bequeathed to them; and is perhaps most satirically treated in *Buffy: The Vampire Slayer*'s lead character, Buffy Summers

(Sarah Michelle Gellar), who defies her superficial image as a blonde all-American girl via her secret identity as The Slayer – a figure given the task of protecting her home town from a range of demonic menaces while constantly yearning for normalcy. A certain misfit status is also held by older women who are contacted by dead females in *The Gift*, *What Lies Beneath*, *The Ring* films, and *Dark Water*, all of whom challenge the genre's tendency to demonise mothers in the heroic role undertaken. The daughter figures presented in the last of these films, Samara (Daveigh Chase) and Natasha (Perla Haney-Jardine), are also misfits, of course, equipped with the power to survive death and cause a great deal of harm to others in their ruthless pursuit of vengeance, thereby articulating a female rage that permeates throughout all the stories we shall look at. The examples chosen run the gamut from the hugely sympathetic to the outright villainous, yet they all have extraordinary abilities – which makes each of them potentially threatening in some way.

Misfit Sisters examines the distinction made between approved and castigated figures (and the complexities that lie therein), asking what significance lies in the focus given to female characters, the powers they are invested with, the ways in which they are variously tested, and the potential modes of identification they offer. A number of critics have noted that active female protagonists emerged in horror at the same time as the women's liberation movement gained prominence and various social changes were making themselves felt. Clover asserts, for example, that the increase of women-headed households and working mothers in the 1960s and 70s made horror's focus on 'sufficient female figures' more plausible,[26] while Pinedo concludes that social transformation, including the second wave feminist movement that emerged in the early 1970s, has facilitated the 'widespread development of female agency, power and self-determination'.[27] Neither is prepared to argue, however, that contemporary horror aims solely to champion powerful females, asserting instead that it provides a mixed response to such changes. Pinedo may claim that 'the horror film speaks both *to* women and *about* them, often articulating the legitimacy of female rage in the face of male aggression and by providing forms of pleasure for female viewers', yet she also asserts that an 'antifeminist backlash' has informed the character of contemporary horror films.[28] In a similar vein, although Clover perceives positive elements in the genre's treatment of gender, she also makes much of Stephen King's remark that *Carrie* was influenced by the women's movement and the fear generated by the possibilities of a 'future of female equality'.[29] King goes on to say, in the same statement she quotes from, that the story would appeal to any victim of high-school bullying, and Clover uses this as the starting point to her analysis of cross-gender identification occurring in the genre, yet nevertheless assumes that a threatened masculinity is what is most at issue in horror of recent decades. Indeed, she subtitles her introduction 'Carrie and the boys' in order to make manifest how an image of female suffering has been primarily utilised for male identification.

Conceived as the foundation to all that follows, *Carrie* is considered to be much more than an early product of antifeminist feeling, or an opportunity for male viewers to experience a masochistic thrill at a female character's expense: it is a complex articulation of a worm that turns, and a powerful evocation of society's intolerance towards such emancipation. However, although there are several male figures that contribute to the protagonist's torment, such as the principal who cannot be bothered to remember her name, the English teacher who ridicules her, or the boy who obtains the pig's blood she is baptised with at the prom, it is principally a female threat that she faces – from her hate-filled mother to the classmates that jeer at her plight in the opening shower scene – characters who refuse to see her as a human being and thus help turn her into a monster. Clover is right to describe her as a 'victim-hero', particularly in highlighting the fact that 'the source of her pain soon becomes the source of her power', and more specifically still when she contends that such power, for figures like herself, 'somehow derives from their female insides',[30] yet the significance of this insight demands greater exploration. Is the implication made that women (and their 'female insides') are fundamentally volatile and therefore need to be watched closely? Or, more progressively perhaps, are we warned that women should not be underestimated because of the latent power they possess, one that has the capacity to transform the world? While Clover fails to say any more about what such films might have to say to women about their potential and position in society, these questions loom large in this analysis.

At its most negative, far from being a metaphor of female emancipation, *Carrie* seems to refute the possibility of progressive female alliances, yet it also rejects feminine ideals. Although she is given two guides in the form of the guilt-ridden gym teacher, Miss Collins (Betty Buckley), and the figurative conscience of the film, Sue Snell (Amy Irving), their attempt to make her better fit into their world pointedly fails to avert the tragedy of the finale. A twisted rite of passage tale is thus provided in which 'Cinderella' is updated, yet the conventions suggested in wearing the right dress or choosing the right shade of lipstick come to nought against the enmity of the wicked sisters plotting against her. Carrie may triumph over them as the narrative turns from wish-fulfilment to revenge fantasy but her victory proves to be short-lived when she eventually chooses self-annihilation. Although some have argued that the film reiterates a misogynistic view of women, particularly in killing off its protagonist, I would argue that it is equally possible to view it as a sympathetic interrogation of the failures of patriarchal myths (including religion and romance), inaugurating a mode of questioning that has endured in horror's subsequent interest in misfit females attempting to negotiate their place in the world.

As Warner has argued: 'Metamorphosis defines the fairy tale'[31] – and the horror narratives discussed here also deal with transformation, not simply in terms of puberty and approaching adulthood, but in female characters trying on various parts, like Cinderella's glass slipper, to see how they will fit. Hence, Carrie's meekness turns to murderous malevolence at the prom when she trades the demeanour of a passive princess for that of a vengeful witch, unleashing her anger at the surrounding throng who are all considered equally complicit in tricking her. Vera Dika has noted affinities between *Carrie* and the slasher cycle because 'both hinge upon the notion of retribution, revenge for wrongdoing',[32] yet Carrie's revenge is problematised by her inability to recognise allies and is tragically mitigated by the fact that she dies at her own hands soon after, seemingly due to a profound sense of guilt. As the other texts evaluated in this study similarly prove, contrary to Pinedo's claims about the genre's ability to articulate a repressed female rage, this is more expressly reproved than approved, with legitimacy only granted in very specific cases. There is clearly more at stake in contemporary horror's focus on women than simply vilifying, or approving, female power, and although the genre engages with feminist politics its response is altogether more complex than existing work in the field has allowed for. Most significantly perhaps, while certain empowered women are shown to be out of control, and even potentially lethal, there is also an increasing insistence made that moral responsibility lies chiefly with women, and they have accordingly functioned to resolve injustices – corroborating traits such as courage and curiosity as necessary survival skills.

The prominence of female leads – and the sympathy with which many are drawn – implies more than a convenient image upon which male anxieties may be projected, marking instead an important shift of narrative focus towards a female perspective. The capacity for women to achieve a sense of identity and assertiveness are key issues in these texts, and although there are limits in the extent to which this is allowed, this in itself tells us a great deal about the conventions the genre continues to insist upon, despite the numerous causes for celebration that this analysis, on the whole, articulates.

Female initiation into adulthood tends to follow the same set of themes. Familial estrangement generally motivates the need to seek independence, with various hazards encountered along the way, including the hostilities of envious female peers. 'Cinderella' stands as a primary model, as is perhaps to be expected from a tale that has long been associated with a female coming-of-age, yet while Warner argues that 'the fairytale transformations of Cinders into princess represent what a girl has to do to stay alive',[33] horror reveals the folly behind such thinking. Far from relying on a fairy godmother to bestow them with gifts, protagonists find what they need within themselves, sometimes with a little help from a maternal spirit, like Sarah (Robin Tunney) in *The Craft*, yet more frequently echoing *Scream*'s Sidney Prescott by rejecting the mother as a necessary step to taking charge of their lives. In addition, while a certain loyalty and interest in men is evidently required from female heroes, they are also advised to dispense with romantic myths, often through encountering dubious male figures who provide a further imperative towards independence. Pinedo suggests that: 'The horror film is an exquisite exercise in coping with the terrors of everyday life . . . including the pain of loss, the enigma of death, the unpredictability of events, the inadequacy of intentions'.[34] What seems particularly interesting is the way in which the genre has drawn upon fairy tale motifs as a means of investigating their continued applicability, while unveiling, at times, their relative inadequacy.

Numerous fairy tale elements inform the tales assessed. As has been noted, a twisted version of 'Cinderella' features in *Carrie*, in which the downtrodden heroine acquires supernatural powers at a time of need yet uses these to take revenge against her antagonists when her aims at initiation fail, concluding the story with mass murder rather than marriage. 'Red Riding Hood' informs most slasher films in terms of the thematic emphasis placed on a female 'innocent' pitched against a dangerous male predator, yet the helpful hunter is notably eliminated from such revisions and the tale is inverted still further in *Ginger Snaps* when the female lead actually becomes the wolf, taking pleasure in forbidden emotions such as carnality and violence, rather than fleeing from them. The murderous spouse in 'Bluebeard' reappears in both the slasher's serial killer and narratives in which women dare to investigate their husbands more closely, as in *What Lies Beneath*, with female characters notably having to protect themselves from danger. The story of 'The Kind and Unkind Girls', in which vice and virtue are divided between two sisters, can be found wherever women are set against one another – with virtuous females proving themselves by their good deeds yet also through disciplining a threatening counterpart – and it is particularly evident in the relationship between Buffy and her alter ego, Faith (Eliza Dushku), in *Buffy: The Vampire Slayer* (which retreads a number of fairy tale conventions, including 'Beauty and the Beast', often with a highly ironic tone).

In all the examples mentioned, traditional fairy tales are not simply repeated but revised, just as folk tales underwent a similar revision during the 19th century, and it is particularly interesting that a number of elements removed during this process appear to have been reinstated within horror narratives. As Tatar notes, female 'curiosity and disobedience came to be highlighted and charged with negative meanings only relatively recently in the history of folk tales', while older versions 'give us daredevils who court danger by entering households that are both forbidden and forbidding' and who, far from being punished for exercising such wilfulness, prove themselves by it instead.[35] Alison Lurie's comparative point that 'strong, brave, clever and resourceful' heroines were omitted by male story collectors in favour of more passive models yields new significance in 21st century horror, which explicitly rewards these outlawed characteristics, albeit within certain confines.[36]

In addition, the genre has resurrected the heroic protective mother that was virtually eliminated from fairy tales. Sibylle Birkhauser-Oeri views this maternal icon as a vestige of goddess worship that existed prior to Christianity, arguing that the notion of a divine female power subsequently took new form in the cult surrounding Mary and a number of female saints in Catholicism.[37] Female martyrs replaced the benign maternal spirit found in early tales, whose supernatural abilities also became eclipsed by malicious mother figures emphasised in later versions. Tatar expresses concern about the consequences of replacing the good mother with evil female entities, particularly in stories that conclude with 'crushing the mother and joining the father', thereby perpetuating 'strangely inappropriate notions about what it means to live happily ever after' by excising the mother from family scenarios.[38] However, she acknowledges the continuing capacity for change, stating that 'we create new tales not only by retelling familiar stories, but also by reinterpreting them'.[39] Horror can be seen to provide this opportunity, and it is striking how far it has gone in re-establishing archetypes that were in danger of being completely eroded, not only in fairy tales, as Tatar notes, but in a society that, as critic E. Ann Kaplan states, 'tries to make us all (men and women) forget our mothers'.[40] The good mother's return in films such as *The Gift* and *The Ring* is significant not only because of the relative absence of positive mother figures elsewhere, but due to the moral responsibility given to these protagonists. Recalling the Greek myth of Demeter and Persephone, in which a female deity forces Zeus to intervene in her daughter's abduction, a burden of responsibility is placed upon mothers to right specific wrongs, legitimating maternal vengeance as a heroic, rather than destructive, force.

This recent acknowledgement of female capacities needs to be considered alongside the maternal ideal in which it is framed – which has always been viewed as the most culturally sanctioned role for women, after all – and is as vital as the accompanying need to question the extent to which these texts can truly be claimed as feminist. In what way are they as compromised and contradictory as the tales from which they have developed? What do these complexities say about our understanding of womanhood, approved 'feminine' traits, and the way that horror allows us to play with these conventions, suggesting alternatives at times and censuring them in others?

Chapter 1 conducts a closer examination of the traits shared by horror and fairy tales, particularly in providing a female rite of passage. It draws on the work of folklorists such as Marina Warner, Maria Tatar, Jack Zipes, and Elizabeth Wanning Harries to investigate the early social function of fairy tales, including their role in preparing female audiences for the responsibilities of adulthood. The factors that contributed to grafting a patriarchal agenda onto oral tales are assessed, and the ruptures within this ideological intent made clear. Female characters depicted by the brothers Grimm and Hans Christian Andersen are contrasted with their predecessors, and compared to examples from contemporary horror, evaluating the roles (and accompanying fears and desires) that are presented for women, and questioning how fairy tale archetypes have been altered, and occasionally extended, today.

The principal area of concern within Chapter 2 is to reassess the moral code underpinning the slasher film and the specific qualities manifested by female heroes. While Clover perceives the slasher's surviving female as an androgyne created to serve male audiences, the chapter asks to what end her traits as an active and assertive figure can be appropriated by female audiences. An assessment is made of key films, from *Halloween* (1978) and *A Nightmare on Elm Street* (1984) to the *Scream* trilogy, evaluating the transitions made by Final Girls in each franchise, and asking whether these stories aim to transform a 'tomboy' into a model mother. *Wes Craven's New Nightmare* (1994) and *Halloween H20* (1998) suggest that the fate in store for the Final Girl is to grow up, get married, and have children, yet these films also disprove the notion of living happily ever after, with each figure being significantly left without a male partner. In proving themselves as single mothers, the chapter asks whether these characters fulfil a destiny that the slasher's ordeals seem to have been designed to both test and prepare them for, particularly in its cautionary attitude to men, and questions the implications of these developments.

Failed initiations govern Chapter 3, which evaluates the competing models of womanhood offered in *Carrie* (1976), paying particular attention to the thwarted rite of passage presented and the ways in which the differing role models given to the protagonist each fail her. In contrast to Barbara Creed's assumptions that horror works to render the threat of monstrous females explicit, the chapter argues that sympathy is fostered for Carrie, rather than condemnation, and suggests certain feminist impulses in the text. The alignment of menstruation and transformation is filled with obvious coming-of-age resonances, yet the film provides a 'Cinderella story with a twist',[41] which is perceived as potentially radical in its implications. Although our downtrodden heroine goes to the equivalent of a ball, and even charms a 'prince' of sorts, the night ends not in betrothal but a blood-bath, including her own eventual death, thereby demonstrating the flawed aspirations invoked by her mentors. The chapter concludes by assessing how the tale is revised in its sequel *Carrie II: The Rage* (1999), which similarly depicts the pathos of failed initiations and the dangers of female rage.

Female kinship and rivalry form the basis for discussion in Chapter 4, in which *The Craft* (1996) and *Ginger Snaps* (2000) present women who refuse conventional femininity, embracing alternate archetypes and clearly transgressing permissible boundaries – only to be punished accordingly. The use of witch and werewolf myths is explored in each film, and both maternal role models and accompanying moral codes are additionally assessed in light of themes discussed in previous chapters. The rejection of specific values and the struggle to control new-found abilities are appraised as 'angry wishes', in line with *Carrie*'s legacy, affecting the transformations these characters undergo, yet the hostilities that result between females are regarded as equally pertinent in the cautionary intent of such tales and the suggestion made that such rivalry is an inevitable result of puberty. A similar narrative trajectory is followed in each film: with those seen to misuse their power either being incarcerated or killed by women who were formerly conceived as their allies, and the significance of this tendency thoroughly questioned.

Buffy: The Vampire Slayer (1997–2003) is the focus of Chapter 5, paying attention to the series' delineation of mother–daughter relationships, as well as continuing the concerns raised in previous chapters by comparing the show's leading female characters – Buffy, Faith, and Willow – in terms of the transitions they undergo, the conflicts they have with one another, and the moral worth attributed to each character. While Buffy (Sarah Michelle Gellar) is presented as the show's virtuous hero, the amorality exhibited by Faith (Eliza Dushku) and Willow (Alyson Hannigan) is compared with powerful yet demonised female figures shown elsewhere in the series, as well as conforming to modes of behaviour that are found to be explicitly punished in previous chapters. The fact that Faith and Willow are ultimately redeemed in the series' finale seems intent on approving the possibilities of female kinship that are largely denied in the other texts we have looked at, and it is this feminist impulse that is deemed responsible for attracting a wider audience than the adolescent demographic the show was seemingly designed for, yet the corroboration of Buffy's heroism through maternal means is also assessed, along with the sacrifices she is asked to make.

Chapter 6 investigates what may be seen as a direct development of the interest women have taken in horror, as is demonstrated in the emergence of a more mature female hero appearing in such films as *What Lies Beneath* (2000), *The Gift* (2000), *The Ring* (2002), and *The Ring Two* (2005). The principal female characters of these films are notably all mothers who are each visited by the spirit of a dead girl and conduct an investigation that not only unearths the circumstances of a wrongful death, but additionally uncovers hidden resources within themselves. Significantly, where the chance of romance is hinted at it, it is quickly snuffed out, reiterating the need for self-reliance. The chapter considers the extent to which the maternal hero has evolved from the Final Girl and themes that have occupied the slasher. Operating as part murder mystery, part scare story, and part family saga, the fact that motherhood has given these women specific qualities is considered relevant, as is the fact that they fulfil their investigative duties in line with proving themselves as good mothers.

The conclusion outlines the concerns laid out in contemporary horror's treatment of women, evaluating how the texts assessed break new boundaries in terms of the female perspective adopted, together with acknowledging the problems women are seen to face and, in many cases, overcome. It reiterates the ways in which folk and fairy tale themes have resurfaced in horror, and suggests reasons why this has occurred over the last decade or so. Above all, it finds reasons to celebrate the unusual women that I have labelled as misfits and the extraordinary abilities they are given, viewing such characterisations as an innovative demonstration of female wish-fulfilment (irrespective of their various outcomes), and questioning whether, even if their ultimate aim is to endorse female values of duty, care, and moral responsibility, they also work to render these conventions transparent. Hence, while *Dark Water* is negatively assessed as an example of maternal sacrifice, recalling yet another fairy tale trope, the film also makes the limited options available to its protagonist clear. The potential degree of identification available to female audiences is speculated upon in the light of the constraints that continue to influence female roles, concluding that, even if female power remains a concern in horror, tending to be upheld where it offers the least threat, and often via domestic concerns, the genre nevertheless offers a potent exploration of themes and ideas that are rarely encountered elsewhere.

The factors that give the chosen texts interest are as numerous as their possible interpretations. In focusing on female characters and their relationships they emphasise the conflicts and difficulties that are encountered in the narrative journey these figures are forced to undertake, difficulties that can be seen to intersect with actual experience, as much as fantasy. The conflation of elements of melodrama and horror is a curious melding of thematic concerns, and testimony to the ways in which genres today are constantly informing one another, yet these texts also prove, as is asserted throughout this book, that we can no longer deny that horror has a female audience and is starting to acknowledge this fact. While the majority of the characters explored are liminal figures, caught between adolescence and adulthood, the potential audience for these films arguably extends to all ages, just as the rites of passage that are outlined are seen to reach beyond puberty alone. The fact that the powers utilised by female figures are frequently restrained, or removed altogether, would seem to confirm that a continued patriarchal dominance operates within contemporary narratives, yet we may not necessarily feel relief at such a denouement, nor even be intended to, and they can still be reclaimed in terms of what they offer: providing an exhilarating alternative to conventional female characterisation, extolling an image of latent strength that audiences might draw upon, with transgressions we may all delight in. This research endeavours to explore this subject as fully as possible and to accordingly make explicit how complex, contradictory, and increasingly contestable the subject of female identity and agency actually is.

1
Telling Tales: Fairy Tales and Female Rites of Passage Narratives

> But can't you give little Gerda something to take so she can gain power over it all?
>
> I can't give her greater power than she already has. Don't you see how great she is? Don't you see how mortals and animals have to serve her, how, in her bare feet, she has come so far in the world? She mustn't be made aware of her power by us. It's in her heart, it's in the fact that she is a sweet innocent child.
>
> – 'The Snow Queen', Hans Christian Andersen

Horror films, according to James Twitchell, are modern morality tales designed to instruct adolescents about appropriate sexual conduct, arguing that 'horror myths establish social patterns not of escape but entry'.[1] In punishing 'deviant' behaviour the genre allegedly serves a conservative function that is used to support such institutions as monogamy, marriage, and the nuclear family.[2] Fairy tales have similarly been viewed as endorsing particular values and modes of behaviour, with psychotherapist, Bruno Bettelheim, arguing that they enable a way of 'coping with confusion, inner turmoil and certain drives which the pubescent ego must learn to control'.[3] They have an expressly moral purpose, in other words, warning against certain drives and desires. However, it is not necessarily the morality of such texts that explains their appeal, but their ability to challenge existing conventions. Fairy tales and horror share a number of elements, including the possibilities and pleasures offered by a fictional domain in which many rules cease to apply – and the path to adulthood is often difficult to find. Far from viewing horror narratives, or the fairy tales that have preceded them, as being solely motivated by aims of conformity and containment, they also offer a vital opportunity to question what we know.

Just as the horror film's audience is not necessarily confined to the adolescents that Twitchell and others assume (and is not necessarily male, for that matter), so the fairy tale demands to be reassessed in terms of its presumed function – which is commonly conceived, in feminist terms, as a means of socialising young women into a patriarchal value system. This chapter investigates such claims by looking deeper into their history. It unearths the warnings that were once given to female characters and the trials they endure in their passage to womanhood, questioning whether there is more to such tales than a simplistic approval of domesticity, marriage, or virtuous femininity – particularly given the spirit and resourcefulness that female characters once exhibited – traits they are seen to share with a growing number of protagonists in contemporary horror.

The origins, intentions, and transitions that fairy tales have undergone are important to note, for while men are more commonly associated with collecting and writing fairy tales, there is much evidence to suggest that women largely assumed the role of tale-telling.[4] Marina Warner argues that this is why so many stories have a discernible slant 'towards the tribulations of women, and especially young women of marriageable age'.[5] A closer investigation is clearly needed if such tales are to be fully understood, which necessitates acknowledging their female sources and appreciating the aims of various tellers over the years.

The epigraph heading this chapter is taken from Hans Christian Andersen's story, 'The Snow Queen', which follows a young girl's quest to find her best friend, Kay. Many interesting female characters feature in the tale: the old 'sorceress' who delays Gerda with enchantments because she always wanted a daughter; the clever princess who wants an intellectual equal in a spouse; the snow queen, who has seduced Kay with kisses and cold rationality, and, of course, Gerda herself. The recognition of her power, made by a 'Finn wife' encountered on her journey, reveals the complexity of such tales. Gerda's innocence is seen as the source of her power, just as her quest is legitimated as 'pure' because it is a selfless pursuit of Kay. Although she suffers a great deal, like many of Andersen's heroines, her quest is vindicated by her strength of purpose and the innocence which compels others to help her.[6] Nevertheless, there is an implication in the Finn wife's words that if Gerda were to know of her power she would instantly lose it. In other words, though she exhibits approved 'feminine' (even 'maternal') traits, such as compassion and responsibility, Gerda cannot lose her innocence, recognise her abilities, and effectively grow up.[7]

This warning is in keeping with Andersen's tendency to graft an overt Christian morality onto his tales, yet the sense of an innate power existing within Gerda invites further consideration, anticipating as it does the question of female agency that is central to this analysis, and which horror has extended via its various adolescent females. It is in attempting to understand the ways in which fairy tales set out to both champion and caution female characters that the chapter concerns itself, recalling a time when they were largely invented by women for the younger females of a given society. Joseph Campbell describes 'rites of passage' as ceremonies that mark key points in an individual's life, including 'birth, naming, puberty, marriage and burial'.[8] His analysis of myths from around the world suggests that similar tales have been used to prepare individuals for their future roles in society – a function that Twitchell claims applies to horror also, particularly in helping male audience members negotiate adolescence. However, the question of specifically female rites remains key. What part does gender play in conceptions of adulthood, and how does the assumption of womanhood differ to that of manhood? How has the meaning of these tales altered over time with respect to female abilities and aspirations and, in particular, to what extent has horror provided a new forum for these concerns?

The part women have played in both writing and relating fairy tales over the centuries has been largely obscured, with male writers, collectors, and film-makers having gained far greater prominence. Mention fairy tales and we immediately think of Jacob and Wilhelm Grimm, Hans Christian Andersen, or perhaps Walt Disney. Those with a more scholarly interest in the subject might add predecessors such as Giambattista Basile or Charles Perrault, yet women's involvement in the field has only recently attracted critical attention and is far from common knowledge. The brothers Grimm exemplify both the cumulative process of fairy tales and the part gender has played in prioritising certain voices. Far from originating the stories in their *Nursery and Household Tales* collection (1812), they compiled them from a variety of (mostly female) sources, getting them into print and thus preserving them for posterity – while simultaneously acquiring enduring fame for themselves. By contrast, their sources are far less well known, as are the myriad anonymous individuals responsible for initiating and developing such tales in their early oral form. Folklorists have asserted that storytelling in pre-literate societies was typically a female domain.

As Warner states: 'Although male writers and collectors have dominated the production and dissemination of popular wonder tales, they often pass on women's stories from intimate or domestic milieux.'[9] Far from simply passing these stories on, however, they also altered them, with the cautionary attitude that was often expressed towards men and marriage frequently removed. Even when women were in a position to publish their own work, such as the educated female writers who used the fairy tale to question ideas of romance and marriage during the early 18th century, they have been largely forgotten. Elizabeth Wanning Harris points out that, 'for more than a century the tales of d'Aulnoy, Lheritier, La Force, Bernard and other women dominated the field of fairy tales',[10] yet these writers have since been eclipsed by the men we mostly associate the fairy tale with today.

Certain examples of contemporary cinema point to this tradition of female tale-telling, as well as revising the cautionary element often associated with oral tales. A grandmother frames the narrative in *The Company of Wolves* (1984), warning her granddaughter about untrustworthy men, while *Edward Scissorhands* (1991) uses a similar device in which a grandmother tells her granddaughter about her own past, and the romance that kindled the jealousy of both her boyfriend and the town's small-minded community – a tale that also warns about a certain type of man: in this case a dim-witted 'jock' who cannot accept the sensitive stranger that enters their lives. Both films play upon established fairy tales, re-telling 'Red Riding Hood' and 'Struwelpeter' respectively, thus proving the enduring interest of such tales, as well as their ability to generate new levels of understanding.

In fact, fairy tales have continuously undergone a process of re-telling, revealing the differing aims of their tellers over the years. In order to draw attention to their alteration of stories, Jack Zipes likens the Grimm brothers to tailors, arguing that 'they kept mending and ironing the tales that they collected so that they would ultimately fit the patriarchal and Christian code of bourgeois reading expectations and their own notion of pure, natural German culture'.[11] This ideological element is important to note in terms of the stories selected, and the meanings they became imbued with, for as Zipes asserts: 'Though we tend to think of fairy tales as part of the female domain, as belonging to the household and child-rearing, it is the tailors who have reigned in the fairy tale tradition'.[12] Although women have played an important part in both devising and distributing fairy tales, they are far less well known, and the tales that have survived, and the moral imperatives they often contain, have therefore been aligned with patriarchy.

Women retain a notable position within the stories themselves however, and it is particularly interesting that the work of Hans Christian Andersen and stories collected by the Grimms all involve a procession of young women – including The Little Mermaid, Gerda from 'The Snow Queen', Cinderella, Red Riding Hood, and Sleeping Beauty – who are each tested in some way. Many such characters, or similar archetypes, extend back centuries prior to their written form, yet their adventures acquired new significance during the 19th century when they were used to instruct young girls about proper conduct and appropriate desires, thereby forming the equivalent of socialisation rituals designed to foster a new set of expectations.

Zipes contends that, as society changed, oral folk tales were appropriated by men in order 'to safeguard basic male interests and conventions'.[13] The assertion made is that oral tales served the interests of a matriarchal, rather than patriarchal, culture, and while some caution must be exercised regarding their 'feminist' leanings, research has revealed that a cautionary attitude towards men and an attendant celebration of female disobedience, cleverness, and resourcefulness feature strongly in earlier versions – elements that were frequently excised as they were adapted for print.

According to Tatar: 'As folk tales dropped contestatory stances and adopted the conciliatory mode of cautionary tales they sought to provide (in however misguided a fashion) models of successful acculturation while supplying women with what conventional wisdom perceived as the correct program for making and preserving a good marriage.'[14] The Grimms, as she notes, aligned female virtue with domestic duties, with Cinderella celebrating hard work, and Snow White's living arrangements with the dwarves reflecting 'contractual relations between men and women', further commenting that 'although fairy tale heroines the world over are often required to labor for their salvation while their male counterparts rely on magic or helpers to carry out their chores, in the Grimm's *Nursery and Household Tales* they work harder than in most other collections of tales', with female roles often consisting of 'toiling beauties and proud princesses'.[15] More insidious than this valourisation of virtue, hard work, and matrimonial submissiveness is the fact that heroic men were invented by the Grimms in order to replace the many heinous examples contained in early tales.

As Zipes points out, the fairy tale 'has undergone and undergoes a motivated process of revision, reordering and refinement',[16] and although it was the sexual element of oral tales that primarily caused concern, it is also the fact that men were portrayed as predatory, if not downright depraved, that makes such revisions interesting. Just as Tatar has noted that incestuous elements of 'The Maiden with No Hands' became sublimated, introducing the devil to explain why a grieving father 'mutilates' his daughter,[17] Zipes confirms that it is the sexual nature of tales such as 'Perceforest' or 'Sun, Moon and Talia', in which sleeping maidens are raped by male intruders, which precluded their inclusion in the Grimm's *Household Tales*.[18] The original Sleeping Beauty was similarly subjected to more than a kiss from her 'prince' before awakening, yet in order to make such stories suitable for genteel society, as much as a newly conceived child audience, this material was erased.[19] In the process, as Zipes asserts, men change from violators to life-givers. From having largely been presented as a menacing presence, they became saviours – with patriarchal authority justified accordingly.

As warnings about men were virtually erased, a distorted emphasis on female villainy resulted, and an attendant investment made in male salvation – both material and spiritual. Noting that tales were further revised in Disney's cinematic versions, Zipes argues that *Snow White* (1937), *Cinderella* (1950), and *Sleeping Beauty* (1959) emphasise male characters who are 'daring, resourceful, polite, chaste, and the conqueror of evil', further observing that

> this evil is always associated with female nature out of control – two witches and a bitchy stepmother with her nasty daughters. The ultimate message of all three films is that, if you are industrious and pure of heart, and keep your faith in a male god, you will be rewarded. *He* will carry you off to the good kingdom that is not threatened by the wiles of female duplicity.[20]

Whether or not this message is as explicit as Zipes suggests, an investment in heterosexual romance is clearly proffered as a means of enabling the heroine to triumph over adversity, with jealous stepmothers and vengeful fairies serving as the cause of her misfortune. Although incestuous fathers feature in early versions of 'Cinderella', and variants of 'Sleeping Beauty' were raped (and often impregnated) while asleep, these negative male figures were substituted with heroic men while female villains became foregrounded. Not only is this an obvious means of legitimating patriarchy, Zipes views this tendency as a means of diverting attention from the true causes of injustice within society, asserting that 'instead of associating evil with the oppressive rule of capitalist or fascistic rulers or with inegalitarian socio-economic conditions, it is equated with the conniving, jealous female, with black magic and dirty play, with unpredictable forces of turbulence that must be cleansed and controlled'.[21]

In aiming to uphold specific ideals regarding appropriate feminine conduct, such texts tend to juxtapose an innocent young woman against an 'evil' (frequently older) female – yet this does not mean that we will necessarily root for the former. Warner asserts that the wicked stepmother in *Snow White*, despite being the most fearsome of Disney's female characters, is more compelling than the saccharine heroines we are given, arguing that 'authentic power lies with the bad woman'.[22] The attractive quality of such characters is that they defy socially approved norms, even if they are demonised in doing so, while demure counterparts exhibit traits such as innocence and forbearance that may be rewarded, but scarcely inspire much interest. The same doubling motif has informed numerous female roles in cinema, setting virtuous women against those who are represented as threatening, including film noir's 'femme fatale', the 'psychotic' females populating thrillers, and many examples in horror, yet this does not predict who we choose to identify with, and horror's depiction of assertive females makes potential affiliations ever more uncertain.

While it is tempting to equate the cinematic tendency to disapprove of powerful women with the castigation of wicked stepmothers and evil witches in the traditional fairy tale, it is also worth considering the ways in which women have been granted greater agency in horror, prompting the need to ask how fairy tale archetypes have been revised. Are prescribed parameters of behaviour the same? To what extent, and in what context, is power given to female characters? What options are presented in terms of female maturity: the roles, ambitions, and modes of behaviour proposed as symbols of womanhood? Finally, what forms the equivalent of a quest for female heroes, what obstacles are faced, and to what extent are other females shown to either help or hinder them?

In the best-known fairy tales protagonists undergo severe hardships, often losing a parent or being threatened in some way. They have consequently been seen to prepare children for difficult experiences as they approach adulthood – a function that is deemed as relevant today as it was in an earlier age. According to Bettelheim, fairy tales are psychoanalytically useful in uncovering childhood traumas, yet he also views them as enabling all children to cope with the inner turmoil and confusion associated with the pubescent ego, arguing that 'fairy tales depict in imaginary and symbolic form the essential steps in growing up and achieving an independent existence'.[23] If fairy tales are intended to prepare children for adulthood then the number of adolescent females featuring in such tales is as notable as the dangers they face and the means of salvation they are given. Far from securing an 'independent existence', maturity for female characters is generally signalled through marriage. Snow White, Cinderella, and Rapunzel all encounter problems as they approach adulthood, either with female rivals aiming to kill or exploit them, or a mother figure who is reluctant to let her charge grow up, yet they eventually overcome these obstacles and gain the love of a prince.

However, while these tales infer an immediate bond between protagonists and their spouse, others suggest more disturbing ramifications to marriage. Stories of forced matrimony to beasts, interpreted by Bettelheim as expressing female fears of sexuality, are situated by Tatar in historical circumstances where marriages were often arranged for material gain, stating that 'the woman who was to make the match had every right to feel frightened by an alliance of such sudden intimacy to a stranger, hence it is no wonder that fairy tales turn the grooms of these unions into beasts'.[24] Ultimately, however, female self-sacrifice is rewarded by what is presented as 'the best of all marriages', one that is based on feelings rather than looks, a denouement Tatar tartly describes as 'a truly gender-specific lesson, for fairy tale heroes are rarely obliged to privilege personality over appearances'.[25] Indeed, Cinderella, Snow White, and Sleeping Beauty manage to make princes fall in love with them by their looks alone, and as with the 'animal-groom' story, by culminating with romance and presumed fulfilment through marriage, sexual monogamy is legitimated as a worthy ambition and the path of socially approved maturity made clear. Nevertheless, it remains the case that fairy tales reveal contradictory feelings towards marriage, with tales of brutish husbands who are never redeemed and alliances that are equated with death. If such tales reflect a fearful attitude towards sex this is not simply born of the repression Bettelheim suggests, but actual conditions in which the high frequency of deaths in childbirth meant that the association of marriage with living 'happily ever after' was already a fantastical premise for women, on health grounds alone.

'Bluebeard' provides an interesting example where marriage to a beast is represented as dangerous and unacceptable. The husband's high status is offset by base morals, forbidding his new wife access to a secret room in his home as a means of testing her obedience and disguising his own murderous nature. Warner argues that 'the forbidden chamber is the tree of knowledge of good and evil – and Fatima is Eve, the woman who disobeys and, through curiosity, endangers her life'.[26] However, she also suggests that the chamber, and its nightmare image of Fatima's dead predecessors, may be linked to the very real equation between sex and death in premodern times, arguing that the new bride sees, and escapes, a vision of her own probable fate. In Perrault's tale Fatima's sister calls for help and their brothers come to the rescue, yet other tales of demon lovers, including 'Fitcher's Bird', 'The Subtle Princes', and 'The Silver Nose', have imperilled wives save themselves through stealth – thereby commending a trait that became virtually outlawed among female characters.

A similar tale of courage and resistance can be found in 'Red Riding Hood', which, like 'Bluebeard', has typically been interpreted as warning about female sexuality, yet has markedly different origins. Although written by Perrault in 1697, an earlier oral version contrasts greatly with the moral denouement he provides. In Perrault's tale the protagonist's cloak symbolises approaching womanhood (its red colour denoting 'menarche' and puberty), yet Red Riding Hood dies a victim of her own disobedience when she ignores her mother's warnings and strays from the path, and is eventually gobbled up, along with her grandmother, by the 'wolf' she encounters, paying a fatal price for dallying with a stranger. The Grimms added a Hunter/Woodsman in their variant, 'Little Red Cap', who enters the story in the final moments, much like the heroic prince in the aforementioned narratives, and despatches the predator. However, they appended this with a second instalment in which, upon subsequently encountering another wolf, Little Red Cap goes straight to her grandmother, who devises a plan to drown him. As Tatar argues, the grandmother and her granddaughter 'do not have to rely on the intervention of a hunter: the two outwit "Old Greybeard" all on their own'.[27] This example of female resourcefulness appears to have descended from the oral version of the tale, which allows the young protagonist to evade the wolf single-handedly. Pretending to need the toilet when she realises who 'granny' is, she goes outside, ties the rope the wolf has placed on her around a tree, and makes her escape. As Zipes states of this early version: 'Clearly, the folk tale was not just a warning tale, but also a celebration of a young girl's coming of age', designed to applaud the fact that she is 'forthright, brave, and shrewd. She knows how to use her wits to escape preying beasts.'[28]

'Bluebeard' and 'Red Riding Hood' may have been 'written' by Perrault yet stem from a much older tradition of tale-telling in which capable heroines refuse arranged marriages, take control of their lives, and exercise traits such as intelligence and capability that are explicitly praised rather than punished. Indeed, although male heroes are often required to be adventurous, cunning, and opportunistic, while females are asked to exhibit forbearance and familial devotion, this was not always the case. Citing instances of male Cinderellas in Germany and a male Sleeping Beauty in Russia, Tatar reminds us that

> we must show caution in drawing generalisations about female developmental patterns . . . And we are obliged to think twice about male hero patterns when we come across a collection of tales depicting heroines who carry out tasks normally put to male heroes alone.[29]

Despite the mutations that tales have undergone, and the ideologies they have been invested with in shoring up certain gender roles, it is as well to remember that women were once required to be as brave and active as their male counterparts. In fact, in what is widely considered to be the first fairy tale, 'Cupid and Psyche', it is the female character, Psyche, who must prove herself by undergoing a perilous adventure. Even among the tales that remain well known today, a degree of cunning is displayed by the likes of Gretel, Gerda, and of course Red Riding Hood – anticipating women in horror who exhibit an equivalent degree of courage and intelligence. Zipes speaks of our continued need to revise and re-tell fairy tales in the modern world to prevent them from becoming myths – as Barthes used the term – which are emptied of history, and made to seem natural and normal.[30] Horror seems particularly appropriate to this endeavour, providing a new format for revisiting established archetypes and reinstating many excised elements in the unusual women that feature within these texts.

While teen horror narratives utilise many fairy tale themes they also confirm that graduating to mature womanhood is altogether more complex than wearing the right dress. The romantic impulse that underlines the traditional version of 'Snow White' and 'Cinderella' is expressly refuted in such films as *Carrie* and *The Craft*, with characters that do not escape the perils of puberty and objects of affection that do not promise a better life. Moreover, the slasher film's numerous male predators arguably return to the early version of the 'Red Riding Hood' story, similarly championing a lone female's ingenuity and cunning. In a clear denunciation of the traditional fairy tale's romantic aims, far from placing her hopes on a prince or hunter for salvation, male figures either let the heroine down or are even exposed as the very threat she is facing.

Contending that the audience switches allegiances between (female) victim and (male) villain, Carol Clover argues that in the horror film's positioning of viewers, 'we are both Red Riding Hood *and* the wolf'.[31] However, as we have seen, Red Riding Hood is not simply a female-in-peril, distinguished by vulnerability and innocence, but has a keen sense of curiosity that may lead her into danger yet also raises her suspicions when she finally gets to her grandmother's house and re-encounters the wolf in disguise. Indeed, this is the most prominent feature of Red Riding Hood's character: the fact that she asks questions, as it is precisely this level of inquiry that makes her alert to change. Just as the oral version the story hailed from allows her to plot her own escape, a similar ingenuity is displayed by the slasher's female hero. Sexual curiosity may mark the downfall of the girls whose names we usually don't care to remember, girls generally distinguished by a weak-willed desire to appease their boyfriends, rather than discover sexual identity on their own terms, but for the 'Final Girl' curiosity becomes a search for truth that proves her courage and ultimately becomes her saving grace.

Isabel Cristina Pinedo suggests that this trait also links the Final Girl to the audience, arguing that 'like the viewer, she directs an active investigative gaze at the events surrounding her . . . like the viewer the surviving female adopts paranoia as a valid position from which to know . . . because the surviving female is conscious of being watched, she becomes watchful'.[32] Furthermore, in being made responsible for saving herself from a male psychotic, she exchanges the role of a conventional heroine (who relies on others for salvation) for that of a hero (who finds the necessary qualities for survival within herself). Although *The Texas Chainsaw Massacre* (1974) and *Halloween* (1978) each culminate with the intervention of a male helper, the slasher usually places the onus on the Final Girl to both fend off and often eliminate her attacker.

If these narratives rework 'Red Riding Hood' by similarly warning against straying from the path of virtuous conduct, they also endorse self-reliance, like the early version of the tale, and we might question what significance lies in the fact that the Hunter/Woodsman is radically removed from these texts. Is this the result of greater cynicism in modern times or perhaps a mixed response to feminism? In effect, the Final Girl is a re-vamped Red Riding Hood who proves that she is capable of the 'independent existence' Bettelheim defines as coming-of-age. It is not simply a realisation that the 'wolf' may potentially symbolise any man, regardless of appearance, that is significant, but the added implication that the good-hearted Hunter/Woodsman is either untrustworthy, severely lacking in his ability to assist, or simply does not exist. Clover and Pinedo have each argued that the impact of the women's liberation movement has been highly influential in horror, and it may well be that the slasher has largely dispensed with the male helper because he was considered either unconvincing or unnecessary to contemporary audiences. Whether this is intended as a progressive gesture is open to question, yet while eliminating him from the narrative emphasises the female's peril, it also forces her to save herself. Greater narrative agency is clearly offered to the girl who makes it to the end of the film by taking a stand against her attacker, rather than simply recoiling in fear or waiting for rescue, and, in doing so, she becomes a hero in her own right.

These examples illustrate the way in which horror has refuted the patriarchal revision of fairy tales, advising female characters (and potentially female audiences) against romantic myths, and thus returning to the warnings that were often elided in the folk tale's transition to literary form. Horror's protagonists are not woken by a prince's kiss, but a rupture of both romantic and familial ideals. Indeed, while love interests often prove to be deceptive or dangerous, a female's coming-of-age is also signalled by a separation from parents, and an attendant need for self-sufficiency. The numerous dysfunctional families that feature in the genre can be seen to aid this process by reflecting, albeit in exaggerated form, actual problems found within the family – an aspect that also has its precursors in the fairy tale, which often portrays the home as a site of violence and danger. As Tatar states, parents 'will look in vain for so-called family values in stories that show us widower fathers wooing their daughters, women lacing up and suffocating their step-daughters; fathers turning their daughters over to greedy kings; and peasants wishing for nothing more from life than the prospect of a good meal'.[33] Again, social conditions need to be borne in mind when considering how themes such as paternal incest, maternal jealousy, arranged marriages, starvation, and child abandonment entered narratives, yet in terms of charting a female rite of passage it is also necessary to ask what role models are presented for young women, in terms of not only fictional peers but older figures.

Parental flaws are mercilessly highlighted in the fairy tale, yet as the 'unnatural' father was omitted from narratives maternal villainy became amplified – resulting in a highly problematic idea of female maturity. The fairy tale's portrayal of motherhood is a very mixed message indeed, as is any idea of how to be a good mother. The high number of deaths in childbirth a few centuries ago not only meant that women could expect only a slim chance of survival if they became pregnant, it also greatly limited the possibility that anyone would ever know their own mother. Mother–daughter relations are thus skewered via circumstances that help to explain the many stepmothers that feature in the fairy tale, with second wives made responsible for their predecessor's children, and bitter rivalries often occurring as a consequence. Despite suggestions by some scholars that the stepmother motif was invented as a means of psychic displacement, allowing negative thoughts about mothers to be voiced without damaging the maternal ideal, Warner maintains that 'the absent mother can be read literally as exactly that, a feature of the cause of female mortality, and surviving orphans would find themselves brought up by their mother's successor'.[34]

'Cinderella' provides a familiar template for rivalries between just such an 'orphan' and her new mother, for in contrast to earlier stories of bereaved heroines who are guided by the spirit of a dead mother, Cinderella's mother does not return after her death, leaving her daughter open to abuse by a resentful replacement. Like other tales, this story has also radically changed from its origins, with various versions around the world explaining the heroine's self-abasement among the ashes as an attempt to flee from a desirous grief-stricken father.[35] Although he is turned into an ineffectual character who fails to come to his daughter's aid when his new wife ostracises and exploits her, this negligence similarly forces Cinderella to abandon any ideas of paternal protection, necessitating that she set out into the world on her own.

Dead mothers were often idealised in early tales as a means of helping children come to terms with a common loss, and in acting as a supernatural guide they provided a source of consolation to the bereaved, yet in substituting the maternal spirit with a fairy godmother in 'Cinderella', Perrault corrupts this intent to preserve the mother's memory. Instead, a mysterious female intervenes in the heroine's fortunes, removing her from her father's house, and the women that have taken charge there, by enabling her to make a good marriage.[36] The fact that this stranger is more inclined to help than Cinderella's biological father infers that vestiges of distrust towards men and their failings are still present in revised tales, yet finding a good man remains the favoured ideal. Zipes draws attention to oral tales of matrilineal societies in which a dead mother provides her daughter with gifts, arguing that in the modern version the tale changes from 'a young active woman who is expected to pursue her own destiny under the guidance of a wise, gift-bearing dead mother, into a helpless, inactive pubescent girl, whose major accomplishments are domestic, and who must obediently wait to be rescued by a male'.[37] 'Cinderella' is thus used to prescribe 'the domestic requirements in bourgeois Christian society necessary for a young woman to make herself acceptable for marriage'.[38] Although Zipes admits that her oral predecessor also marries a prince, qualifying, to some extent, the feminist reading made, the mother's total elimination from what is arguably the best-known female initiation story is notable indeed, for in her absence the protagonist is left without any model to follow other than the matrimonial ambitions advocated by both the fairy godmother and the wicked stepmother.

Any aims beyond marriage are hard to discern among the fairy tales we are most familiar with, yet the numerous mothers that die in childbirth also present a foreboding image of marital affairs, leaving their daughters at a loss. Indeed, the primary quest for many fairy tale heroines is having to grow up by learning to cope with death. Providing a fascinating reading of 'Red Riding Hood', Cristina Bacchilega argues that three stages of womanhood are presented in the tale, with the mother issuing her daughter with a task that is intended to instruct her about the real facts of life. As she puts it: 'Just as the protagonist must enter and exit the older woman's house successfully, she must also negotiate the older woman's changing nature and death.'[39] This bears some comparison with 'Baba Yaga' tales in which a girl is sent to the home of a fearsome witch – a woman who, in earlier versions, was simply an older female relative – and proves herself by confronting her fears of death. As older female characters became transformed into fearsome witches these lessons are sadly forgotten, taking any progressive notions of female kinship, and maturity, with them. However, if the good mother (or grandmother) has been written out of the text, like the active female protagonists that once featured in the fairy tale, this does not mean that such characters disappear completely.

Joseph Campbell identifies a key function of myth as a means of negotiating 'the regions of the unknown' which are held to be 'free fields for the projection of unconscious content'.[40] Myth thus offers a way to acknowledge taboos, yet also to potentially question existing conventions. Horror may equally be seen to tap into subconscious fears and fantasies, as well as provide an outlet for criticism, and, like stories of abandoned and abused children in the fairy tale, the genre may therefore admit to realities that are otherwise ignored or repressed. In fact, horror narratives are less eager to provide the same level of reassurance, seeming more intent on provoking unease and uncertainty. This has allowed certain assumptions to be tested, particularly as horror has similarly adapted to suit changing times, as the emergence of the heroic female (and the 'maternal' ideals invested in such figures) exemplifies.

Just as young women take a central role in the best-known fairy tales, undergoing specific trials, including the loss of a parent or being tormented by enemies, contemporary horror also prioritises a female protagonist who is threatened in some way. However, rather than wait for a fairy godmother, handy woodsman, or group of benevolent dwarves for assistance, she must find qualities within herself to survive. Her coming-of-age is not initiated by marriage, but self-reliance. This is in marked contrast to the traditional fairy tale convention in which female maturity is primarily signalled by securing a romantic relationship. Cinderella escapes hostile female siblings through marrying a handsome prince. Snow White, having learnt how to be a good housewife through looking after her dwarf protectors, is carried off to a better life by another prince, far away from the enmity of her wicked stepmother. Sleeping Beauty is woken from her coma, the result of further female malevolence, by yet another prince – suggesting that life only begins for women when they have won a man's heart. Beauty of 'Beauty and the Beast', having entered into an arranged marriage for her father's sake, learns to love her seemingly aggressive husband and makes a human of him, just as the spoilt princess with the golden ball in 'The Frog Prince' learns to love her own beastly husband, in another arrangement her father insists upon. As we have seen, these tales have been adapted to fit specific ideologies, yet interesting exceptions are still in evidence. Red Riding Hood remains alluring precisely because she has no such marriage tacked onto her story. Like Gretel – who is quick-witted enough to fool the witch threatening to kill (and cook) her brother, Hansel; or Gerda – who assumes narrative agency in the dangerous journey undertaken to save Kay, it is tenacity, rather than passivity, that makes these characters the evident predecessors of horror's female heroes, women who also have to resist danger, and are similarly asked to exhibit a sense of responsibility towards others. The same combination of courage and compassion thus resurfaces among horror's heroic females, investing in a maternal ideal that has largely been forgotten.

As for horror's more negative representations, it is all too easy to see how the cannibalistic witch of 'Hansel and Gretel' serves as the archetype for horror's numerous bad mothers, how the angry fairy of 'Sleeping Beauty' adopts the guise of the thriller's various female psychotics intent on destroying happy families, and how the vanity expressed by Snow White's rotten stepmother can be seen in every woman on screen that looks in a mirror and admires herself – and is particularly evident in horror's cautious incarnations of female power, signalling a self-centred ruthlessness that is explicitly denounced.[41]

Nonetheless, horror has also shifted narrative perspective to allow repressed or abject elements of female subjectivity to resurface, not only in terms of providing some positive maternal figures, but in additionally utilising witch and werewolf identities to symbolise forbidden emotions such as power, lust, and rage. Even if such figures are invariably punished for their transgressions, the genre's stereotypes are subverted when seemingly 'villainous' females gain our sympathy, or are shown to reflect the misogyny that has been placed upon them. In the oval mirror that seems to symbolise the fairy tale's denunciation of female vanity and self-interest, do we see reflected our own self-image and insecurities, or distorted reflections that have been imposed on us over centuries?

Of the female characters that are best known today, such as Cinderella, Sleeping Beauty, Snow White, Rapunzel, the miller's daughter in 'Rumpelstiltskin', and the princess in 'The Frog Prince', Zipes contends that 'for the most part these heroines indicate that a woman's best place is in the house as a diligent, obedient, self-sacrificing wife. In the majority of these tales and their imitations, the male is her reward, and it is apparent that, even though he is an incidental character, he arrives on the scene to take over, to govern and control her future.'[42] While romantic comedies have uncritically revised the 'Cinderella' motif in films such as *Pretty Woman* (1990), *Never Been Kissed* (1999), *Miss Congeniality* (2000), and *My Big Fat Greek Wedding* (2002), enabling protagonists to secure a love-match by enhancing their appearance, horror has tended to promote self-sufficiency over finding a 'prince'. The fairy tale's conventional ending of a couple living happily ever after has additionally been interrogated, with narratives that explicitly question the reliability of men. *Scream* (1996), *The Gift* (2000), and *What Lies Beneath* (2000) appear to serve the function of cautionary tales in much the same way as Warner suggests that stories on the 'Bluebeard' theme were once used to warn younger females in the community not to expect too much from marriage or men.

Revisions of this kind indicate the extent to which fairy tale archetypes continue to inspire new variations, and it is especially interesting that former 'villains' have been re-appropriated, such as the witch or sorceress. Barbara Creed perceives witches as the most prominent example of the 'monstrous feminine' to appear in the horror film, drawing on a long historical legacy,[43] yet such figures were not always culturally reviled, having once commanded respect within their communities as healers, herbalists, and 'wise women' before circumstances caused them to be demonised. Lyndal Roper has examined how the witch was used as a convenient scapegoat in German 17th century agrarian culture – pointing out that older women were often targeted as witches (and blamed for all manner of ills) when food was scarce and ignorance and illness reigned, arguing that these prejudices would later be distilled in the villainous witches populating the Grimm's collected tales.[44]

Given that those accused of witchcraft tended to be older women (typically seen as a drain on resources), it is notable that a more glamorous youthful image of the witch has recently appeared on screen. Furthermore, in contrast to the 'snarling toxic hyper-pregnant'[45] utterly abject portrayal of female satanic possession portrayed by the adolescent Regan (Linda Blair) in *The Exorcist* (1973), the supernatural female has become a celebrated figure, appearing in both television and cinema as a symbol of female empowerment.

The three sisters in the long-running series *Charmed* (1998–2006), who inherit occult powers from their dead mother – like the main protagonist in *The Craft* (1996), the misfits sisters of *Carrie* (1976) and *Carrie II* (1999) whose burgeoning talent dies with them, and Willow (Alyson Hannigan) in *Buffy: The Vampire Slayer* (1996–2003) who learns to temper her abilities after almost ending the world, all have an obvious connection to the witch of fairy tale tradition. While such figures do not enjoy their powers without constraint, neither are they presented as monstrous aggressors, but complex sympathetic characters who struggle to use their abilities 'wisely' before they are destroyed by them. Mothers figure prominently in these texts not simply as a threatening abusive figure, but often as an important role model, and although they are sometimes dead, continuing a motif from early fairy tales, they similarly manage to assert their guidance from beyond the grave.

Equally interesting is the avenging mother that appears in *The Gift*, *What Lies Beneath*, and *The Ring* (2002), each of whom is contacted by dead female spirits and given the responsibility of revealing a murder in their midst (while the protagonist of *Ring Two* (2005) finally enters a supernatural realm to prevent any further deaths); indicating that communing with the dead, seeing visions, and casting spells are no longer forbidden territory, and may even be used for 'good'. This may not redress centuries of murderous vilification but is a curious development nonetheless. Horror cinema has provided a number of variations on the theme of supernaturally gifted women – from those who use their powers to help others to figures portrayed as psychotic – offering a means to reassess these archetypes and question their use. Indeed, although far from unproblematic, the genre arguably allows the greatest freedom to subject conventional depictions of femininity and gender roles to closer examination.

The slasher's Final Girl may not have any supernatural abilities but is resourceful, intrepid, and courageous – traits that importantly enable her to survive. However, her abilities have also been tested to breaking point, with Robin Wood asserting that she is 'always apparently reduced to insanity' by the end of her ordeal.[46] The *Scream* trilogy (1996, 1997, 2000) follows its protagonist's journey to adulthood and 'normalcy', finally allowing her to move beyond grief – and to trust men – when she learns enough about her mother's past to reject her formerly cherished memory. She thus overcomes her trauma through separating (somewhat questionably) from her mother. In other characterisations, the Final Girl's sanity is more explicitly tested. Mothers take centre stage in *Wes Craven's New Nightmare* (1994) and *Halloween H20* (1998) where the more mature 'Final Girl' in each scenario must fight to save both her sanity and her son, equipped with no greater power than the ability to perceive the threat faced. Madness or 'hysteria' (a term deriving from the idea that the womb had physically moved) has long been used as a means of castigating women and both films question how suggested mental problems and attendant notions of poor motherhood are shown to be damaging and distorted misconceptions. If fairy tales offer little insight into the problems facing mothers, preferring to harshly judge them instead, these films place their sympathy with troubled maternal figures who are given the task of surviving with both their sanity and their children intact. Self-reliance is thrust upon them, rather than chosen, with supportive male partners rapidly killed off in yet another blow to the fairy tale's traditional ending.

In *What Lies Beneath* the notion of a female neurotic is again raised in order to be disproved, thanks to a progressive counsellor who suggests that Claire (Michele Pfeiffer) investigate her 'disorder' (believing that she is being haunted by a female spirit) rather than ascribe a textbook pathology to her symptoms. Although the viewer is initially encouraged to believe that she is simply experiencing an 'empty nest' syndrome when her daughter leaves home, events confirm that her house is genuinely haunted. As a result of her investigations and her possession by the spirit of a dead girl, the idea of her seemingly loving marriage is shattered as a necessary move to saving her own life. While her position as a mother makes her vulnerable to social forces that threaten to undermine her, like the other figures mentioned, any accusations of 'hysteria' are ultimately obliterated in the face of a narrative truth that only certain exceptional women seem able to perceive. These tales not only provide progressive images of mature females, they also indicate that a rite of passage is not secured through marriage or giving birth, but in undertaking specific responsibilities.

What Lies Beneath and *The Gift* each portray being visited by the dead as having a benign purpose, one that expressly warns against the threat of male violence, recalling the gift-bearing dead mother of fairy tale tradition. That the 'woman who warns', in both cases, is a former rival of those they guide is a notable affirmation of female kinship, particularly given the rivalries shown in many such narratives. The protective role undertaken by screen witches is equally interesting, proving their relative virtue compared to more threatening figures. The Halliwell sisters in *Charmed* function as supernatural guardians against the forces of evil. Willow performs much the same function in *Buffy*, yet also highlights the malevolent possibilities of witchcraft by turning 'evil' for a season through grief. A similar ambivalence informs the contrasting representations of powerful young women in *The Craft*, with the insecure and unhappy Sarah (Robin Tunney) being guided and protected by her dead mother, and finally proving herself as a 'good' witch by punishing unhinged rival, Nancy (Fairuza Balk). Just as Willow indicates the parameters allowed in overstepping permissible boundaries, insanity and mental imbalance are implicated where such powers are seen to be misused. Hence, the supernaturally empowered Faith (Eliza Dushku), who acts as an alter ego to the eponymous hero of *Buffy*, is similarly implied to have psychological problems, lacking the restraints that make Buffy (Sarah Michelle Gellar) the legitimate 'Slayer'. Female power and maturity are thus aligned with moral responsibility, with a future maternal role often implied as the ultimate goal.

Significantly, not all such figures are allowed to survive. The abused protagonist in *Carrie* acquires the ability to defy her mother and defend herself against hostile peers through realising her telekinetic powers, yet she also destroys herself in the process, like her half-sister in *Carrie II*, and for all the sympathy extended to these girls the threat they pose must seemingly end with their deaths. Despite her relative rehabilitation, the 'witch' clearly remains a formidable adversary, as is demonstrated in Nancy's insatiable lust for power, the furious anger unleashed by Willow when her lover is killed, and, perhaps most terrifyingly, in Samara (Daveigh Chase), the inhuman figure at the centre of *The Ring* films, who has the power to inhabit people's minds and even exist beyond death. Such images indicate a continuing fear of women with supernatural abilities, questioning how such power might be abused, and returning us again to the fears and fantasies presented in the fairy tale.

The fact that fairy tale archetypes persist in contemporary forms may be explained by the fact that they are the earliest narratives we are told, and thus evoke an almost primal memory. Female horror fans interviewed by Brigid Cherry claim that a childhood interest in fairy tales, and the fear they generated, was a decisive formative experience – an insight that not only confounds the critical assumption that women gain no pleasure from horror, but which also makes the fearful nature of fairy tales, and their link to horror, explicit.[47] Yet the fantasies these tales evoke are equally as interesting as the fears they may engender. Per Schelde reminds us that 'traditional folklore was typically composed in rural settings by poor people' and provided a level of wish-fulfilment to help them escape the drudgery of their lives.[48] It might be argued that the unlikely hero, who triumphs over adversity, is equally appealing today. Campbell describes the hero of the fairy tale as 'the youngest or despised child who becomes the master of extraordinary powers [and] prevails over his personal oppressors'.[49] Horror's explicit championing of a female hero who triumphs over danger, despite her relative size and strength, clearly challenges gender assumptions, yet the anxieties manifested towards her 'evil' counterparts indicate that the fairy tale's legacy is a complex one.

In horror's updated version of fairy tales, sibling rivalries are transmuted into peer-group conflicts, attempted initiations into conventionally approved 'womanhood' generally fail, and wish-fulfilment fantasies that seek to transgress such conventions are, at basis, severely cautioned against. Downtrodden female characters who acquire power with adolescence are warned against making angry wishes, and only virtuous conduct is approved. Wicked stepmothers are substituted with a range of flawed maternal figures – who similarly get their just desserts, while fathers occupy a marginal role as failed protectors. Dead mothers return to offer solace (in most cases) to their daughters, yet their elimination is also presented as necessary for them to mature. Most notably, perhaps, male love interests prove to be unworthy of the rivalries they engender, and sometimes acquire explicitly dangerous overtones, including the threat of sexual violence. Many elements attributed to the oral tradition thus resurface in contemporary horror texts, urging self-reliance yet also cautioning against both treacherous females and duplicitous men. Despite invoking powerful women who gain a new level of confidence as they approach puberty, clear restraints are imposed. No sooner do we get a tantalising glimpse of female agency and independence than this is abruptly curtailed, with a contradictory impulse that champions trangressions, but cannot permit them to go too far.

Zipes argues that 'the fairy tale provides us with the verbal power and narrative skills to inscribe our hopes and wishes in the world. It conceals and simultaneously reveals our underlying motives and drives that we cannot articulate in a totally rational manner'.[50] This claim seemingly contradicts the idea that these tales are solely the result of ideological processes that have been reinterpreted over the years, suggesting instead that there are innate drives which certain tales 'speak' to. The same explanation has been applied to horror, with the oft-expressed idea that they function as a 'return of the repressed', sublimating certain fantasies and anxieties within an acceptable format, yet whose fantasies are voiced and whose anxieties are provoked in their fictional realisation?

Ample conflict can be seen in terms of the desires that are both expressed and suppressed in horror, resulting in a mixed message that testifies to the uncertainty that surrounds gender roles and expectations, yet the genre has also shown itself able to question its own conventions, and test audience assumptions, rather than simply repeating specific formulas. Warner notes how 'fairy tales often attack received ideas: monsters turn out to be handsome young princes, beggars princesses, ugly old women powerful and benevolent fairies', acknowledging the degree to which they tend to champion 'lost causes, runts of the litter, the slow-witted and malformed'.[51] Like the trial presented in the fairy tale, horror films often place female protagonists in peril, with a narrative goal that becomes a quest for survival, yet they also force us to rethink assumptions about female abilities, identities, and expectations – even if certain females are also presented as a threat. Warner expresses concern regarding the vilification of women in the fairy tale and its transition within popular culture, arguing that 'the danger of women has become more and more part of the story, and correspondingly, the danger of men has receded'.[52] However, the horror texts evaluated here can also be seen to reconstitute fairy tale myths, foregrounding female experiences while questioning the romantic ideals that have long attracted feminist scorn. In many ways they reflect significant changes. No longer are women reliant on marriage as a means of deliverance, and although female maturity remains linked to a maternal ideal these narratives also question the social structures that often condemn these figures.

Campbell has argued that: 'It has always been the prime function of mythology and rite to supply the symbols that carry the human spirit forward, in counteraction to those other constant human fantasies that tend to tie it back.'[53] The opportunity provided by horror is particularly notable in this respect, especially in charting the difficult passage to female adulthood. He concludes that 'there is no final system for the interpretation of myths, and there never will be any such thing'.[54] The same might be said about both fairy tales and horror, and the interpretations they have generated, yet the task remains to pose new questions, evaluating how puberty and the loss of innocence have each informed contemporary horror's understanding of female identity and maturity, and to ask what these texts might mean to women.

Paul Wells makes a distinction between adolescent and adult horror films, describing the former category as the product of an increased phenomenon of 'McDonaldisation' – utilising audience familiarity and mechanistic formulas in a manner he describes as 'highly conservative and reassuring', with a mode of address intent on playing out 'adolescent issues and pre-occupations'.[55]

By contrast, as he puts it:

> the horror text that remains 'adult' still carries with it the complex psychological, emotional, physical and ideological charges of ancient folklore, fairytale and myth. In illustrating and commenting upon deep-seated anxieties of its time, the horror film thus performs a necessary social function, for to challenge and disturb is to insist upon a liberal democratic purpose that both reflects and critiques its socio-cultural moment.[56]

While the analysis that follows agrees that horror both reflects and critiques prevailing cultural concerns, and is capable of being both reactionary and radical in its assessment, it takes exception to the idea that such a clear-cut distinction can be made between 'adolescent' and 'adult' films. Instead, what Wells describes as 'adolescent issues and pre-occupations', which might include questions of identity, peer pressure, familial conflict, cynicism about the world, and a reluctance to grow up, are held to be more commonly experienced than in puberty alone, with 'deep-seated anxieties' being clearly voiced in the seemingly 'adolescent' texts evaluated. For female audiences, in particular, the requirements of mature womanhood remain highly contested, for while the same factors of 'separation, initiation and return' identified by Campbell as central to the hero's journey are present in many of the narratives investigated, those who fail such initiations are arguably just as alluring as heroic counterparts, and may have something equally important to say.

Campbell describes the hero as 'the man or woman who has been able to battle past his personal and local historical limitations' and 'return to us, transfigured, and teach the lesson that he has learned of life renewed'.[57] The acknowledgement that women can occupy this heroic role is one that horror has importantly articulated, yet it has also invited a reassessment of other roles given to female characters, and an accompanying evaluation of their intentions. In Campbell's view: 'The tribal ceremonies of birth, initiation, marriage, burial... and so forth serve to translate the individual's life-crises and life-deeds into classic impersonal forms. They disclose him to himself not as this personality or that, but as the warrior, the bride, the widow, the priest, the chieftain; at the same time rehearsing for the rest of the community the old lesson of the archetypal stages.'[58] But archetypes alter, particularly as societies evolve, and they can be re-written also. In Campbell's estimation 'the differentiations of sex, age, and occupation are not essential to our character, but mere costumes which we wear for a time on the stage of the world'.[59] Is gender as unimportant as he assumes? It is a question that underlies the analysis that follows, informing the differing roles female characters are asked to play.

2
Sex and the Final Girl: Surviving the Slasher

> There are certain rules that one must abide by in order to successfully survive a horror movie. For instance, Number 1: You can never have sex. Big NO NO. Big No No. Sex equals death, ok?
>
> – Randy Meeks, *Scream*

The slasher film's punitive response to sex is so familiar it has assumed the status of cliché. When horror buff, Randy Meeks (Jamie Kennedy), spells out to his fellow high-school friends in *Scream* (1996) that staying alive means staying virgins he confirms the idea, culled from avid viewing of his favourite genre, that sex and death are closely equated. Moreover, although young men are often targeted as much as young women, it is the woman's death the camera tends to linger over. By extension, it is female sexuality that tends to be viewed as the principal concern of such narratives. Adam Rockoff summarises the usual detraction as follows:

> Those who find the morality of slasher films distasteful generally hold as evidence what they take to be these films' prevailing mantra: good girls don't die, but loose ones do. To simplify it further, the girls who refrain from having sex survive, the ones who indulge in their passions die.[1]

The legacy can be traced from *Psycho* (1960) in which Marion Crane (Janet Leigh) introduced to us having had sex outside marriage, shortly dies thereafter, just as a host of sexually active females in the slasher are destined to die soon after copulation. That the girl who tends to survive such films is distinguished by her relative virtue may accordingly be seen to endorse a specific morality – rewarding restraint and responsibility. This chapter questions whether this convention is as misogynistic as many have assumed, asking whether the slasher offers more to young women than simply demanding sexual abstinence.

A case in point is the virginal Laurie Strode (Jamie Lee Curtis) in *Halloween* (1978). Despite being presented as a sexually naïve bookworm who is mocked by her female peers, Laurie affirms that boys are intimidated by her intelligence and it is this trait that contributes further towards saving her than her piety. Indeed, although numerous critics have seen the slasher as an attempt to regulate female sexuality, it is equally possible to argue that it provides a positive affirmation of female capability, non-conformity, and a refusal to 'put out' simply to keep a man (as sex is generally portrayed in such films). Reynold Humphries makes an apt comment in this regard, arguing that while '*Halloween* suggests that virginal girls are socially superior to sexually experienced ones . . . I would argue that it is progressive (and politically incorrect) to suggest that a girl of eighteen might wish to give greater priority to her studies over sex.'[2] Although Humphries betrays a confused understanding of what constitutes political correctness, Laurie's characterisation obviously extols self-realisation above conformity, displaying a maturity, like other Final Girls, that refutes any simplistic equation between sexual 'liberation' and independence. In endeavouring to understand what these films might mean to a female audience this point is fairly crucial, as our sympathies are clearly invited towards the girl whose disposition sets her apart from friends who are seemingly interested only in having sex, girls who are typically presented as 'airheads' that deserve neither admiration, identification, or pity. Rather than interpret the Final Girl's abstinence as puritanical and the deaths of her friends as punitive, there seems to be equal, if not greater, scope in perceiving the message progressively: be true to yourself, and act responsibly, or pay the consequences – providing a cautionary attitude to sexual relations that might seem reasonable, rather than repressive, in an era of high teen pregnancies, STDs, and a continued threat of violence against women.

Not that things are as clear-cut as the apparent narrative formula suggests. As Rockoff argues: 'The truth is that in the slasher film both "good" girls and "bad" girls are killed with equal gusto',[3] additionally providing examples where 'bad' (sexually active) girls survive, and even instances where 'not only does the "pure" Final Girl survive, she turns out to be the killer'.[4] While these are obvious exceptions to the rule, the slasher nevertheless demands reconsideration. Although it has been commonplace to argue that it represents a patriarchal backlash against female emancipation, firmly reproving 'loose' women just as liberation was linked to sexual freedom, this chapter questions this account, assessing the criticisms that are frequently made of men in these films, the cynicism expressed regarding their efficacy as protectors (or even partners in many cases), and evaluating the degree to which slasher narratives champion strong independent women – even as they promote abstinence.

The slasher was once considered too lowly to be taken seriously, deemed as unimaginative exploitation fare routinely churned out for dumb teenagers. As sequels reached double figures and plots became ever more hackneyed, the sub-genre's reputation seemed forever doomed to merit only marginal interest, yet slashers have since acquired new appreciation, thanks in part to *Scream*'s witty self-commentary and its acknowledgement of a critically informed fan-base. As Rockoff states: 'It had tapped into an unexploited and fertile market, at the same time reinventing and deconstructing the genre for a smart, jaded and appreciative audience which, until now, no one really knew existed.'[5] The film's success was not simply among teenagers but among an older generation that had grown up with these films, whose familiarity with conventions was ably utilised by screenwriter, Kevin Williamson, and director, Wes Craven. If the 'teen' tag had kept interest in slashers fairly quiet, *Scream* proved that their audience was much wider, inviting the question of what motivates this appeal. Noted horror connoisseur, Kim Newman, may seem somewhat dismissive in describing the 'coming-of-age, getting laid, getting killed, death of childhood themes that run throughout the whole teenage body-count genre',[6] yet it is precisely such themes that are considered of interest here, arguing that there is more to be said about the ideals underlined in such texts, and the misgivings they share about growing up, than has been critically acknowledged thus far.

It was with the publication of Carol Clover's essay, 'Her Body, Himself', later collected in her book, *Men, Women and Chainsaws*, that the likes of *A Nightmare on Elm Street*, *Friday the 13th*, and *Halloween* first gained academic legitimacy. Clover perceived interesting gender games being played out in the sub-genre, particularly via the 'Final Girl' – a figure chiefly characterised by her ability to survive. Transcending the role of mere 'scream queen' by dint of the courage and ingenuity used to outwit her homicidal assailant, the Final Girl emerges triumphant by the end of the film and thus assumes heroic proportions. However, Clover argues that she is only nominally female, asserting that the Final Girl is deliberately given 'masculine' qualities to appeal to the audience she claims typify such films, arguing that 'the Final Girl is, on reflection, a congenial double for the adolescent male'.[7] Contrasted against dim-witted friends who prioritise establishing a relationship with boys, the Final Girl appears 'tomboyish' by comparison, and Clover argues that she was chiefly created so that adolescent males can both share her fear and enjoy her ability to fight back without feeling unduly threatened.

According to Clover, the Final Girl is given features such as a lack of sexual activity, an androgynous name, and a refusal to behave like the 'typical' female victim in order to provide male audiences with an acceptable figure to root for. Clover thus argues that the Final Girl (and her conflation of both 'masculine' and 'feminine' characteristics) demonstrates the permeability of gender in terms of audience affiliations, yet while this idea extends Laura Mulvey's work on gender identity in cinema spectatorship, she crucially ignores potential female identification, failing to consider how the Final Girl might be viewed by female audiences. Clover's assumption that the majority of the horror audience is comprised of male adolescents is itself based on rather flimsy evidence. Asking a video store clerk to note the age and gender of those checking out certain films hardly offers conclusive proof that young men make up the main audience demographic.[8] Her attendant claim that the slasher is primarily marketed at this group is equally uncertain, as is the question of who sees these films, and the potentially diverse meanings they might generate. Although Clover acknowledges that gangs of female viewers also form horror's audience, she negates them entirely, which is partly what motivates this chapter, exploring the appeal the Final Girl might have for women, and assessing what kinds of behaviour are approved and reproved in such narratives. Since *Men, Women and Chainsaws* was published, new films have emerged, and the Final Girl has altered accordingly. These changes require consideration in terms of horror's representation of women and its attendant exploration of female heroism.

Because certain young women survive the traumas of the slasher, over-coming physical and psychological adversity, they provide an image of self-sufficiency and resilience that sets them apart from female characters generally seen in cinema. Indeed, it might be argued that the slasher allows women to transcend the usual parameters of proscribed female behaviour by exhibiting a degree of violence and cunning in order to fend off their attackers.[9] Rather than rely on anyone else, their own resources are tested and proven, yet despite acknowledging that the slasher's emergence in the 1970s significantly coincided with the women's liberation movement, Clover evaluates the sub-genre as a manifestation of male fears regarding female emancipation.[10] The politics of such films are admittedly complex, yet there is arguably more to gain from celebrating the Final Girl as a woman who learns to defend herself against violence, in line with the wider climate of dissent in which she originated, than viewing her as a pseudo-male.

What mitigates against unreservedly championing such texts, however, is the fact that women number more greatly as victims than as heroes. These films essentially revolve around killing, with a plot largely distinguished by the range of murders featured, and although men are often included in the procession of victims slaughtered on screen, attractive young females are the primary focus. This has instigated claims that these women are punished because of their desirability, with any signs of sexual activity marking them out as easy prey. That the killer in question is almost always male adds further implications of patriarchal control, but before making too large an ideological leap in this regard it is important to bear in mind that the supposed patriarch is far from vindicated in their actions – and virtually always defeated by a capable young woman.

Psycho is a notable antecedent of the slasher, not only in placing its horror in a contemporary setting, but in presenting a 'monster' who is not a supernatural entity but an awkward young man with a sexual hang-up. Having become intensely jealous/desirous of his mother, Norman Bates (Anthony Perkins) kills her with her lover, and subsequently punishes any attraction towards other women by despatching them also. However, the sexual repression and abnormal familial relationships presented seem to parody Freudian psychoanalysis, as much as question conventional sexual mores. The film's female lead, Marion Crane, engages in an 'illicit' sexual liaison and absconds from her office with stolen money later that day. While she exhibits elements of independence that make her an interesting precursor to the Final Girl, Marion's sexual conduct also marks her out as a victim in standard slasher typography, and she is killed by the 'psycho' of the title within hours of meeting him – seemingly as a form of cosmic retribution for her sins. Her killer's distorted desires seem to parallel the relative failures of her lover. While Norman is unable to control his mother's apparent influence over him, Marion's lover, Sam (John Gavin), is unwilling to take responsibility for making their affair more concrete, which is what motivates her to steal. Although Marion aims to give their relationship greater legitimacy, her card is seemingly marked from the moment she attempts to take responsibility for her life, setting off a chain of events that leave her in the wrong place at the wrong time. After having been caught sleeping in her car by a suspicious policeman she stops at the Bates Motel for the night, which effectively seals her doom.

A connection is formed between herself and Norman as they eat supper together, with 'mothers' and 'traps' forming a key theme in their conversation. We have already been alerted to the fact that, although Marion's mother is dead, she continues to exercise a degree of power over her daughter, provoking guilt over her relationship with Sam. Marion consequently sympathises with Norman when he presents himself as the victim of a similarly domineering mother, yet is targeted nonetheless when he becomes attracted to her, and in one of cinema's most notorious scenes she is stabbed to death while taking a shower. As Clover notes of this surprise twist: 'The monster is an insider, a man who functions normally in the action until, at the end, his other self is revealed'.[11] However, Norman's ostensible normality is offset by various factors, including his gruesome display of stuffed birds. As Barbara Creed has pointed out: 'The birds in his parlour are birds of prey; they hover menacingly overhead as if about to pounce on one of their victims. Norman has frozen them in time at the very moment when they are most dangerous, most threatening.'[12] It transpires that he has similarly preserved his mother as a means of maintaining a perverse level of control over her. Indeed, although the pat psychological explanation given for Norman's 'condition' at the end of the film attempts to blame his mother, it is his attempt to control her that is most evident – both in having killed her and in his subsequent denial of her death, preserving her corpse with skills honed from his bird collection. This hobby may also be seen to symbolise an attempt to preserve outmoded sexual mores. The film was made at the beginning of the 1960s, a period of sexual liberation which would culminate in both a lessening of censorship restrictions in cinema and changing attitudes to sexual behaviour, yet the Bates Motel, particularly Norman's 'parlour', is more redolent of the Victorian era, owned by a family who are out of step with progress (a new road having diverted their clientele), with a sensibility that contrasts heavily against the decade in which it is set.

Comparisons may be drawn between Hitchcock and Norman Bates in the control they seek to exert upon women, particularly as the director famously delighted in torturing 'cool blondes' such as Tippi Hedren (*The Birds*), Ingrid Bergman (*Notorious*), and Grace Kelly (*Marnie*) on set.[13] It is also part of Hollywood legend that Hitchcock himself wields the knife in *Psycho*'s shower scene, yet rather than read such tendencies as evidence of his misogyny, it may be more productive to assess the degree of assertiveness Hitchcock gives his female characters, and to question whether he does more than simply punish them.[14] It is in wanting to cement her relationship with a somewhat listless lover that propels Marion to take the initiative when an opportunity presents itself, notably stealing money from a lascivious client who feels free to demean her and then go on to enjoy a private joke with her boss. Despite such relatively transgressive qualities, however, Marion's independence is swiftly curtailed when she encounters Norman. It is her death, as much as her sexual activity, which prevents her from being attributed Final Girl status, which actually rests with her sister. Norman's crimes may well have continued unabated were it not for the fact that Marion has a younger sister who is intent on finding her. Having hired a private detective who fails to report back, Lila (Vera Miles) goes to the motel, accompanied by Sam, where she exhibits qualities that would become a mainstay of the slasher's surviving female. Clover perceives her as a conflation of the film's murdered detective (Arbogast) and its rescuer (Sam), describing Lila as a 'spunky inquirer' who willingly enters 'the Terrible Place' (Norman's private residence) in order to know the truth.[15] She may scream upon discovering Mrs Bates' corpse, and rely on Sam to physically apprehend Norman, yet it is Lila who exhibits sufficient daring to discover what happened to her sister and thus prevents the killer from striking again.

Made two decades later, *Halloween* revises many of the same ideas, particularly in terms of a psychotic male killer and the young woman that helps to defeat him.[16] A series of students are murdered one Halloween, generally just after having sex. Laurie, by contrast, is a virgin whose insecurities are capitalised on by a friend claiming she will fix her up with a boy from school if she will assume her babysitting responsibilities. As it turns out the friend will be dead by morning, killed by another male psycho, who Laurie eventually helps capture. Clover argues that Laurie is motivated (and saved) by what she has in common with the killer: arguing that both share the experience of intense sexual frustration.[17] The killer is, like Norman, a deeply repressed young man, yet the disturbing twist in this scenario is the extremely young age at which he first kills. As is shown in a flashback at the beginning of the film, the mask unveiled by parents returning home one Halloween reveals a smiling young boy, their very own son, to be responsible for killing his teenage sister. We are later informed by his psychiatrist, Dr Sam Loomis (Donald Pleasance), that at only 6 years of age Michael Myers decided to punish his sister for having sex in their parent's bed, brutally killing her with a knife. What is frightening about this concept is not only his young age, but that he should feel such rage about this indiscretion. It is suggested that he is no ordinary boy but a dangerous sociopath who is not considered truly human. As Loomis states: 'I spent 8 years trying to get through to him and another 7 trying to keep him locked up.' This endeavour fails when Michael breaks out of the asylum one Halloween, inaugurating a new series of murders.

In contrast to *Psycho*'s isolated motel, where hardly anyone happens to drive by, *Halloween* is set in a suburban town called Haddonfield where the cops know the kids by name. Yet despite the seemingly idyllic nature of this community, it has produced a psychopath in Michael Myers, and a sense of estrangement when he returns. Laurie's relative alienation intensifies as her friends are successively killed, and becomes pronounced still further when she knocks imploringly on neighbour's doors only to find that no one comes to her aid. The entire street seems improbably devoid of anyone but herself and her antagonist. In fact, Clover points out that 'neighbours hear her screams for help but suspect a Halloween prank and shut the blinds'.[18] The implication made is that although everyone seems to know each other, no one can be called upon in a time of crisis.

In being left alone to face Michael, Laurie must rely on her intelligence and ingenuity to fend off his attacks, utilising domestic items such as knitting needles and coat hangers as weapons. Although clearly terrified, she overcomes her fear in order to defend herself, demonstrating the courage and resilience that would become trademark characteristics of the Final Girl. In *The Texas Chainsaw Massacre* (1974), even the terrified perpetually screaming young woman at its centre, Sally Hardesty (Marilyn Burns), is distinguished by a commendable force of will that leads to her eventual escape. As an extension of the same 'flee or fight' instinct, Laurie knows that she must face the enemy in order to survive. There is no handy pick-up truck that will drive by and take her away, forcing her to fend Michael off until Loomis eventually comes to her aid. As with *Psycho*, a familial catastrophe is inferred, by some critics, to have caused Michael's insanity, yet his murderous rage largely remains inexplicable, creating a compelling nightmare figure who would return in successive sequels – and influence a host of similar killers.[19]

Halloween was followed by a variety of films that focus on teens in peril, each providing girls like Laurie who survive by facing the enemy, yet the intervention of a Loomis figure would also be removed, with male helpers, the equivalent of the hunter/woodsman figure in 'Red Riding Hood', noticeably disappearing in order to concentrate on a lone female's heroism. As Clover argues, the 'comic ineptitude and failure of would-be "woodsmen" is a repeated theme in the slasher film',[20] and it is only when stripped of the notion that she will be saved that the Final Girl comes into her own, undergoing a transition from passive victim to active aggressor when under attack. Clover identifies such narratives as rites of passage tales, arguing that: 'When the Final Girl stands at last in the light of day with the knife in her hand, she has delivered herself into the adult world'.[21] However, she problematically perceives this transition as requiring the 'assumption of the phallus', arguing that 'the passage from childhood to adulthood entails a shift from feminine to masculine'.[22] Equating assertiveness and narrative agency with masculinity is a common error in film criticism, yet even Clover is forced to admit that because of the Final Girl's achievements 'one of the markers of heroism, triumphant self-rescue, is no longer strictly gendered masculine', affirming that the slasher consequently constitutes 'a visible adjustment in terms of gender representation'.[23]

Equally apparent within such films is the way in which domestic relations come to the fore, with slashers often attacking the family, as much as adulthood itself. Many such texts are framed as nightmares in which the innocence and relative safety of childhood are shattered, and while normality returns at the break of day there is also a sense of a path having been crossed, from which there is no way back. *Halloween* is no exception. By morning, the adults have returned to Haddonfield, yet now that we have been permitted to see what terrors can take place, even at home, things would never be the same again.

A Nightmare on Elm Street (1984) plays on a similar theme, exploring the dark secret of a suburban neighbourhood in the shape of the bogeyman at its centre, Freddy Krueger (Robert Englund). In an invocation of the idea that the sins of the parents will be visited upon their children, Freddy has returned from the dead to stalk and kill the town's teenagers in their sleep. Final Girl, Nancy (Heather Langenkamp), experiences the same collective nightmare as her friends, yet finally battles the enemy, and gains mastery over her existence in doing so. As the film's director, Wes Craven, has commented: 'If you can bring this thing that is threatening you out into the light of day, you will have a way of coping with it. And in a sense, that's how humans deal with their nightmares.'[24] The ability to confront her fears is provided by Nancy's mother, Marge (Ronee Blakley), who drinks as a means of trying to forget her problems, yet gives Nancy the information she requires to fight her enemy. When Nancy brings Freddy's hat back from the dream-world her mother can no longer conceal the past and tells her Freddy's history. The film explains him as a child murderer (although originally written as a child molester) who was freed by police on a technicality after his arrest. The town's parents traced him to the boiler room where he committed his crimes and burnt him to death. Only when she learns the truth is Nancy able to devise a plan to kill Freddy – by luring him out of the dream-world, yet although her mother finally comes through for her, and commends her ability to face reality, the film concludes by forcing Nancy's separation from her. In the film's final moments Freddy returns, this time in broad daylight, and kills Marge as she waves to her daughter from the doorway.

This conclusion seemingly marks Nancy's assumption of adulthood, which her greater level of maturity has indicated throughout. Sex is a clear sub-text in this regard, with Nancy's difference to her best friend, Tina (Amanda Wyss), indicating the moral code underpinning such films. While Tina is portrayed as overly dependent on pleasing her boyfriend, Rod (Nick Corri), Nancy is much more assertive in her relationship with Glen (Johnny Depp), and calls the shots in deciding when to have sex. In a sleep-over at Tina's house, she assumes the role of chaperone when Tina, prior to retiring upstairs with Rod, asks Nancy to stay and look out for her (thereby raising concerns over his trustworthiness). By refuting Glen's advances, reminding him 'we're here for Tina', Nancy proves her good character and the scene implies that, while Nancy may not be a virgin, she is a moral figure nonetheless. Humphries argues that what differentiates the Final Girl from the more promiscuous girl that usually winds up dead is a matter of individualism versus altruism, arguing that the Final Girl is more 'socially responsible'.[25] Moral maturity and a social conscience are placed with Nancy over any of the adults we see, proving her integrity and heroism.

Tina's relative lack of confidence can be attributed to a background in which a father is non-existent and her mother apparently prefers spending time with her new boyfriend. Such instances of negligent or corrupt parents are repeated throughout the *Nightmare* films. Indeed, Nancy's parents are also far from ideal. Her mother is a drunk for whom she shows little affection while her father, local cop Lt. Thomson (John Saxon), becomes an equally bitter disappointment. Nancy may initially show her maturity by putting her friend's welfare before her own pleasure, yet she truly starts to grow up when her father uses her to frame Rod as Tina's killer. 'You used me daddy!', she states incredulously, and although Humphries suggests an incestuous relationship between them, this merely reiterates Twitchell's claim that incest is the dominant sub-text in horror, while totally missing the point.[26] Nancy may seem closer to her father than her mother, yet the film notably distances her from him when she sees that he is equally flawed. The lesson is a coming-of-age realisation that when you can no longer trust your parents you must rely on yourself.

The parents of Elm Street deceive their children as a means of protecting themselves, as much as their offspring. Craven sees this as a general tendency towards deceit that he views as characterising American society since Vietnam. Speaking of his own upbringing, the director has argued that 'there was an enormous amount of secrecy in the general commerce of our getting along with each other. Certain things were not mentioned... if there was a feeling it was repressed. As I got older, I began to see that as a nation we were doing the same things.'[27] Maturity comes from understanding Elm Street's past, including her parents' failings, and in Nancy's ability to both rationalise and face her fears, rather than allow them to consume and destroy her. If Freddy Krueger stands for the ultimate 'bad father', judgemental and punitive in turn, Nancy's refusal to believe in him appears to be a progressive gesture. As a quintessential Final Girl she exercises sufficient strength, self-discipline, and intelligence to not only assert herself at a time of crisis but to free her community from the spectre that haunts them. The Final Girl is not a languid princess waiting to be saved, but an active protagonist who becomes a hero in her own right. Although such narrative agency is admittedly short-lived, with most Final Girls failing to survive beyond a single instalment of any franchise, young women are still made responsible for vanquishing foes such as Freddy and Michael, and are championed in doing so.

Does this parallel a perceived 'battle of the sexes'? Are they fighting patriarchy or re-negotiating its boundaries? Relations with men are clearly high on the agenda, yet the slasher's articulation of sex and the Final Girl is by no means clear-cut territory. It is not simply a case of total abstinence from sexual activity that defines the surviving female, as Nancy indicates, but an insistence that sex is conducted on her own terms. To argue that she is motivated by sexual frustration is a grave misunderstanding. In contrast to the generation that grew up reading books such as Erica Jong's *Fear of Flying* (1973) and believing the equation made between sexual availability and sexual freedom, strength and status are derived from the ability to exercise genuine choice. Later films similarly reward female heroes for not submitting to the idea of 'putting out' in the hope of gaining normalcy, acceptance, and protection. In fact, they often isolate the Final Girl via the death of a male love interest, or expose seemingly innocuous men as potential threats, fostering self-sufficiency by highlighting either male inadequacy or even their outright enmity.

As the source of Freddy's power lies in the illusions held by Elm Street's teens, and their reluctance to look reality in the face, the need for demystification is key. Nancy thwarts Freddy by refusing to believe in him, which one might extend to accepting patriarchy. As Clover argues: 'Nancy kills the killer by killing her part of the collective nightmare.'[28] It is also when she learns that she cannot rely on either her father or boyfriend to protect her that she finally does so herself. However, as one generation of teens grow up a new one takes their place, and as Freddy returns in subsequent films it becomes the task of other adolescent females to fight him. In *A Nightmare on Elm Street II: Freddy's Revenge* (1985) a boy becomes the means by which Freddy continues his killing and his girlfriend Lisa (Kim Myers) must defy him. In part *III: Dream Warrior* (1987) Nancy returns as a graduate psychologist, trying to help teenagers in a mental hospital faced with the same foe. We learn that Freddy's mother, Amanda, was gang-raped in an asylum prior to conceiving him, thus portraying him, in a twist of *The Wolf Man* plot, as the son of a 100 maniacs. Nancy's attempts to help the teenagers in her care prove futile when she is killed by Freddy during a moment of weakness, leaving other females to assume her role. In part *IV: The Dream Master* (1988), Kristen (Tuesday Night) and Alice (Lisa Wilcox) fight off his evil influence, in part *V: The Dream Child* (1989) Alice's pregnancy takes the Final Girl to a new dimension when impending motherhood brings new responsibilities, and by part *VI: Freddy's Dead: The Final Nightmare* (1991) Freddy himself is shown to be a parent, with a daughter, Katherine (Lisa Zane), now known as Dr Maggie Burroughs, who is finally given the task of despatching this figure in a contest between father and daughter.

Clearly, the films deliberately appoint young women to fight this bogeyman, and the strengths and qualities evidenced by each character challenges the idea that women are simply victimised in such films. Neither are they tomboyish figures, as Clover has contended, but girls who set themselves apart by being more grown-up, serious, and responsible than their friends. Indeed, they must oppose the demon in their midst because the adult world has failed to protect them – a fact made evident not only by the apparent disbelief they face from parents and police alike regarding Freddy, but because it is their parents' actions that has increased the threat he poses, having burned him alive when legal means failed to punish him. While some might argue that they were only trying to protect their children, it is knowing their parents are not the simple suburban folk they had imagined that widens the gulf between parents and their children, revealing the hypocrisy and deceit by which they have attempted to deny the all-too-real traumas their offspring are experiencing.

Freddy's evil conduct, formerly insinuated to be a consequence of his mother's rape, is later explained, in *Freddy's Dead*, as the product of a dysfunctional upbringing, and in having suffered at the hands of a sadistic stepfather he is seemingly destined to continue the cycle of abuse. Far from putting a stop to the danger he poses, his threat becomes exacerbated in death. Freddy is reborn with virtually invincible powers, threatening Elm Street's teenagers by breaching the divide between the dream-world and reality – a liminal state that is paralleled with adolescence, and which most adults are unable to enter. Indeed, rather than being solely motivated by vengeance, he seems additionally intent on instructing adolescents about parental follies. The troubled teenagers in *Dream Warrior* are victims of abuse, like himself, yet Freddy punishes any who attempt to deny this fact and thus fail to make the separation that is necessary for adulthood. Despite her relative maturity, Nancy dies when Freddy assumes her father's guise because she fails to differentiate truth from illusion (her father being dead by this point in the narrative), confirming that painful facts have to be faced in order to grow up.

However, the actress that played Nancy would return in a postmodern postscript to the cycle, *Wes Craven's New Nightmare* (1994), in which Heather Langenkamp plays herself. With an older female at its centre, the film presents the Final Girl in a new stage of maturity, and when the happy nuclear family she is now part of becomes targeted a new means is found to test her fortitude and courage. Heather begins to have nightmares, like her character in the *Nightmare* films, and after her husband is killed early in the narrative she is left with a young child who is at risk from Freddy. Having largely preoccupied himself with teenagers, Freddy now stalks a young child – a departure which is seemingly used to address concerns about horror cinema's alleged effects upon underage viewers. Accordingly, a psychologist blames Heather for her son's disturbed behaviour, claiming that because she allowed him to see her performances in the *Nightmare* films, despite being well below the age approved for certification, he has become psychologically damaged. Clearly, this is the standard 'video nasty' argument, a topic that was very much in the public eye at the time of the film's release, with James Bulger's death in 1993 having been attributed to violent videos supposedly viewed by his 10-year-old killers.[29] Craven ridicules similar accusations made at himself and other film makers via these criticisms of Heather's mothering abilities, yet he also evinces concern at the adulation given to Freddy over the years, which evidently surpassed his intentions or expectations.

In his article, 'Spectacles of Death: Identification, Reflexivity, and Contemporary Horror', Jeffrey Sconce has explored the fascination Freddy has for teenage audiences, arguing that they 'perversely' identify with Freddy over the screen teens he annihilates due to a combination of his wit and the spectacular way in which each murder is committed. The world he inhabits is viewed as crucial to this appeal, for as Sconce puts it 'the very premise of the *Nightmare* series (Freddy's ability to enter dreams and kill the dreamer) ensures repeated confrontations . . . where a wise-cracking Freddy, much to the viewer's delight, has the absolute power to manipulate time, space and matter'.[30] Sconce concludes that Freddy is the 'star protagonist and chief point of identification' because 'he is all powerful while the teens are just so much fodder for Freddy's gory choreography'.[31] It may be that teenagers simply side with the winner during such confrontations, as Sconce assumes, because of the pleasure he provides and the relative disdain with which his victims are presented, yet Sconce crucially ignores the Final Girl, who manages to triumph against this powerful figure, even if she is successively replaced in sequels – no doubt so as not to vie too much with his established status. Who does the audience root for when it is a figure such as Nancy that Freddy is placed up against? Is the Final Girl intended to remind us of our humanity and morality, and thereby contrast against the sadistic pleasure offered by spectacles of death? The fact remains that for all the power at Freddy's disposal, and the awesome abilities others of his ilk are capable of, a young woman effectively challenges such foe, armed with nothing more than an exceptional degree of courage.

Such figures may initially have no greater motivation than the will to survive, yet as slashers have progressed motherhood provides an additional level of commitment in confronting the threat posed. Interestingly, even when Final Girls pass beyond adolescence and become one of the adults that are so suspiciously viewed in such films, they are re-visited by dangers they have proved unable or unwilling to forget, as is inferred by Vera Dika's comment that, while the slasher typically ends with a surviving female, 'the heroine is not free'.[32] The question of psychological 'damage' is explicitly investigated in *Wes Craven's New Nightmare* when Freddy acquires a life of his own and it is left to the actress that once thwarted him to attempt to do so again – at the possible cost of losing her child or, as some suspect, her mind. Although Robert Englund is shown to be markedly different to his best-known role, Heather exhibits similar traits to her screen character, including the fact that, although she has grown up, she still has limited control over her life, as her husband's unexpected death proves. A sub-text of mental illness and accusations of being a poor mother are used to query what scars she might carry through acting in the *Nightmare* films and she struggles to protect her young son against a menace she is only too familiar with, yet which other adults cannot comprehend. Heather eventually proves capable of defeating Freddy, and additionally proves herself to be a good mother. The implicit idea is that only through facing her demons can she devote herself to raising her child alone.

Similar concerns are raised in *Halloween H20* (1998), which revisits Laurie Strode 20 years after the events of the first film, trying to make a new life for herself with a new name (Kerri Tate), a teenage son, and a job as headmistress of a private school. Beneath the surface normality, however, she is scarred by her past and particularly nervous as October 31st approaches. A fun moment of intertextuality occurs when the school secretary, played by Janet Leigh, turns to Jamie Leigh Curtis and says: 'If I can be motherly for a moment, we all have bad things that happen to us' – clearly referencing the parts that catapulted each actress to fame, as much as their real-life relationship as mother and daughter. As with *New Nightmare*, the theme is past trauma and the need for psychological closure. The notion of maternal neglect is also at the heart of the film, with Laurie's son, John (Josh Hartnett), seemingly smothered by his mother's anxiety and claiming to be at risk of psychological damage by her. As he says in response to being banned from attending a Halloween sleep-over: 'Some of your shit is leaking out on me.'

The 'shit' in question is the neuroses she has been left with as a result of her experiences. Although well enough adjusted to have reached an advanced position in a prominent school, Laurie is shown to have a secret drink problem. The school shrink she becomes involved with dies the very moment she confides to him, after making love, about who she really is, and only when she is alone again, confronted by her demons, and physically under attack, does the old Laurie begin to re-emerge. She learns to fight, rather than evade her problems, rescuing John when half-brother, Michael, looms again on the scene. Having realised that she must prioritise her son over skeletons in her family closet, and think of the future – in a piece of cod family psychology – rather than remain hung up on the past, she effectively matures into the mother he needs.

In the film's final sequence Laurie lovingly calls to her sibling with her hand outstretched before chopping his head off. This would seem to end his life once and for all – literally, as well as psychologically, slaying the demons of her past – and would have been an effective means of concluding the franchise, particularly in making the only person capable of killing Michael Myers the one who is closest to him. However, another sequel emerged in the shape of *Halloween: Resurrection* (2002) in which the person Laurie beheaded is revealed to have been someone else. Michael is finally electrocuted, yet the greatest shock occurs when Laurie dies early in the narrative. Cinema's ultimate Final Girl, distinguished by her ability to survive a number of slashers, finally proves incapable of doing so, yet her demise is inevitable, and seemingly needed to reiterate the fact that, despite the remarkable qualities displayed by all Final Girls, they are also all too human. Indeed, it is this humanity, as much as her mortality, which makes the Final Girl so compelling.

The continuing focus placed on such figures as they mature offers further proof that females occupy a privileged position in horror narratives. Yet if the Final Girl undergoes a journey of self-discovery, one that can be approximated with fairy tales, her fate refutes the usual conclusion of such tales. By refusing the possibility of a prince who will end her tribulations, and making her responsible for herself instead, the slasher might be read as a feminist twist on such fables, offering a sobering antidote to the dream of romance as a woman's ultimate source of fulfilment. Indeed, in slasher morality, to believe that romance, or sex, is the ultimate goal for womanhood is to effectively fail the test.

Molly Haskell argues that:

> For women, unlike men, adolescence is not the time of awakening, the moment of crossing the threshold into womanhood. Sex is more a terror than an opportunity (witness the huge popularity with girls of the slasher . . . in which the tartish 'fast' girl is violently punished); it is not until a young woman goes out into the world, leaves the 'womb' of friends and family, marries (or gets a job) and has her wings clipped, discovers the split between the nurturing woman and the free spirit, that her consciousness is stricken – and raised! Until then, she believes she can have it all – hence the natural gulf between the adult women who have cut their feminist teeth on the world, and the next generation, their daughters and friends, who take feminism's gains for granted.[33]

The trials of the slasher, one might argue, demonstrate a narrative means of cutting one's 'feminist teeth on the world', principally via the self-reliance thrust upon heroines. With male helpers despatched, the only person the Final Girl has to rely on is herself, and the rigours she endures are seemingly designed to equip her with the strength and resilience not only to bring up a child, but to do so on her own.[34] Whether this is necessarily positive is another matter. Some might argue that it offers a more realistic account of female prospects than the 'happily ever after' myth of marriage and motherhood, yet it might also be seen to support the contention that maternity is an inevitable destiny for women, perhaps even their sole purpose. In Laurie's case, having raised her son to adulthood, and crucially learning to let go, her 'role' is seemingly fulfilled in a manner that is reminiscent of Sarah Connor's exit from the *Terminator* franchise once her own son becomes a man. Given the shadow cast by *Psycho*, the suggestion is that such separation is necessary to enable men to develop unhindered, and while films such as *Carrie* demonstrate that an oppressive mother can be equally damaging to women, it remains the case that paternal responsibilities are only given minor consideration in such films.

If horror narratives present a rite of passage, the choices given to women seem to offer little divergence from a carefully established norm, with a greater tendency to prioritise the 'nurturing woman', to use Haskell's terms, over that of any 'free spirit'. The Final Girl may distinguish herself from her peers, yet independence is far from unconstrained. Is her proven responsibility and self-sufficiency a means of testing her character as suitable mother material? Could it also be seen, perhaps quite cynically, as a means of letting men off the hook regarding their own responsibilities as both nurturers and protectors within the family? Do such tales function to warn female audiences against specific myths, like living happily ever after?

Robin Wood sees the Final Girl as providing a new twist on the 'Beauty and the Beast' tale, substituting refusal and resistance over the acquiescence and understanding this story seems designed to foster. In the original narrative a young woman is forced to marry a stranger (through an agreement made by her father), yet eventually falls in love with him, despite his gruff exterior, by seeing what he is like underneath. The tale thus serves as both a warning to women and a treatise on marriage, arguing that forbearance is necessary to make marriages work. In contemporary terms it resembles a masochistic response to male aggression, supporting the well-worn cliché that violent men will change if given sufficient tolerance and understanding. However, while Beauty feels sympathy for the Beast, and succeeds in 'taming' him, slashers rebuff any such solution. That the sub-genre originated at a time when women were campaigning against sexual violence and organising 'Take Back the Night' demonstrations seems more than coincidental,

particularly given the fact that, in the slasher film, 'Beauty' rejects physical assault and even commits violence in the name of self-defence (as
is also seen in the spate of rape-revenge films that appeared during this
period). Beauty bests the Beast, in Wood's terms, not through acquiescence but through resistance.

In their anger towards women the slasher's male murderers might
also be compared to another monstrous male figure of traditional folklore, Bluebeard, a man so intent on controlling women that he kills a
succession of wives when they break his rules (and expose his crimes).
Where does the psycho killer's hostility come from? Is he impotent, as
suggested by Clover, not a 'real' man, like the Final Girl is apparently
not a 'real' woman? Does he kill with his array of phallic weaponry
because he is incapable of having sex? Has he been warped by a dysfunctional upbringing, like *Psycho*'s Norman, *Nightmare*'s Freddy, or *The
Texas Chainsaw Massacre*'s Leatherface? Or is he simply born psychotic,
as is implied in the case of *Halloween*'s Michael Myers? Whatever the
reasons, the Final Girl knows better than to try and understand him
and perceives him to be beyond redemption. Like Fatima, the last of
Bluebeard's wives, she finally puts a stop to his reign of terror.

She also grows up in the course of her experiences. Already more
serious and responsible than her contemporaries, the Final Girl gradually discovers what she is capable of. Such narratives accordingly extend
the suggested project of the fairy tale, placing an intrepid young woman
in danger in order to prove her ability to survive. Marina Warner has
pointed out that fairy tales were often told to young girls by older
women of the family in order to destroy any illusions they might have
about love and matrimony.[35] In some ways the slasher can be seen to
perform a similar function. Indeed, it is deeply ironic that although film-
makers such as Wes Craven have been accused of misogyny, they can
also be seen to produce cautionary tales for the modern age, warning
female audiences that men are potential beasts who are not to be
trusted. This point is explicitly made in the trilogy of films with which
Craven followed *New Nightmare*, for if Freddy Krueger is presented as an
inhuman monster, the killers in *Scream* (1996) are literally the boys next
door.

The twist in this tale is not only that there are two killers at work,
but that one turns out to be the heroine's boyfriend, Billy Loomis (Skeet
Ulrich). Despite appearing to be an ardent love interest, his courtship of
Sidney (Neve Campbell) is ultimately shown to be motivated by hatred.
From the beginning of the film Billy wants to have sex with her, and
even accuses Sidney of being a repressed tease. She eventually complies,

just as Randy delivers his warning about not having sex if you want to stay alive, and by relenting to Billy we are invited to assume that she will become the next victim of the killer in their midst. Yet Sidney survives beyond their love-making and the act serves to shatter her remaining innocence, for it is after she loses her virginity to him that Billy starts to reveal his 'true' self. We eventually learn that he killed her mother, Maureen (Lynn McRee), a crime for which another man was convicted. The reason given for doing so, interestingly enough for a boy who complains about Sidney's unwillingness to 'put out', is sexual immorality, and his animosity is clear: 'Your slut mother was fucking my father. She's the reason my mom moved out and abandoned me. Is that motive enough for you?' Billy's torment of Sidney, and his murder of other teens, is attributed to the same logic of the typical slasher psycho, seemingly propelled by sexual repression combined with an 'unnatural' attachment to his mother. Despite causing Maureen's death, he fails to find fulfilment in this act, and believes that Sidney must also suffer. In addition to Billy's intensely personal motives, as well as satirically responding to contemporary qualms about media violence (as in *New Nightmare*), he and his accomplice, Stuart Macher (Matthew Lilliard), have clearly seen too many scary movies, which have seemingly warped their view of reality. Although Billy protests: 'Movies don't make people killers, they just make killers more imaginative!' he is clearly a product of his favourite genre, even down to his excuses.

This helps to explain why Casey Becker (Drew Barrymore) is so chillingly murdered at the outset of the film, as she not only fails the scary movie trivia quiz, but flirtatiously lies about not having a boyfriend. Once again, the sexually active female is punished, alongside the wisecracking best friend, Tatum (Rose McGowan), the school principal (amusingly played by Henry Winkler, former cool guy, The Fonze, from *Happy Days*), and anyone else who gets in the way.

The film acknowledges that audiences, far from being the dumb teens that tend to be portrayed in slashers, are discerning connoisseurs who appreciate the subtleties of such films, and draws on every cliché in the book, yet although it is an open parody of slasher conventions, as is exemplified by the 'scary movie rules' laid out by Randy, *Scream* also revises established rules. Hence Sidney is allowed to have sex and survive – and although her initial instincts in abstaining are vindicated, this is nevertheless presented as an important step in facing her fears. As she states, in explanation of her aversion to sex, it is her mother's legacy that she dreads: 'I think I'm really scared that I'm gonna turn out just like her ... like the bad seed or something.' While it is obviously lamentable that she loses her virginity to the very man who killed her mother, Sidney is quickly forced to recognise that her view of him, like that of her mother, and of sexuality for that matter, are all equally flawed. Billy, despite seeming so charming and caring, is not who she thought he was. In fact, in a case of 'Beauty and the Beast' in reverse, his outward attractiveness and demeanour conceal a warped mind, intent on causing as much mayhem as possible. Yet far from being doomed by having sex, the film breaks rule Number 1 and allows Sidney to save both herself and her bloodied and beaten father, who the boys have planned to frame for their murders. She turns the tables on her treacherous ex, dismissing him as a 'pansy-ass momma's boy' before shooting him in the head. Interestingly enough, it is Billy's over-attachment to his mother that she finally uses to define and deride him, a fault which the trilogy finds her equally guilty of.

Scream 2 (1997) relates Sidney's transition to college, where a killer is again at large, and although she initially suspects her new boyfriend, Derek (Jerry O'Connell), this is shown to be 'baggage' from her first disastrous relationship. The killer is revealed to be another double-act, comprising of Billy's mother, who has adopted the name Debbie Salt (Laurie Metcalf) and seeks vengeance for his death, assisted by college student Mickey (Timothy Olyphant), motivated simply by glory. In a nod to *Psycho* (and, of course, Jason Voorhees' mother in *Friday the 13th* (1980) – the trick question Casey gets wrong at the beginning of *Scream*), a mad mother is blamed, yet again, for warping her son. Mrs Loomis is shown to have been behind the death of Sidney's mother, having led Billy to murder her rival as punishment for breaking up her marriage. Relations as twisted as a Jerry Springer show are thus given black humour treatment, and Sidney's mother even makes a curious posthumous appearance in the final instalment of the trilogy, evoking Sid's worst fears, yet also ultimately working to reject her maternal misgivings. As Randy Meeks states in the third instalment, when it comes to trilogies the rules change, all bets are off, and the franchise ends by questioning the very cliché it has built itself on: the idea of the monstrous mother.

Scream 3 (2000) ups the ante on postmodern self-referencing, with the action located on a film-set where the third part of a group of films based on the murders at Woodsboro, *Stab 3*, is being made. In another case of life imitating art, the cast are stalked by an unknown assailant who is killing each character off, in line with the script, and leaving a picture of a young Maureen Prescott at the scene. This moves Sidney to emerge from her life as a virtual recluse, joining the cast and crew on set to try and determine what is going on. In doing so she is visited by frightening images of her mother which play on her fear that she might resemble her, for as this apparition states: 'You're poison. You're just like me', As a video message from Randy explains: 'True trilogies are all about going back to the beginning and discovering something that wasn't true from the get go', and Sidney's final journey is to delve deeper into her mother's past and question how much she really knew her.

Her investigation provides a crude explanation for Maureen's later indiscretions, and the murders that resulted, which is seemingly intended to force Sidney's emotional separation from her. We learn that Maureen worked in horror B-movies as an aspiring actress and became involved in a director's licentious party. In getting pregnant as a result, and abandoning her child, the final treasured memories Sidney has of her mother become irrevocably tarnished. It is the child in question that turns out to be the killer, and Sidney's newly discovered half-brother also happens to be the director of the film being made, Roman Bridger (Scott Foley).

Roman claims to have been motivated by the attention the murders will bring his film. He also reveals that he engineered the events of the entire trilogy by filming a tryst between Maureen and Mr Loomis which was later used to incite Billy's fury. Although Roman is obviously insane, much like Billy, the errant mother is still partially held accountable for her failings, and Sidney must become totally disillusioned in her, it is implied, in order to mature, yet she must also reject Roman's account of her mother as a monstrous figure – an image that she has herself projected upon her, and which has evidently caused so much damage.

Maureen's apparition, refracted through Roman's anger and Sidney's fears, is negatively presented as a vain and destructive figure, and although the film goes some way to correcting this notion, with its revelations of her innocence having been stolen from her as a young woman, she is nevertheless seemingly punished for desiring to be a star, and for her refusal to be a mother to the resulting child. This revelation marks the culmination of the trilogy's narrative journey for Sidney: from grieving over her murdered mother and fearing that she will resemble her, she ultimately achieves a sense of separation from her.

Far from the fairy tale convention in which a dead mother exists as an empowering force in her daughter's life, protecting her from harm as she matures, Sidney's mother appears as a sinister spectre who betrays any such ideal, coldly saying to her daughter: 'I lied, fool! I can't protect you at all.' Sidney's evident disappointment in her mother is born of conflicting emotions that she is forced to work through. Maureen

Prescott is ultimately presented as a woman with a murky past whose failures as a mother extend to rejecting her illegitimate offspring, yet while the suggestion is made that maternal abandonment turned Roman into a psycho, much like Billy, this claim is finally refused by Sidney. Just as Laurie Strode seemingly murders her own half-brother at the end of *Halloween H20*, Sidney must kill her sibling before he can do any more harm. Like their mother, she rejects him, along with his excuses, prior to ending his life, stating: 'Do you know why you kill people Roman? Do you? Because you choose to. There is no one else to blame. Why don't you take some fucking responsibility?'

The finale thus elects to acquit Maureen, yet while Sidney learns that she too cannot blame her mother she also opts to put her memory behind her. The 'closure' she achieves through accepting that Maureen was less than perfect is seemingly intended to make her death easier to handle, correspondingly allowing Sidney to 'move on' and trust people again. At the outset of her investigations, LAPD detective Mark Kincaid (Patrick Dempsey) seems to be another likely suspect in the detailed knowledge he has amassed about her life, as well as sinisterly describing his own life as 'a scary movie', yet the denouement suggests that a relationship may form between them. Sidney's passage to womanhood is ultimately signalled by putting aside her grief (and anger) for her mother, allowing her to form relationships with men, and perhaps even to become a mother in her own right. The house Sidney formerly occupied alone with her dog and a mass of security equipment is finally opened to the surviving friends she has made over the course of her experiences, including Duey (David Arquette) and another surviving female of the trilogy – Gale Weathers (Courtney Cox), while detective Kincaid seems to be a likely love interest. What lies in store is anyone's guess. Now that she has faced her demons, and put aside her grief, Sidney is seemingly able to pursue matrimony and motherhood, yet her story may not necessarily end with either state, for the fate of the Final Girl is never as pat as this would suggest.

Wes Craven's New Nightmare, *Halloween H20* and *Halloween: Resurrection* each confirm that growing up, getting married, and having children does not provide a fairy tale ending. Both Heather and Laurie are ultimately forced to raise their families single-handedly and have their sanity called into question as they battle to obliterate demons of the past. Although they seemingly fulfil their journey to womanhood by demonstrating appropriate maternal responsibility, whether this is progressive remains open to question, particularly as Laurie is so swiftly killed off in the last of the *Halloween* films. Nevertheless, the fact that these Final

Girls fight more than a resident bogeyman or lunatic brother, but the idea that they might themselves be bad mothers, indicates an interesting development. Clearly, mental illness is simplistically discussed in such narratives, with the inference made that past traumas may have 'damaged' them in some way, yet the continued testing of such characters remains curious. While they heroically rise to the challenge of protecting their families, the accompanying notion suggests that because they have transgressed specific boundaries, they must deal with the emotional fall-out. Clover's assertion that the Final Girl has something in common with her psychotic antagonists is accordingly corroborated, yet not in terms of sexual frustration, but mental instability, with the suggested fear that these women might harm their children. The Final Girl is thus charged with the responsibility of defending not only her community, but a future generation. While Nancy's mother drank because she could not face reality, and Laurie's parents were virtually invisible, like the other adults in her midst, these women show they can offer a better example.

This is just as well because horror reserves a special price for poor mothers, which is equivalent to the fate frequently given to the many sexually active girls presented in the slasher: death itself. The following chapters will further explore how maternal discourses are played out in teen horror, including positive and negative examples. The qualities exhibited by the Final Girl will be reprised in Chapter 5 (where Buffy is evaluated as a variation on this theme) and in Chapter 6 (where the Final Girl's maternal responsibilities are combined with elements of the supernatural in the mother avenger cycle). However, it is upon less overtly heroic females that attention now turns, young women who, while extraordinary in their own ways, do not possess the ability to survive that is granted to the Final Girl. Female maturation remains a key question, including painful initiations into adulthood. The victim/villain axis of femininity is explored in greater depth, together with the question of female power, its perceived abuse, and accompanying containment. Beyond the slasher, and its hymn to virtue, lie narrative explorations of witches and werewolves, and themes involving infatuation, jealousy, and rage – emotions and experiences that are equally vital to understanding how contemporary horror has conceived impending womanhood, and the shadowy fate it yields.

3
Maternal Monsters and Motherly Mentors: Failed Initiations in *Carrie* and *Carrie II*

> The girl's relationship with her mother remains forever unresolved, incomplete. In heterosexuality she is forced to turn away from her primary love object and is destined never to return to it.
>
> – E. Ann Kaplan[1]

> Please see that I'm not like you mama!
>
> – Carrie White to her mother, *Carrie*

Described by one critic as 'a straightforward Cinderella story with a twist',[2] it is the 'twist' itself that makes *Carrie* (1976) such an interesting take on the familiar tale of a young woman's desire to transcend her difficulties and achieve a better life for herself, as telekinesis is substituted for magic in this version, and no happy ending is provided. This chapter asks how the film, and its later sequel, subvert the ideas epitomised within 'Cinderella' in terms of female aspiration and initiation, arguing that, in terms of mother figures, female rivals, and romantic interests, *Carrie* provides a curious retelling of the fairy tale, from an altogether more cynical perspective.

The film opens with school misfit, Carrie White (Sissy Spacek) starting her first period in the school shower. The cowering, terrified, uncomprehending young woman is pelted with sanitary towels by jeering classmates and then slapped by her sports teacher, who shouts at her: 'Now grow up! Stand up and take care of yourself!' The first sign of Carrie's new-found power is to make a light-bulb shatter overhead, miraculously turning the teacher into a sympathetic mentor who soothingly strokes her hair. From this moment on, Carrie will indeed attempt to 'grow up' and assert herself, and is given a number of helpers and hindrances in this task, including the teacher, who takes it upon herself to guide her charge through the trials of puberty. Ultimately, however, Carrie fails to be initiated into womanhood, and dies by the end of the film, taking her tormentors – and the teacher – with her.

It is this spectacular failure to be accepted (indeed, even to survive) that makes the film so interesting, exemplifying as it does the monstrous nature of an unbridled female power. As we shall see, its protagonist is caught between two contrasting perceptions of womanhood offered by very different mother figures; one promoting apparent liberation through romance, the other intense repression and denial – neither of which are adequate to help her realise her unique abilities. *Carrie*'s unhappy ending reveals the failure of both models, and exposes the extent to which existing constructions of 'femininity' are themselves deeply flawed.

The senior prom serves as the contemporary equivalent of the fairy tale ball – and should mark our heroine's transcendence – yet ends in a blood-bath; the date Carrie has imagined to be her prince charming is knocked out with an upturned bucket; and both the teacher serving as fairy godmother and the menacing mother she seeks to escape each die at her hands – along with the romantic myth that is effectively demolished by the end of the film, thereby radically rewriting the traditional 'Cinderella' story. Yet perhaps the most astonishing deviation of all is the transformation our protagonist undergoes, making the transition from shy schoolgirl to pretty princess and, ultimately, a female fury. *Carrie* is, in fact, a Cinderella story with a number of twists, as this exploration will reveal.

Narratively, the film updates 'Cinderella' within a contemporary setting, one in which the ineffectual father is written out of the story, the girl's biological mother is the one tormenting her – rather than a 'wicked' replacement, and the ugly sisters are transmuted into bitchy schoolgirls. In addition, the heroine's response to her experiences are more realistically developed via emotions that encompass not only pain, frustration, and shame, but also, ultimately, rage – that most censured of female emotions. Carrie's late menstruation becomes a potent symbol of her finally beginning the journey to womanhood, marking the emergence of a new power that allows her to begin standing up for herself.

It is only when she starts her period, and finally understands, through her new mentor, what is happening to her, that she begins to realise how her mother has deceived her. Carrie bravely reproaches her: 'You should have told me, Mama!' – followed by a pitiable attempt to gain her sympathy by explaining how the other girls laughed at her ignorance. Although this admission is met with aggression, it nonetheless signifies an important turning point in their relations. Now that she is also becoming a woman Carrie begins to see her mother with adult eyes, acknowledges her failings, and starts the arduous task of trying to differentiate herself from her. She even attempts to rebuff her fervent religious beliefs, saying 'no' when her mother tries to imbue her with feelings of shame towards her own sex. Convinced as she is that the onset of menses implies that her daughter has had 'sinful' thoughts, Margaret White (Piper Laurie) incarnates the irrational misogyny of Christian rhetoric, and tries to indoctrinate her daughter in the same manner. Despite her initial protests, Carrie finally repeats the incantation, 'Eve was weak', in order to appease her mother, and it is this warped view of women as inherently corrupt and threatening that will partially be corroborated in her eventual transformation. In the shifting power relations that follow between mother and daughter, Carrie changes from a submissive child to a defiant teenager and, ultimately, an altogether more frightening figure, turning the tables on the woman who has stifled her development – even as she fulfils her monstrous image of womanhood.

Carrie's difficult relationship with her mother lends great pathos to the unfolding narrative, describing a conflict that has been made familiar through a number of fairy tales. 'Snow White' has often been viewed as a template for fractured mother–daughter relations during adolescence, providing a wicked stepmother who resents her foster daughter's existence and does not want her to grow up, primarily because she threatens to displace her position as 'fairest of them all'. Their lack of blood ties is used to explain the murderous hatred that results, freeing the queen from any maternal affiliations. For Margaret White, however, it is the very fact that Carrie is her biological daughter that creates resentment towards her, being a living reminder of her 'sinfulness' – even in procreation – and the pleasure she took from having sex. Far from wishing to be the most beautiful woman in the land, she has an equally unrealisable aim: that of purity. However, she can never attain the virtuous state the Bible has foreclosed against women, which necessarily demands that Carrie herself can never mature and become a woman in her own right. Indeed, just as Snow White's stepmother attempts to eradicate her, Margaret White endeavours to kill her daughter in the film's climax, yet is killed by Carrie instead. Tanya Krzywinska has argued that 'it is common for teenagers to exact a fantasy revenge on a mother for her disciplinary actions by imagining, for example, that she is an evil witch bent on the persecution of an innocent'.[3] The film may adopt the narrative perspective of the abused daughter, and present Margaret

White as a cruel monster, yet there is no sense of triumph for Carrie in her mother's death, only loss, and it is additionally significant that she cannot bear the thought of living without her.

The fairy tale's exploration of a troubled mother–daughter relationship has conventionally been seen as a means of preparing children for an inevitable separation from their mothers, one that is necessary for maturation; a reading that our analysis of the slasher may be seen to corroborate, with Nancy and Sidney each having to lose their mothers, it is implied, to become fully adult. The 'bad mother' archetype has also been critically perceived as a means of psychologically acknowledging the fact that mothers are imperfect, and potentially capable of cruelty or selfishness – an acknowledgement that may be seen as helping in the task of separation. Negative characterisations of the mother have become a mainstay of fairy tales, it is argued, because they tap into universal experiences in our development, and they have also provided horror with one of its most enduring narratives.

From *Psycho*'s Mrs Bates to various other maternal figures the genre has given us over the years, if the mother is not abusing alcohol or drugs, or otherwise absorbed in herself, she inflicts damage on her children through over-involvement in their lives. Significantly, many such characters are single mothers who are shown to be unfit in some way. Although heroic examples also exist, as we have seen, they generally attempt to define themselves against poor predecessors, showing that they will not repeat the same mistakes. It is because mothers tend to be presented as excessive, destructive, or distorted individuals, often providing a convenient hate figure for audiences to focus on, that we need to look closer at what these stories say about female identity and power – and specifically the daughter's story in these scenarios – particularly in terms of finding an appropriate role model to follow.

The prominence of the bad mother in horror has led a number of theorists to argue that it is a resentment of maternal power in the early stages of our development that is played out in these scenarios. As is typical within psychoanalytic analysis of this kind, the focus tends to be placed upon male subjectivity. Accordingly, Barbara Creed draws on Julia Kristeva's theories of 'abjection' in assessing horror's images of maternity as a reflection of male fears. The 'abject' is a term which Kristeva applies to ideas and images that fail to 'respect borders, positions, rules', and consequently disturb 'identity, system, order'.[4] Abjection is therefore a means of identifying difference, and creating monstrosity, of justifying the exclusion of particular subjects within the 'symbolic order'. Those who fall outside the perceived classification system are deemed Other, and the example typically used by Kristeva, and reiterated by Creed, is the mother's body.

Despite attempting to use a psychoanalytic approach for feminist purposes, the result is highly problematic, not least in terms of threatening to entrench the very ideas that are seemingly opposed. Female 'Otherness' becomes normalised through 'the abject', rendered explicable even as it is exaggerated. Furthermore, and equally frustratingly, female subjectivity tends to be ignored altogether in the prominence given to an assumed male audience. Mothers are not seen through the eyes of a hypothetical daughter, but an imagined son – with attendant inconsistencies evident therein. Freud's Oedipal theory, for example, argues that all boys feel sexually attracted to their mothers and resent their fathers accordingly, while his Castration theory asserts that mothers are feared because they lack a penis, and that boys possess a subconscious belief that their mothers intend to remove this item from them. These theories not only conflict with one another, they also remain highly contestable, and although Creed attempts to reinterpret castration fears, she still assumes that it is the threat of powerful women that principally motivates horror.

Following Kristeva, Creed contends that the mother is used in horror cinema to evoke repressed male anxieties. The genre supposedly reveals 'the abject at work' and invites the audience to 'eject the abject',[5] with maternal figures used as a central target. Various examples are assessed in Creed's analysis, including *Psycho* and *Carrie*, in which she claims that 'the maternal figure is constructed as the monstrous-feminine',[6] asserting that, in refusing to allow their children to grow up and attempting to induce feelings of shame, sexual repression leads to deviance – with each mother warping her child's development.

In fact, both figures are near-parodies of traditional psychoanalytic tendencies towards maternal blame, their offspring demonstrating the disastrous consequences of over-identification in a society that encourages both emotional and physical separation. If Norman's psychotic persona is explained through being unable to differentiate himself from his mother, or the guilt that she has apparently induced within him, Carrie also fails to transcend her mother's repressive influence. Far from confirming the monstrosity of the mother, might such characterisations not be used to question why such demonisation takes place, and what impact this potentially has? The mother's suggested role in forming subjectivity has provoked much interest within psychoanalysis, and it is particularly notable that women have been taught to disassociate from their mothers both as a means of entering the patriarchal order and as a means of asserting their feminism. Nancy Chodorow's *The Reproduction of Mothering: Psychoanalysis and the Sociology of Gender* (1975) and Nancy Friday's *My Mother, My Self: The Daughter's Search for Identity* (1988), for example, each argue that women must evaluate the role their mothers have played in shaping their identities and expectations in order to break free from repeating negative models. If fairy tales work to underline the need for separation from our mothers as we mature, such writers insist upon the same project, yet how we define a positive model of femininity remains pressing, particularly given the fact that virtuous womanhood is usually defined through sacrifice, both in the fairy tale and beyond.

Counterbalancing the 'wicked stepmother' in such stories as 'Snow White' and 'Cinderella' are mothers who avoid criticism through their death, many of whom, in their early versions at least, subsequently reappear in their children's lives via supernatural means. Whether the split between good and bad incarnations is motivated by psychological or actual historical factors, the resulting narratives are especially interesting in the contrasting representations of motherhood provided, and the conflicts that are detailed between women. These motifs often resurface in horror films, particularly in terms of female rivalry, yet the distinction made between maternal virtue and villainy has also been increasingly questioned within the genre. Indeed, despite three decades since its release, one of the most interesting aspects of *Carrie* is that it rejects both mother figures presented.

As Kristeva and Creed have noted, horror cinema is keen to explore the fascination and anxiety generated by monstrous females, yet these figures may inspire more than revulsion, potentially allowing us to re-evaluate the values they attempt to shore up. Although Lucy Fischer has argued that motherhood in cinema has always been a 'site of crisis', with mothers either blamed or absented altogether, she also notes that the horror film *Rosemary's Baby* (1968) provides an opportunity to express legitimate female concerns surrounding pregnancy.[7] While Fischer opts to explore what this film has to say about a young woman's sense of powerlessness during impending motherhood, the two films examined in this chapter are used to ask what happens when marginalised females acquire power, in what ways do their failed attempts at normalcy challenge cultural expectations, and to what extent are they accordingly deemed monstrous?

Carrie White and her half-sister, Rachael – who appears in the sequel *Carrie II: The Rage* (1999) – are outcasts who clearly inspire more than fear and loathing. They are given mothers who pointedly fail to nurture them, acquire mentors whose well-intended advice backfires, and undergo transformations that subvert the ideals by which we usually measure the female coming-of-age parable immortalised by the likes of 'Cinderella'. If Rosemary's ordeal provides an opportunity to see maternity from the perspective of a disempowered young woman, one whose attempts to gain control over her pregnancy avowedly fail, Carrie and Rachael explode other myths in their exploration of female identity and empowerment, refuting the fantasy that a benign mother figure will initiate them into womanhood, or that romance will alleviate all their troubles. In their thematic exploration of familial disharmony, social alienation, and female rivalry, they not only update and rewrite 'Cinderella', they also touch upon areas that will resurface in other texts explored in this book, with *Carrie* serving as an important textual touchstone that has been continually revisited.

The fact that both figures are 'gifted' with telekinesis – the ability to move objects with one's mind – is viewed as a symbolic manifestation of inner power that is offered as a form of compensation for the relative deprivations of their upbringing, not least in terms of the mother each has been given. However, while they struggle to assert themselves, their ability to control this power is also tested in each narrative, twisting the traditional 'Cinderella' tale out of shape as they each ultimately fail their initiations in becoming women, yet also providing a powerful criticism of the ideals that inform a female coming-of-age.

Carrie charts the remarkable transformation of 16-year-old high-school student, Carrie White; an ill-treated misfit, tormented both at home and at school, who ultimately exacts revenge in spectacular fashion through an ability that arrives with the onset of puberty. If Laurie Strode is portrayed as a sexual innocent, then Carrie's total lack of knowledge, even about female physiology, takes such innocence to disturbing new dimensions. As the film's opening sequence makes clear, her first period terrifies her into thinking that she is bleeding to death – a terror that is greeted with mocking humiliation by her female peers. However, while the film conspicuously targets female animosity as a whole, it is Carrie's relationship with her mother, and the effect this has on a sensitive and deeply insecure young woman, that makes the story both moving and disturbing.

Margaret White is one of cinema's most memorable depictions of the mad mother, with insane eyes, unruly hair, and incessant ranting. Religious to the point of mania, she believes sex to be a sinful act and curses the day her daughter was conceived. Abandoned by her husband, Ralph, Margaret was left to raise Carrie on her own, and openly abuses the power she has over her. Caught within the confines of her mother's religious belief, Carrie is punished for every perceived misdeed with psychological and physical abuse, being locked in a closet-cum-shrine under the stairs for hours at a time. Indeed, her life closely resembles a living hell, with a hate-filled dominating mother at home and peers that routinely deride her at school, yet this changes in the few days charted in the film's narrative, for with her first menstruation comes a realisation of who she really is, and an awareness of the exceptional power in her grasp.

Telekinesis is a mysterious psychic phenomenon which Carrie seemingly acquires in order to compound her difference from other girls. However, it can also be seen as a metaphor of empowerment, for it is in discovering this ability that she takes her first steps in resisting the wrongs that have been made against her.[8] She begins by putting her mother in her place when she attempts to bar her from attending the school prom, reminding her, with a demonstration of her new power, that she is no longer under her control. Carrie's decision to go is prompted by two events that boost her self-esteem: being asked to attend by a boy she likes and reading about telekinesis in the school library – events that significantly occur within moments of each other. While her new abilities vindicate her sense of uniqueness, and allow her to defend herself against her mother, it is the chance of normalcy suggested by the prom that motivates her most. Believing that the devil is working through her daughter, Margaret White implores her to resist, stating: 'You must renounce this power. You must give it up. You must never use it.' Her daughter is calmly adamant in her response: 'I'm going mama. You can't stop me. I don't wanna talk about it any more.'

Writing in respect to the slasher, Vera Dika has observed that events such as 'Halloween, prom night, graduation day and fraternity initiation rituals actually form the basic situation of many of the films.'[9] The prom's significance in marking the assumption of adulthood is nowhere more powerfully presented than in *Carrie*, where it forms the equivalent of the ball where Cinderella reveals herself in all her glory. Perhaps more importantly, as an inversion of this tale, the prom reveals the fallacy behind the idea that the accoutrements of femininity (having the right dress, hair, make-up, and date) are the only desirable goals for a woman – and this is what makes it such an important revisionist fable.

Having denied her daughter any understanding of the world because she sees it as intrinsically sinful, Mrs White is clearly reluctant to allow her to go to the prom, cruelly laughing at her preparations for this event, and even attempting to physically prevent her attendance on the night – an attempt her daughter is now able to curtail with a simple demonstration of her growing powers. Equally important is the fact that Carrie has a crucial ally in Miss Collins (Betty Buckley), the high-school gym instructor who comes to her defence in the shower at the beginning of the film, who later seeks revenge on her behalf through her position at the school, and who attempts to give Carrie the confidence and self-respect she lacks. She thus acquires a sympathetic mentor who genuinely seems to care for her, and who endeavours to offer an alternative image of womanhood to that presented by Mrs White. While her mother punishes her for having her first period, insists that she wears dowdy home-made dresses, and attempts to prevent her from going to the prom, Miss Collins tries to bolster Carrie's self-image by informing her that she is a 'pretty girl', suggests that she do more to improve her appearance, and even oversees her first date.

In many ways then, Carrie has two mothers in the film, one who obstructs her journey to adulthood because she is filled with a pathological hatred towards women, as much as patent distrust of the 'unbelievers' in their midst, while the other attempts to encourage her to make more of herself physically and thus 'fit in' better with the other girls at school and their superficial world of dates and dances. Interestingly, an older woman is cast to play the teacher than is presented in the book, which gives her character added ramifications. Some have read her as a lonely figure whose reminiscences about her own first date on prom night are offset by her single status. Serafina Kent Bathrick, for example, labels her a 'lonely romantic' who is haunted by her inability to 'keep that high school sweetheart'.[10] The significance Miss Collins invests in prom night is made explicit when she punishes the other girls for bullying Carrie, threatening anyone planning to skip her detentions by withholding their prom tickets. As she knowingly states to the shocked group of girls: 'That would really get you where you live, wouldn't it?'

Like Mrs White, Miss Collins is alone, frustrated, and intent on ideas of punishment and redemption – which is partly fuelled by the sense of guilt she feels for having initially understood the girl's actions in reviling the outsider in their midst. It is in response to this guilt that she elects to help Carrie, yet events will prove that she is deluded in her belief that Carrie's main problem lies in how she looks.

Miss Collins attempts to instil her charge with feminine ideals by suggesting that she curl her hair, put on lipstick, and stand up straight, yet despite these ideas being followed to the letter they fail to provide a solution to Carrie's troubles. Shelley Stamp Lindsay suggests that the film consequently explodes the myth of femininity by proving it to be both misguided and untenable, asserting that 'promising Carrie a femininity achieved through good posture, lip gloss, and curls, the gym teacher offers the teenager a route to mature womanhood apparently free from the repression enforced by the girl's mother', yet deems the 'culturally sanctioned femininity' she proffers to be just as 'repressive' as her mother's puritanical beliefs, ultimately labelling her feminine aspirations to be a 'hopeless charade'.[11] Reynold Humphries is similarly suspicious of Miss Collins' motivations, arguing that although 'she is clearly maternal in the way she protects – or thinks she is protecting – Carrie, and therefore seems to function as the "good" mother as opposed to the "bad" mother. Just how good she is, however, is a moot point.'[12] In Humphries' view, in advising Carrie to make more of herself she simply turns her into an object of the 'male gaze' – arguing that she ultimately uses Carrie 'as a way of reinforcing her own narcissism', as well as supporting a 'masculine discourse' of female beauty.[13]

While her advice may ultimately be unhelpful, and is clearly intended to mould Carrie in her own image, Miss Collins nonetheless attempts to help her gain acceptance through what appears to be genuine concern for her, as well as seeking to appease her own conscience. Both book and film provide a key scene in which the teacher discusses Carrie's abuse by the other girls with the embarrassed headmaster, crucially admitting: 'I knew how they felt.' Underwriting this comment, although undisclosed to her boss, is an awareness of the fact that she physically attacked her charge, slapping her in her hour of need, seemingly due to the fact that, in reaching out to her, Carrie soiled her teacher's pristine white shorts with a bloody hand. It is guilt over this act that apparently motivates Miss Collins, who takes it upon herself to punish the other girls' cruelty as a means of making amends. Like Sue Snell (Amy Irving), who also feels a sense of contrition at the part she played in the shower room, and seeks to make up for it in both loaning her date and forfeiting her own attendance at the prom (thus sharing the role of fairy godmother), the 'good' woman is identified with having a conscience and being prepared to act on it – traits which, as we have seen, distinguish the Final Girl also.

Yet perhaps there is something more in Miss Collins' attitude than guilt alone, more than fear that she has acted unprofessionally, because she goes above and beyond the call of duty in punishing the girls' wrongdoing. The shower scene seems to be a pivotal moment for Miss Collins, as much as Carrie, as her ability to nurture and protect another person is initially found wanting, resulting in a noticeable change in her after this event. A girl like Carrie White would never have met with the tough gym instructor's approval through excelling at sports, but makes a more intense connection on another level, gaining her sympathy and friendship. While Miss Collins admits to identifying more readily with the other girls, she also endeavours to distance herself from them, and offers Carrie the protection and encouragement that she was initially incapable of. The fact that De Palma chose to cast an older actress to the naïve young teacher imagined by Stephen King adds an extra level of pathos to the fact that Miss Collins, clearly unmarried, and despite being an attractive woman still, seemingly has no life outside the school. The date she tells Carrie about, when serving as chaperone at the prom, is little more than a fond memory, yet one she elects to share with her charge as another romantic nudge in what she perceives to be the right direction. Even if the advice given to Carrie is ultimately unhelpful, her attitude towards her is infinitely more caring than her mother, whose desire to 'protect' her daughter is far more excessive than the zeal with which Collins presides over her detentions. Furthermore, although telling Carrie that she is a 'pretty girl' clearly subscribes to patriarchal values, by which women are judged by their physical attractiveness, it is a world-view that the film's narrative will fatally undermine.

The senior prom marks the end of school life and the succession to adulthood. For Carrie it is additionally significant because, although the occasion is intended to demonstrate her attempted graduation to normalcy, it ultimately confirms her radical difference to those around her. Thanks to Sue Snell, Carrie gets to go on a date with Tommy Ross (William Katt), the boy she has admired in English class, and, taking Miss Collins' advice, she prepares for the night by sewing a beautiful pink satin gown, curling her hair, and wearing lipstick. Seemingly the result of all this effort, as much as her shy innocence, is that Tommy appears genuinely attracted to her, and they share a touching kiss while they dance. Yet if she defies his expectations Carrie also discovers that her initial idea of Tommy is a sham. As they dance together she learns that he did not write the poem in class that she had considered 'beautiful'. Although surprised, and seemingly disappointed, when asked if this matters, she simply shakes her head and smiles. It is enough just to be with him. Carrie thus happily assumes the appropriate reaction of loyalty and unchecked devotion, appearing to have gleaned more from the women's magazines seemingly pored over in preparation for the big night than make-up tips alone. They appear perfect together and for the first time in the film she looks happy, as if this is the culmination of a long-desired fantasy, yet this is the calm before the storm, and if she is briefly allowed the 'Cinderella' dream of dancing with her prince, it is not long before events take a sudden turn.

While Miss Collins is juxtaposed against Mrs White as contrasting images of mature womanhood, two adolescent females continue the same doubling motif, and although Sue seeks atonement for her cruelty to Carrie by letting her take her place at the prom, the spoilt and spiteful Chris Hargensen (Nancy Allen) refuses to accept any such responsibility, is accordingly barred from the event, and seeks vengeance by aiming to humiliate Carrie still further. After being elected prom queen and king in a ballot that looks only partially rigged, to judge from the applause they receive, a malicious prank dreamed up by Chris serves to break the reverie when a pail of pig's blood is thrown over Carrie and her date, heralding yet another transformation as shock and betrayal turn to rage.

Carrie can be seen to wear two costumes on this fateful night. The pink satin dress, sewn herself, that earns her the admiration of both her classmates and her date, is a triumph of textbook femininity, along with the lipstick and curls that accompany her makeover. Yet the dramatic red hue this fairy tale gown acquires, with the addition of pig's blood, places Carrie in another league altogether – one which is no longer reliant on the approval of her peers, but which sets her apart as a woman they have all underestimated, and who proves this with the ferocious power unleashed.

The red filter and split screen are stylistic devices used to exacerbate the surreal quality of what transpires, yet a carousel shot of the laughing audience effectively deceives us. In King's novel, an eye-witness testimonial claims that everyone is complicit in laughing at the hapless couple.[14] In the film, however, something more subtle occurs as De Palma shows the onlookers both *through* Carrie's eyes and how they *actually* are. We thus experience the shock of apparently seeing Miss Collins laughing uproariously with other staff and pupils, yet this does not gel with earlier shots of the teacher looking upset for Carrie and moving sympathetically towards her, and there are also intercuts of one of Tommy's friends looking shocked and outraged at what he sees. De Palma thus shows that there were exceptions in the crowd who found nothing humorous in Carrie's plight, even if, in her embarrassment, anger, and dismay, Carrie is seemingly unable to distinguish them. Her mother's prophecy is deemed true and her warning – 'They're all gonna laugh at you!' – echoes in her ears amid the ensuing carnage to reinforce her sense of being unanimously vilified. No one is spared, not even Miss Collins, and despite her earlier wistful recollections about her own prom, and the intimacy with Carrie that led Billy to comment about her trying to steal his date, Miss Collins meets a particularly grisly death via Carrie's telekinetic powers, as if she has let her down more than anyone.[15]

Having dispensed with one (apparently false) mother figure, as well as killing the majority of pupils and staff at the school, Carrie returns home, seeking comfort from her mother. She runs a cold bath, washes the blood off herself, dons a childish night-gown, and kneels to pray with renewed reverence and compliance with her mother's wishes. Pitiably, however, Mrs White has nothing but further violence to offer her daughter, in the form of a large knife with which she intends to sacrifice her to God, viciously plunging it into her back as she kneels. In shocked reaction, Carrie then kills her mother in grand guignol style, impaling her with knives in the same cruciform pose as the Christ statue to which she was so often forced to pray. Immediately consumed with guilt over this, Carrie lets out a heart-rending cry of 'Mama!' as the foundations of the house begin to self-destruct. Her power is finally used to destroy herself as, rather than flee outside into a world that has tormented her, she drags her mother's corpse into the punishment cupboard, either to protect them both from the falling masonry, or to meet their maker together. Carrie is thus killed, just as she became more than a mere victim, like a monster who cannot survive the threat it poses. However, while it may be argued that her death is used to punish female aberrance, it may also be seen as an indictment of those who tormented her, for the true monster of the text is the ignorance of an entire community, including her mother, for treating her as they have.

Ultimately, the film can be read in a number of ways: as part of horror's usual denunciation of the dysfunctional family (Tony Williams); as a sympathetic portrayal of a misunderstood 'monster' (Robin Wood); or as a misogynistic reaction against womanhood in which menstruation (and being female) is truly shown to be a 'curse' (Serafina Bathrick). In some ways all these readings are accurate because Carrie's upbringing is as blameworthy as the small-minded school crowd responsible for triggering her rage. Even Bathrick's evaluation has a degree of truth as it is female figures that are principally targeted as villainous, yet there are also more favourable examples, such as Sue Snell and Miss Collins, and I would contend that there are feminist gains to be found in the film, particularly in perceiving Carrie's transformation as a rite of passage that allows her to try on the traditionally approved model of virtuous and desirable femininity only to show its ineffectuality. In the contrasting images offered the film exposes the animosities that exist between women, with female characters simplistically delineated as good and bad, yet Carrie herself defies this simple dichotomy as, far

from being portrayed as evil, she is a pitiable figure whose transformation into a force to be reckoned with, no matter how short-lived,
provides a radical wish-fulfilment for any audience members that might
identify with her situation. Even if Carrie is not allowed to survive, she
nevertheless represents a dramatic breaching of borders – even beyond
that permitted the Final Girl – as, rather than neatly becoming initiated
within the conventional realm of maturity offered by Sue Snell and Miss
Collins, she disrupts these conventions where they stand.

The film's impact on horror would have long-lasting repercussions,
not least in focusing on a female misfit's tribulations at school, and
a range of ideas concerning class and gender would also be reprised
in subsequent narratives. The Whites are not only poor, they seemingly live in another era. Their house is a simple wooden shack that
is notably up for sale, while their clothes are home-made and equally
old-fashioned. Although she is a single parent struggling to make ends
meet, little sympathy is offered to Margaret White, whose only apparent
contact with her neighbours is going from door to door selling religious
pamphlets and preaching of the Apocalypse to come. She is a repel-
lent image of mental instability and religious fervour later emulated in
similar characters found in 'soft horror' examples such as *The Witches of
Eastwick* (1987) and *Edward Scissorhands* (1990), with Felicia (Veronica
Cartwright) and Esmeralda (O-Lan Jones) both stemming from the same
mould in their pious, hostile, and accusatory natures.[16] Equally repel-
lent is Carrie's school nemesis, Chris, whose lack of morality is given
some economic explanation in the novel. When Chris is slapped by the
gym teacher during detention, her lawyer father reveals a similar tendency towards bullying, threatening to sue the school for reprimanding
his daughter. Unlike Mrs White's excessive and unmerited punishments
there is no sense of shame regarding his daughter's conduct, and no
discipline seemingly required in her upbringing, with the accompanying
notion that the rich can behave as they want to. All that survives in
the film version in terms of this economic discrepancy is the contrast
between the White house and the elaborate property belonging to Sue
Snell's family – partially explained by reference to her father being a
doctor – as well as the cosy domesticity of the Snell family meal prior to
the fateful prom. Chris's father is notably removed as a figure of blame,
with no mention made of a mother, leaving her cruelty inexplicable.

Situated as the most positive female figure in the film, Sue serves
as a symbol of morality and conscience in her attempt at contrition.
She also demonstrates an interesting degree of foresight in perceiving,
and attempting to unmask, the plot hatched by Chris in humiliating

Carrie at the prom (an attempt Miss Collins rashly misinterprets, ejecting Sue from the premises and thus unwittingly saving her life, while also allowing the tragedy to unfold). In contrast to Sue, Chris thinks she is beyond reproach in engineering Carrie's downfall, and seemingly feels no pity for her at all. Interestingly, she also seems to have a penchant for bad boys who treat her with contempt, suggesting a masochistic streak in her otherwise callous demeanour. In line with the moral code under-written in the film, Chris dies while Sue Snell survives, although she is tormented with nightmares after having lost virtually everyone she cared about, aside from her family. Indeed, some have argued that Sue's family, although clearly more affluent than Carrie's, is not without prob-lems of its own. When visited by Mrs White earlier in the narrative, her mother is seen drinking in the middle of the afternoon as she watches daytime soaps, hurriedly paying her off with a 'donation' in order to be rid of her. Tony Williams asserts that: 'Sue Snell's mother (Priscilla Pointer) presents no positive image . . . her solitary afternoon drinking and light-headed attitude reveal her to be an ineffectual parent.'[17] This is seemingly confirmed by the fact that Sue is inconsolable when Mrs Snell attempts to comfort her in the film's closing scene, saying 'It's all right. I'm here' – as her daughter continues to scream.

Although Mrs Snell unconvincingly affirms that Sue is young enough to eventually forget her trauma, Carrie is fated never to grow up, never to have sexual relations, or a child of her own, and thus escapes having to prove herself as a mother. Her legacy endures, however, in similar misfit characters that have appeared in recent cinema and television, not to mention the sequel *Carrie II: The Rage* (1999) which presents her with a much younger half-sister, Rachael (Emily Bergl), in order to continue the theme two decades later.

Although they are born of different mothers, Rachael is condemned to have a similarly unhappy upbringing. With a father she never knew and a mother who is in an asylum, she is adopted by a neglectful 'white trash' couple and becomes a depressed teenage Goth.[18] She is saved from isolation at school through having a like-minded friend, Lisa (Mena Suvari), yet she commits suicide at the outset of the film, leading to a chain of events in which Rachael, now alone like older sister Carrie, ulti-mately learns of her own dormant powers. As a plot necessity to explain the sisters' link, telekinesis is said to be inherited from their mutual father, Ralph, yet it is the maternal line that is stressed in King's novel, and which is largely emphasised in the host of narratives about female powers that have followed. Partly because of its tenuous explanation of her powers, as much as the derivative nature of its plot, *Carrie II* is at best a dismal unimaginative film compared with the original and looks like a crude attempt to cash in on the revival of interest in horror wrought by *Scream*, yet if Clover is correct in asserting that all horror sequels are, in fact, re-makes, then closer analysis is quite revealing, particularly in the way in which it serves as a thematic bridge to later films.[19] In fact, a number of female telekinesis films followed *Carrie*, including *The Fury* (1978), *Firestarter* (1984), and *Friday the 13th VII: The New Blood* (1988), with *Carrie II* serving as one of the most obvious, and lacklustre, examples.

Perhaps the film's most interesting element is that Amy Irving reprises her role as Sue Snell, who is now a counsellor at Rachael's school. We learn that Sue had to be admitted to a mental hospital in the events that followed Carrie's blood-bath, and that she is still haunted by what happened. (A similar fate occurs to Laurie Strode after her ordeal in *Halloween*, while Nancy's work at a mental hospital for disturbed teenagers in *Nightmare III* is also possibly a reference.) As a response to her experiences Sue is determined to help others and, offering a parallel of the relationship between Miss Collins and Carrie, she becomes the equivalent of a mentor to Carrie's half-sister, and the nearest thing Rachael has to a mature female she can relate to. Rachael is much tougher and more cynical than Carrie, stating in her English class that she does not believe in love, and even writes her half-sister off as an urban myth.

Sue: You've heard of Carrie White, haven't you?
Rachael: Supposedly she set the fire as some sort of revenge-suicide thing, Elvis was her date, and they escaped in a UFO.

Rachael learns the truth about her sister from Sue, who is anxious that history should not repeat itself, yet, once again, fails to avoid tragedy. Reluctant to believe her, Rachael seeks conformity as a means of dealing with her grief for Lisa, yet in trying to be like other girls, and overcome her misfit status, she embarks on a relationship with one of the high-school jocks implicated in her friend's death, Jesse Ryan (Jason London), losing her virginity to him. Seemingly befriended by the school in-crowd, she is then lured to a 'frat' party – the contemporary equivalent of the prom – only to be humiliated with the knowledge that her new boyfriend has only slept with her in order to add her name to a list, making her part of the very same game that effectively made her best friend kill herself.

For all its relative failings *Carrie II* derides the male culture in high school, and the class system that supports it, as blameworthy. With the same commitment as Miss Collins before her, Sue Snell tries to force the school principal into criminally prosecuting the boys implicated in Lisa's death, arguing that, as they engaged in underage sex, they are guilty of statutory rape, yet the school authorities are reluctant to press charges because of the boys' affluent parentage and their status as school sports stars. Rachael sets about teaching them a lesson because no one else is prepared to, but only undertakes this mission when she herself has been placed in the same humiliated position as Lisa. The ridicule she faces at the frat party incenses Rachael, and she kills the assembled jeerers as well as Sue Snell (who is locked outside, vainly trying to intervene once again, yet is impaled through the door by the very person she is seeking to help). Rachael then tries to eliminate Jesse, yet the film cannot allow her to maintain this murderous anger against him and adds a dubious romanticism in order to let Jesse off the hook. He is spared because the video he made of them in bed together, which happens to be playing in the background when she confronts him, has the all-important detail of showing him whisper 'I love you' while she is asleep. Seeing this tender moment on screen makes her realise that Jesse's love was pure after all, yet the house starts to fall down as a result of the destruction her rage has already unleashed, and her final act is to save him before she herself dies, like her similarly ill-fated sister, amid the ruins caused by her fury. However, in perhaps the corniest ending imaginable, particularly given the famous shock ending to *Carrie*, Rachael returns to haunt him, romantically living on in Jesse's memory as a love that could never be. Arriving as a ghostly presence a year later, in his university bedroom, in a scene reminiscent of *Wuthering Heights*, her image glides towards him alluringly . . . only to shatter the moment after he kisses her.

Although it is a very pale shadow of its predecessor, *Carrie II* similarly suggests that normalcy lies in getting it together with a boy – even as it refuses its protagonist any lasting romance with the object of her devotion. It also contains the same themes of parental neglect, yet while Carrie's mother was tyrannical in the control she had over her daughter, Rachael's biological parents are notable in their absence. Her foster-parents are reminiscent of the trashy dead-beats given to the young John Connor in *Terminator 2* (1991), neither appearing to care about what she is going through, or inquiring into what she does. The notion of ineffectual adults at school is equally apparent. Sue Snell may be well-meaning in trying to counsel Rachael but her efforts to help her, like Miss Collins' endeavours with Carrie, ultimately backfire. The school is again shown to be run in the interests of a corrupt patriarchy. Just as

Chris Hargensen believed she was above school discipline because her father was a rich lawyer, the boys linked to Lisa's suicide are excused the crime of having underage sex because they are prominent athletes for the school, with equally prominent parents. Sue's attempts to vindicate Lisa's death thus prove futile in a climate where class issues may never be explicitly stated, yet have a profound effect on the status of differing pupils nonetheless.

However, despite some progressive elements, the film is more intent on a conservative denouement than its predecessor. The former misfit quickly finds romance to replace the close female friendship so recently lost, and problematically forgives her beau the part he played in using other girls sexually, because his avowal of love for her supposedly proves that he is different to the rest. Furthermore, although her latent power allows her to punish the in-crowd for humiliating her, there seems little justification in this act of genocide, for Rachael was never as deeply unpopular, or tormented, as big sister Carrie, and grants Jesse a reprieve that no one else is allowed. The implication made is that a 'mad mother' – represented as a paranoid schizophrenic – and the telekinetic powers supposedly acquired from her father have each provided her with a doomed inheritance, and like her equally ill-fated sister, she pays for her transgression and hasty temper with her life. That she was propelled to her fate partly because of her friend's suicide is notable, for while Carrie was singularly without friends, isolated from everyone around her, much like her mother, Rachael's closeness to Lisa is shown to have created an important source of ballast against heedless foster parents and the hostilities of fellow adolescents, the absence of which leads to her greater vulnerability – and a relatively undiscerning interest in getting herself a boyfriend.

That school-life is just as nasty and adolescence remains an equally arduous experience three decades on is scarcely any surprise, yet it is also notable how much this subject has increased in popularity since *Carrie* was first released. While *Carrie II* greatly resembles an unimaginative exploitation vehicle, it contains many elements that would be further explored in successive narratives. Among the prominent themes revised are the dilemmas experienced with dawning maturity: including the conflicts faced in trying to balance conformity with individuality; the struggle to come to terms with dysfunctional family relations; the fight against low self-worth; and the attempt to negotiate both the tenuous nature of female friendships and relationships with boys – both of which cause evident problems. Above all, the journey undertaken to achieve a sense of self-realisation becomes a key feature of numerous narratives involving female misfits, assessing the available options and obstacles faced on the path to adulthood, while allowing an aberrant female agency to be briefly glimpsed, yet also decisively curtailed.

As we shall see, the mother remains a potent image in horror narratives, including more positive portrayals of mothers as a source of empowerment, rather than the negative figures we have mostly looked at thus far. While the spectre of maternal monstrosity serves as a means of presenting females exceeding permitted bounds, the final chapter will examine how maternal figures have become invested with a heroic capacity in more recent films. It additionally evaluates changing trends in the representation of female rage – which remains a constant concern in the chapters to follow – generally represented as a highly disapproved of emotion, yet with some very interesting exceptions. Burgeoning female identity and power remain a central preoccupation in teen horror, as we shall see, with specific 'gifts' and abilities being both championed and punished. *Carrie*'s legacy is thus interestingly revised by the narratives that follow, yet the extent to which female kinship is frequently undermined by sexual jealousy, competition, and conflict remains most notable. Indeed, if the neglectful, abusive, or otherwise flawed mother is taken off the hook or moved to the background in later narratives, female rivalry between peers is shown to be a far greater menace than any other factor. The extent to which women are represented as either empowered or cursed is accordingly questioned, for just as a latent 'rage' haunts Carrie and her half-sister (almost as much as their dysfunctional upbringing), the powers given to other adolescent females are either validated or repudiated in interesting ways. The host of expectations that surround growing up female are thus assessed, particularly as an emerging sexuality is seen to cause conflict between women.

Writing in reference to the two symbolic mothers presented in *Carrie*, Bathrick argues that 'neither Miss Collins nor Carrie's mother feel anything but loathing for the sexual awakening that takes place among the adolescent girls who surround them. Their mistrust forms the basis on which we are asked to accept the impossibility of positive female relationships.'[20] It is a reading that I would contend with respect to Miss Collins, as she seems more than happy to guide Carrie through her perceived understanding of sexual awakening, yet her single status and carefully preserved white shorts also suggest a certain level of prudishness that might be equated with Mrs White's heightened repression, with both women exhibiting an intense sense of frustration that is focused, in differing ways, upon Carrie. That she ultimately eliminates both the wicked mother and seemingly treacherous godmother is seemingly due to the fact that each has apparently failed her, offering a fable in which maternal monsters and motherly mentors are both proved to be lacking.

It is additionally interesting, in yet another twist of this 'Cinderella' story, that romance is replaced by revenge as the dominant motif, with Tommy Ross ultimately figuring as quite an insignificant figure, who Carrie ceases to give another thought to once he is knocked unconscious – perhaps even regarding him as being complicit in her humiliation. While Sue Snell is the sole person to escape Carrie's wrath, this is shown to be more by luck than design. Sue's sense of compassion and concern are further demonstrated in the sequel, when she subsequently meets and befriends Carrie's half-sister, yet her attempts to help Rachael to both acknowledge and control her powers ultimately fail. Like Miss Collins before her, she cannot help her charge, and similarly pays with her life. Rachael, it seems, must repeat the same fate as her sister – and confirm the falsity of placing one's faith in the redemptive power of conformity – a fate which also ends in her death, and which no maternal mentor can seemingly help her avoid.

While this chapter has presented failed initiations into socially approved womanhood, the next chapter looks in greater detail at young women who prefer to remain at the margins, rather than join the herd, and revel in their outsider status. It evaluates the camaraderie and comfort that is briefly formed through female friendships, as well as the animosity and conflict that invariably emerges, both uniting and fatally dividing the misfit sisters that follow.

4
Misfit Sisters: Female Kinship and Rivalry in *The Craft* and *Ginger Snaps*

> But when will women really come into their own power, or when will the evidence of this power be felt?... Where, oh where, is the camaraderie, the much vaunted mutual support among women?
>
> – Molly Haskell, *From Reverence to Rape*[1]

> You know, in the old days, if a witch betrayed her coven, they would kill her.
>
> – Nancy, *The Craft*

The previous chapter evaluated two misfit sisters in *Carrie* (1976) and its sequel *Carrie II: The Rage* (1999), who, despite never knowing one another, are fated to lead similar lives. Both are hampered by a 'dysfunctional' upbringing in which each is abandoned by the same father and cursed with a different 'mad' mother. Telekinesis is discovered with the onset of puberty and serves to compensate for the additional suffering these characters experience at school; making them a force to be reckoned with, yet also proving to be their undoing. A thwarted rite of passage is thus set forth, in which each heroine seeks to transcend her difficulties, yet expires upon doing so. Despite the narrative sympathy extended towards them – and the obvious pleasure taken in the vengeance unleashed against their antagonists – their powers are decisively curtailed, along with their lives. The potential mode of identification fostered is thus odd indeed, seeming to advance and then withdraw approval in a manner that appears both confused and contradictory. Both outsiders fail in their attempts to fit into the status quo, and while some idea of female kinship is suggested, the nastiness that triggers their fatal rage destroys any hopes of belonging.

The cruelty of adolescence, particularly in terms of bitchy girls and sexually manipulative boys, would become a prominent theme in horror films and TV series during the 1990s. Haskell's question, cited above, and framed very much as a lament, becomes increasingly pronounced in such texts, with female power and the very notion of 'camaraderie' frequently undermined by sexual rivalry and a narrative impetus towards punishing 'wayward' girls. The difficulties of establishing female solidarity, and the greater tendency to depict women in competition with one another, is one of the main concerns governing this chapter, drawing parallels between two key films in order to re-evaluate Haskell's question.

As we shall see, similar themes are explored in *The Craft* (1996) and *Ginger Snaps* (2000) such as teen suicide, the uncertainty of female friendship, and boys that serve as a catalyst for rivalry. Supernatural powers enhance the degree of agency demonstrated by female leads, yet are also seen to be misused. The protagonists accordingly follow the legacy of the White sisters, to some extent, in their alienation and transgressions, and a fundamental question posed is whether they are equally seen to be cursed as much as celebrated by being 'different' from other girls, by having negligent or absent parents, indeed, simply by being female?

While normalcy and self-worth is falsely linked to forming a romantic relationship with boys in *Carrie* and *Carrie II*, the protagonists in *The Craft* gain a sense of mutual affirmation through their friendship with one another. Four misfit students unite to bolster their troubled egos. Sarah (Robin Tunney) is guilt-ridden due to her mother's death in childbirth; Nancy (Fairuza Balk) is inferred to have been sexually abused by her stepfather; Bonnie (Neve Campbell) is afflicted with scars from a childhood injury; and Rochelle (Rachel True) suffers racist taunts at school. Together they gain strength and acceptance, yet an intense rivalry soon forms between them – with a boy serving as a crucial divide. Far from providing us with four downtrodden heroines, as initially seems to be the case, *The Craft* places greatest sympathy with newcomer, Sarah, who undergoes several trials over the course of the film, including starting at a new school, a troubled relationship with high-school jock, Chris Taylor (Skeet Ulrich), and betrayal by her female friends. The film's title refers to witchcraft, which the girls dabble in through performing rites together, and which Sarah is shown to have an innate ability for – attracting both awe and envy from her new friends. Her arrival brings the established threesome a new level of confidence as they set about transforming their lives through magic, yet a rift occurs when the most charismatic member of the group, Nancy, becomes carried away with her augmented power and growing jealousy, killing Chris when he rejects her over Sarah, and uniting Bonnie and Rochelle against her. Nancy is thus presented as a dangerous villain, and it is left to Sarah, for whom 'the craft' is revealed to be her birthright, to ultimately put Nancy in her place, providing a moral tale in which 'good' is seen to triumph over 'evil'.

As we have seen, how young women prove their virtue is a familiar sub-text within horror, as is the function given to mothers in providing the 'right' upbringing. *The Craft* interestingly reprises the folk tale's use of the dead mother as a positive presence, yet shows actual living mothers to be far from ideal. Nancy's mother is a drunk who dresses too young for her age and prioritises her unsavoury new husband over her daughter; Bonnie's mother is a worrier who hovers in the background of her sleep-overs and skin treatments – possibly suggesting that it was her prior negligence that caused her daughter's horrific burns; while Rochelle's mother does not appear at all. Even Sarah's mother has unwittingly damaged her daughter by dying while giving birth to her, leaving Sarah with a profound sense of guilt which the film works to erase. However, unlike the examples we have seen, far from insisting that she reject her mother in order to mature, *The Craft* insists that Sarah must discover her maternal inheritance and draw upon the power bequeathed to her. Sarah's mother is the weakness Nancy targets when relations sour between them, yet also becomes a source of strength. Preserved in the form of both a photograph and a ring kept by her daughter, her spirit is finally called upon in Sarah's hour of need, filling her with the power required to fight Nancy. The narrative thus provides another twist on the 'Cinderella' fable; in which female enmity is transferred to high-school peers, the prince they fight over ends up dead, and the heroine triumphs through gaining a much-needed sense of self-esteem – while additionally learning that supernatural powers are more trouble than they are worth.

The film opens with Sarah's arrival at her new school. Following a failed suicide attempt, she has moved with her father and stepmother to a new community as a means of starting her life again. Her shy demeanour and the scars on her wrist swiftly impress the other outcasts, snidely dubbed by Chris as 'the bitches of Eastwick', yet jealousy soon rears its ugly head. Although the conflict between Sarah and Nancy is ostensibly about leadership of the 'gang', what really comes between them is a boy who does not seem to merit either one's attention. Chris is an arrogant youth who Nancy is somewhat masochistically infatuated with. His promiscuous ways are referenced by her warning Sarah that 'he brings disease' – suggesting that he has passed a sexually transmitted infection to her in a past liaison – yet, rather than feel any animosity about this, Nancy is fuelled by an obsessive crush that increases when he becomes attracted to Sarah. Nancy's obsession is consistent with the faith she has devised for the circle of misfits she leads, for despite being an all-female ensemble it is a male spiritual guide called 'Manu' they invoke, with Nancy clearly attempting to use this source as a substitute for romantic longing:

Nancy: It's like . . . it's like you take him into you. It's like he fills you. He takes everything that's gone wrong in your life and makes it all better again.
Sarah: Nothing makes everything all better again.
Nancy: Maybe not for you.

Nancy's faith in Manu is offset against Sarah's maternal guides, which include both her mother and the owner of the local magic shop, Lirio (Assumpta Serna), who recognises the significance of her mother's ring – informing her that she was a witch – and perceives Sarah's own inner power. However, it takes a long time for Sarah to admit this inheritance, being initially more drawn towards her attraction to Chris and the presumed normality a relationship with him presents. He behaves like no prince charming however. On their first date together she proves her virtue by refusing to have sex with him. Chris responds by spreading lies at school that she not only put out, but was a lousy lay. In order to teach him a lesson Sarah places a love spell on him, yet she also seems to genuinely desire a relationship with Chris, agreeing to go on another date with him when her friendship with the other girls becomes strained. Out in his car, his enchanted devotion turns ugly, causing Sarah to fight him off when things get physical. She appears for comfort at Bonnie's house and is met with some sympathy from her estranged friends, yet Chris's attempted rape causes Nancy's jealousy to take a still more disturbing twist. Going to a party at his house, ostensibly to exact revenge, what Nancy seeks instead is to have sex with Chris by magically adopting Sarah's appearance. The likelihood of such an experience being unpleasant is not even considered – proving the extent to which Nancy's infatuation seems to be steeped in self-loathing. Still more strangely, Sarah arrives to protect Chris – apparently considering herself to blame for his attempted 'seduction' – and exposes Nancy as her true self. Chris's subsequent rejection ends in his death as Nancy's fury pushes him out of a window. This creates the ultimate rift between both women as Sarah's allegiance is posthumously given to the boy who tried to rape her. Blaming herself for having placed an infatuation spell on him, and thus apparently 'leading him on', she ignores Chris's track record at school and maintains to her father that 'he was basically a good guy underneath'.

In response to her disapproval, Nancy and the remaining coven turn against Sarah, tormenting her with nightmares and eventually coming to her house to drive her insane. Her deepest fears are then played upon with spells cast by her former friends, from swarms of insects filling the house to the dread of losing her remaining parent apparently realised when a news broadcast informs her that the plane her father and stepmother were travelling on has crashed. It is at this moment that Sarah confronts her bullies, drawing on powers that she has, up until now, largely denied. She easily overpowers Bonnie and Rochelle by turning their fears against them and causing them to flee the house, leaving the final confrontation between herself and Nancy. Showing a willingness to stoop to any depths, Nancy attempts to coerce Sarah into killing herself by reminding her of her guilt about her mother, yet Sarah finally refuses this position and her mother's photograph acts as a talisman by which to draw hidden reserves of strength. Conjuring what magic they can in the ultimate bitch-fight (which became an MTV video favourite), the two fight it out until Sarah triumphs. Assuming a moral responsibility that her former friend is so clearly devoid of, she places a binding spell on Nancy that seemingly drives her insane: we last see her strapped to a bed in an asylum, ranting about the power she once had.

The film interestingly relates female insecurities and attendant desires, yet while the four use 'the craft' to invoke a powerful sense of wish-fulfilment this ultimately backfires. Bonnie's intense self-consciousness evaporates when her burn scars are magically removed by a pioneering medical treatment that far exceeds expectations, but her new confidence soon turns into vanity and a careless attitude towards others, being all too ready to reject Sarah at Nancy's urging. Rochelle is very much in the minority as a black girl at school and suffers the racist taunts of another girl, Laura Lizzie (Christine Taylor), who she punishes with a magical dose of alopecia, yet while she exhibits some compassion in watching her former adversary lose her blonde locks by the handful and, with it, the arrogance that made her such an unfeeling bully, Rochelle also becomes a bully herself in turning against Sarah. Nancy's greatest fear is that she is worthless and unimportant, the way Chris made her feel, yet although the occult helps her attain a degree of power, with the death of her slimy stepfather providing the money needed to escape her trailer-trash life, this clearly does not bring happiness. Despite its initial sympathy towards them, the film is intent on demonising Nancy and disbanding the circle she leads. The moral message is that each has abused their power, for as Lirio states, bad magic will return three times as powerfully, necessitating that all three of the 'bitches of Eastwick' are punished.[2]

Only Sarah is deemed 'pure' enough to wield such power, her sense of guilt after Chris's death having seemingly set her straight, yet after using her power to defeat her former friends she seemingly relinquishes it.[3] While Hollywood comedies such as *I Married a Witch* (1942) and *Bell, Book and Candle* (1958) portray witches forsaking their powers for love, Sarah seemingly does so in order to be normal, events having shown how easily 'the craft' can be abused. However, she also arguably forsakes the legacy her mother gave her. Sarah achieves both revenge on Chris's behalf and self-worth for herself by incarcerating Nancy – but refuses to take her place in the coven. When Bonnie and Rochelle sheepishly ask if she still has her powers at the end of the film she warns against trying to befriend her again, seemingly closing this chapter in her life. Normality ensues with the safe return of her father and his second wife, their 'deaths' being shown to be a mere charm, yet her dad is left unaware of who he was once married to – or the powers his daughter has. Most disconcertingly, although the film briefly provides a sympathetic view of female kinship, it chiefly warns against rivalries and the disaster that female power can bring. Like *Scream*'s Sidney, who is also forced to get over her mother's death, Sarah is placed on the 'right' path of emotional development, yet one that is rooted in a denial of her power, having proven her virtue and sanity in contrast to Nancy's malevolence.

The relationship between Sarah and Nancy is reminiscent of the main protagonists in *Girl, Interrupted* (1999), who meet in a 1960s mental hospital. Based on a biographical novel by Susan Kaysen, the story is narrated by Susanna (Winona Ryder), a young woman experiencing low self-esteem and depression whose attempt at suicide places her in Claymore – an upmarket institution for women with mental problems. Susanna meets the irrepressible Lisa (Angelina Jolie), an assertive and insightful figure who is as charismatic as she is cruel, and the scene is set for a similarly intense female friendship that also deteriorates into hostility. Like Randall P. MacMurphy in *One Flew Over the Cuckoo's Nest*, Lisa has a force that intensifies those around her and operates in clear contrast to Susanna's languid self-interest. She frequently absconds from the institution, only to be given new shock treatments on her return, yet refuses to give in. Captivated by her, Susanna is warned by

Dr Wick (Vanessa Redgrave) against imitating Lisa too closely, and just as Sarah distances herself from Nancy in a bid for normality, Susanna ultimately rejects her former friend. Despite bohemian airs, her cynical attitude, and beatnik clothes, Susanna wants to conform to 'the system' in operation around her, happily sacrificing Lisa in her bid for freedom. Despite having been given the opportunity to express herself, to defy the authorities, and even to escape Claymore via the interest Lisa takes in her, Susanna calculatedly turns against her.

The most uncomfortable scene occurs at the end of the film when Lisa and Susanna psychologically lay into one another, with Lisa reading Susanna's diary to the other inmates, including the bitchy comments she has made about them. Susanna's response is to retort that there is nothing unusual about Lisa – a remark that cuts her to the quick, despite seeming patently absurd, for what sets Lisa apart from the others is both an indomitable energy and an ability to see life more clearly than the others. However, like *The Craft*'s Nancy, Lisa is bound over to keep the peace, finally shown strapped to a hospital bed in punishment for her refusal to tow the line. When Susanna leaves the institute, having jumped through all the hoops required of her to be deemed sane, she proves that there was nothing wrong with her other than a self-interested cry for attention, while the true hero of the film is the one left bowed and seemingly beaten. Like Nancy, there is seemingly too much of Lisa to allow her to roam free in the world, and just as a seething resentment fuels Nancy to commit deeds that put her dangerously beyond the pale, so Lisa is deemed too much in the clarity of her vision and her refusal to conform.

Another interrogation of female adolescent outsiders is offered in the Canadian independent film *Ginger Snaps*. Functioning as an inverted 'Red Riding Hood' – linking pubertal transformation with violent teen angst – the film innovatively makes a female the aggressive force in question, rather than its victim. Werewolf films are a staple feature in horror yet have predominantly featured men infected by the 'curse'. Female variants include two features that followed the success of the *Cat People* films in the 1940s, *Cry of the Werewolf* (1944) and *She-Wolf of London* (1946); Italian exploitation film *The Legend of the Wolf Woman* (1976); *An American Werewolf in Paris* (1997); and, more recently, *Dog Soldiers* (2002) and *Cursed* (2005), yet none have equalled the gravity with which *Ginger Snaps* treats its subject – presenting its transformation as a sub-text of female adolescence. As the tag-line for the film reads: 'They don't call it the curse for nothing' – and menstruation is melded with lycanthropy in a witty, scary, and very original film.

The two misfits at its centre, the Fitzgerald sisters, are set apart from their peers in their dress, attitude, and fascination with death. The sisters have made a pact – 'Out by 16 or dead on the scene but together forever' – indicating their intent to either leave home or not grow up at all, with suicide considered as a means of refusing conformity in their average hometown suburbia of Bailey Downs. It is seemingly symptomatic of their reluctance to grow up and become women that both are late in menstruating, being 15 and 16 respectively without yielding to 'the curse'. As Linda Ruth Williams puts it, the film provides a 'complex view of that moment when girls hover on the brink of womanhood and would rather not take the next step'.[4] Typically perhaps, it is the more dominant of the two, Ginger (Katherine Isabelle), who starts her period first and she voices evident displeasure at doing so, complaining: 'Kill yourself to be different and your own body screws you.' The fact that this occurs during a full moon adds obvious supernatural elements, as is being bitten by a werewolf almost immediately afterwards, and Ginger duly starts to change.

Boys have already started to notice her maturing figure and, although previously hostile towards them, Ginger's attitude alters, ignoring younger sister Brigitte (Emily Perkins) as she starts to take a greater interest in boys. She also focuses more on her appearance and in a scene directly reminiscent of *The Craft*, in which the four girls make their way through the school cafeteria filled with a new-found confidence and sexuality, turning heads as they go, Ginger makes a similar entrance at school, with due appreciation from her male admirers. Underneath, however, physical changes prove less appealing, such as the tail she is growing and the hairs sprouting from wounds caused by the werewolf attack. As Brigitte states: 'Something's wrong. Like more than you just being female.'

Playing on the 'Red Riding Hood' theme still further is the boy responsible for having inadvertently killed the initial werewolf with his van, Sam (Kris Lemche), a plantsman who works at a local nursery yet also hangs out around the school dealing dope and looking for fresh conquests. Sam is what the school bitch, Trina Sinclair (Danielle Hampton), refers to as a 'cherry hound', inferring that he is interested only in virgins, and we see Trina regularly humiliated by his subsequent dismissal of her. However, the film also reverses the usual high-school scenario of avaricious boys and submissive females – a fact that is probably best explained by its screenplay having been written by a woman, Karen Walton, who subverts a number of conventions. Hence, while Sam is accused of being a sexual predator, like the symbolic wolf of 'Red Riding Hood', he also acts as a helper (if not quite saviour) to Brigitte – sharing her knowledge that there is a lycanthrope in their midst and helping her find an antidote for its 'infection'. The 'real' wolf, clearly, is Ginger – transforming from petulant misfit to a dangerous beast once bitten. Equally interesting, and refreshingly different, is Jason McCardy (Jesse Moss), the boy Ginger decides to have sex with, for in contrast to the male characters we have seen, he is the more passive party when she takes the initiative to have sex. Already going through 'changes', Ginger's intensity causes alarm on his part, as is revealed in the following exchange:

Jason: Don't we need protection?
(*Ginger pushes him down and viciously opens his shirt.*)
Jason: Stop! Wait a second . . .
Ginger: You're fucking hilarious, cave boy.

That Jason is *not* acting like a Neanderthal makes a welcome change to the typical image in horror of young men fuelled only by an interest in having sex and women generally coerced into going along with things. When he advises her to 'lie back and relax', Ginger shows her dominance by reversing the instruction. Although Jason escapes the exchange relatively unscathed – and seemingly having enjoyed every minute of it – he becomes infected and goes through changes of his own, including destroying his own dog. Ginger admits the same fascination to her sister, as well as her relative disappointment in her first sexual encounter. Having killed the neighbour's dog, she states: 'I get this ache . . . and I thought it was for sex, but it's to tear everything to fucking pieces!' Violence and physical pleasure are clearly equated, as is made evident in the way Ginger describes the joy of a kill: 'It feels so good, Brigitte. It's like touching yourself. You know, every move, right on the fucking dot. And after . . . you see fucking fireworks, supernovas. I'm a goddamn force of nature! I feel like I could do just about anything!'

Despite such exhilaration, a form of binding must obviously ensue. To feel you can do 'just about anything' without adequate moral restraint is clearly to exceed permissible boundaries for a female, and, as with Nancy and Lisa, it is another woman, the one Ginger is closest to, who is charged with curbing her.

Ginger's aggression causes a rift between the sisters, behaving in an ever more reprehensible manner in her heedless cruelty, yet it is also inferred that she has always been the more dominant of the two and the film foregrounds Brigitte's need to define herself as a separate individual. Although she does her best to help her sister, they are obviously moving in different directions, and when Ginger murders both the school councillor and the janitor, Brigitte knows she has crossed a line that she is not prepared to follow. Although Ginger coaxes her to 'turn' with her, in the same vein that she has previously urged her towards a suicide pact – saying 'this is so us, B!' – Brigitte will have none of it, and when emotional blackmail is used by her older sister it meets a swift retort.

Ginger: I said I'd die for you!
Brigitte: No. You said you'd die *with* me – 'cause you had nothing better to do.

The level of control Ginger tries to exact on her sister is unnerving, and reaches frightening levels when sexual jealousy reveals itself. Not only does Ginger kill the kindly school janitor, stating 'I don't like how he looks at you' as explanation, she also seems jealous of Sam's interest in her younger sister. This is one of the most compelling elements of the film, for although Sam informs Brigitte that he does not feel 'that way' about her, it is the complete disinterest she exhibits towards this seemingly 'cool' character that sets her apart from other girls, disarming him entirely. When he arrives at the school stating that he has spent the last week looking for her she is unimpressed, and when he returns while she is in hockey class she rebuts him with a laconic: 'Are you on drugs? I mean *right now*?' Although he is evidently trying to help her, she makes him do all the running, and there is clearly more implied in their relationship, whatever he may say. Intelligent yet sullen, awkward and unusual, Brigitte seems a long way behind her sister in terms of dawning sexual maturity, and it is this prepubescent state that also makes her one of the most interesting female figures horror cinema has yet seen. Brigitte is at an age and mindset where no one else's opinion matters, including the need to fit in. She is not interested in drugs or boys or her looks, and, despite ostensible appearances, she is by far the stronger force of the two sisters, without whose common sense and indefatigable reasoning Ginger would clearly be lost.

Their uncommon closeness is a bond that is far from easily broken, yet, as with Sarah and Nancy, rivalry increases through jealousy. However, while Ginger accuses Brigitte of always wanting what she has, the truth seems to be the reverse. As Brigitte exclaims shortly after discovering that Ginger has attempted to seduce (and possibly kill) Sam: 'You wrecked everything for me that wasn't about you . . . ' (and after cutting her palm and exchanging blood with Ginger in an extension of the pacts they have previously made together) 'Now I am you'. Ginger's response is the usual sardonic riposte employed by school kids when an insult has come their way, stating: 'I know you are, but what am I?' It is dialogue of this kind, its depth of meaning, as well as the outstanding performances of its protagonists that won the film a number of awards and accolades. Ginger's identity is truly in question and Brigitte's response, for all her anger towards her sister, remains fuelled by love.

In forming a new blood pact with Ginger, Brigitte exposes herself to the curse, doing so as a means of gaining her trust and luring her home in order to give her the antidote created by Sam, yet she clearly endangers herself in the process, as there is only enough monkshood for one of them. As Ginger's transformation into a beast becomes ever more complete, the two face their final showdown in the family home. Again, the fixation with dying is all too oppressive, recalling a time earlier in the film when Ginger attempts to use emotional blackmail to coerce her sister, stating:

Ginger: You said we'd go together, one way or the other.
Brigitte: When we were *eight*!

Brigitte's reply indicates that she has not romanticised the idea of dying to the same extent as her sister. Despite her similar interest in 'death projects' – a collection of photographs the girls have taken of each other posed in a variety of suicide or fatal accident scenes – she is still able to make the distinction between fantasy and reality. Furthermore, and no doubt surprising herself in the process, she also indicates that she truly does want to be alive. However, when Sam suggests that they give her the antidote instead and 'take off', Brigitte refuses, still adamantly placing her sister first – although it is becoming increasingly clear that this loyalty would not be reciprocated.

When Ginger kills Sam and rounds on her sister in their bedroom, Brigitte is ultimately forced to make a separation, exclaiming to a beast that is now incapable of speech: 'I'm not dying in this room with you!' Finally cornered with a syringe of monkshood in one hand and a knife in the other as Ginger descends upon her, it is the knife that is eventually used to defend herself. In a beautifully shot ending Brigitte holds her dead sister, arms wrapped around what is clearly more wolf than human, corroborating Ginger's claim that they are 'not even related any more', finally alone.

The mother's role in the film is also refreshingly innovative. Pamela Fitzgerald (Mimi Rogers) delights when she finds Ginger's blood-stained underwear in the laundry, presenting her with a cake and happily exclaiming to her husband: 'Our little girl's a woman now!' Although this is obviously embarrassing for Ginger, it is particularly endearing compared with the punitive response encountered by Carrie White when she also starts menstruating considerably later than normal and is greeted only with malice by a hate-filled mother. For Margaret White 'womanhood' signifies that Carrie has lost her innocence, seemingly wanting to keep her as a child under her control forever. The open pride displayed by Pamela offers a touching contrast, and her devotion to her daughters makes her much more than a comic figure. Not only does she inadvertently supply the monkshood needed to cure Ginger (presumably used for flower arranging), she also suggests to Brigitte, having discovered Trina Sinclair's dead body in the garden, that the three run away together, leaving their father at home. Her seeming antipathy towards men in general is made clear earlier when Brigitte asks what boys want (as a means of distracting her attention) and she responds by giving her daughter a sex talk that concludes by saying 'some of them may seem cool or different but they're all pretty much the same'. In her view her husband would only blame her for their daughters' involvement in Trina's death (which may have been accidental but looks very bad all the same), and she seems to agree. When Brigitte attempts to reassure her that events are not her fault, she replies solemnly 'yes it is', yet interestingly seems to anticipate going on the run, stating: 'It's one thing if you leave home, that's normal, but no one's taking my girls away from me. We'll start fresh, just us girls.'[5]

Although Pamela resembles the overly nurturing mother, Beverley Sutphin (Kathleen Turner) parodied in *Serial Mom* (1994), her loyalty is clear. Despite her daughters' embarrassment, testified by Ginger's line: 'I hate our gene pool!', she is infinitely preferable to the many negative mothers populating horror, yet the sisters are locked in their own world, and the enemy at large seemingly includes their mother, who represents an image of maturity they would rather die than emulate.

Ginger's reasoning for thinking they can get away with Trina's accidental murder aims to capitalise on the way women have been reduced to stereotypes (particularly in the teen horror genre), arguing: 'Nobody thinks girls do shit like this... We're either slags, bitches, teases, or the virgin next door. We'll just go by how the world works.' However, the film is also at pains to equate monstrosity and freakishness with womanhood, joking about PMT and sexual maturation while portraying female adolescence as a deeply unpleasant experience. Ironically, despite starting her period, Ginger is not initiated into becoming a woman, but becomes a wild animal instead. Her metamorphosis accordingly emblematises 'abject' theories of female abhorrence as teats and a crone-like face accompany increasingly nasty behaviour – confirming an animalistic notion of women that horror has long been fascinated with. Furthermore, contrary to werewolf myths established since *The Wolf Man* (1941), transformation does not switch between human and beast forms but is a permanent condition that infers the ultimate loss of humanity. Becoming a wolf does not occur on a monthly basis, like moon and menstrual cycles, and as the film's sequel shows, it does not even have a cure, yet neither is the 'curse' presented as wholly undesirable, but is potentially empowering if one is willing to forsake conventional morality. Indeed, the idea that dehumanisation is a transgressive experience provides *Ginger Snaps* with one of its darkest fantasies.

Angela Carter, rewriting fairy tales in her collection, *The Bloody Chamber and Other Stories* (1979), imagines just such a possibility, with female characters in 'The Tiger's Bride' and 'Wolf-Alice' experiencing tremendous freedom in their bestial transformations. Carter was disappointed by the film version of another story taken from the collection, *The Company of Wolves* (1984), despite collaborating on the project, stating that she felt a sense of 'difficulty' in the fact that 'the film has been about a girl coming to terms with her libido, and yet when confronted with the pure "libido" of the wolves, she screams! She could have just smiled, that would have been all right . . . She could handle the wolf.'[6]

Ginger Snaps fulfils such sentiments by presenting a young woman who can not only 'handle', but literally *becomes* the wolf. Ginger's awakening libido initially seems to be the prime motivation behind her transformation yet, as she later informs Brigitte, the hunger she feels is not simply for sex but a desire to cause harm, attesting to only feeling good when she's 'tearing living things apart'. It is this destructive rage and violence for its own sake that cannot be tolerated by the more mature, and moral, Brigitte, and which finally brings their close relationship to a head. To kill the neighbours' pets is one thing, yet in killing humans a line is crossed that Brigitte cannot accept. If Nancy crosses a similar boundary in *The Craft* when she kills Chris, and if *Girl, Interrupted*'s Lisa does likewise in contributing to the death of sexually abused Daisy (Brittany Murphy) by brutally naming her secret and showing no remorse at her death, then a lack of conscience also sets Ginger apart, and when she snaps it is Brigitte's task to end her life before her own is taken.

A sequel, *Ginger Snaps: Unleashed* (2004) takes up the narrative after Ginger's death. Brigitte has gone on the run yet is found by the police, overdosing on a syringe of monkshood. She has learned how to prepare and administer the herb to herself yet has also discovered that it can only delay a person's transformation, rather than cure the curse. Brigitte has been cutting herself in order to track her metamorphosis by timing how quickly she heals. Her marginal status is thus aligned with troubled behaviour such as self-harming and drug addiction – the two misconceptions made by the police when they find her. Assuming that she is on drugs, Brigitte is sent to a rehab clinic, where she is without the monkshood needed to offset her descent into animality, and the film follows her attempt to both escape the institution and avoid the sexual interest taken in her by another werewolf in Bailey Downs and a lascivious male nurse. Indeed, it is Brigitte's negotiation of her sexuality that the sequel is intent on documenting, albeit with much less impressive results than the original.

While Brigitte is just as compelling in her cynicism and self-possession as the previous film, by being incarcerated in an institution that is far darker and more menacing than anything *Girl, Interrupted* had to offer, an all-pervasive gloom is set up that tests her in new ways. Furthermore, in contrast to the refreshing departures of the original, it is the predatory side of male sexuality that is focused on, with male nurse, Tyler (Eric Johnson), trading drugs for sexual favours with female inmates, including Brigitte herself. That her 'addiction' to monkshood makes her submit to this deal is lamentable indeed and, given her situation, Brigitte's continued determination *not* to become wolf lacks its former justification. Ginger's ghost occasionally appears to ask why she is fighting wolfdom, yet is a goading rather than comforting presence, reiterating their conflict:

Ginger: We can't help what's in us, B
Brigitte: I'm not like you, Ginger. I'm stronger.
Ginger: (*laughing*) That's not how I remember you the first 15 years of your life.
Brigitte: It's how I remember the last 15 minutes of yours.

While she was the evident hero of the first film, within the context of the sequel Brigitte's determination to remain human seems self-defeating rather than admirable, particularly as she engages in a sexual trade-off with Tyler that demeans her integrity. Despite her efforts to avoid her sister's fate, like the elongated ears that grow back each time she cuts them off, her attempts to delay her transformation are ultimately futile, and instead of the amoral empowerment enjoyed by Ginger, Brigitte seems destined to suffer instead. She mistakenly aligns herself with another inmate, known as Ghost (Tatiana Maslany), who Brigitte defends against bullies in much the same way that Ginger once defended her against Trina Sinclair, yet her new friend proves to be deceitful – as well as psychotic – providing yet another cautionary message about the perils of female friendship. Although she helps Brigitte escape the clinic, Ghost's duplicity is revealed in their new hiding place – the house in the woods (in yet another inversion of 'Red Riding Hood') where she once lived with her grandmother – and deliberately set her alight.[7] The Beast of Bailey Downs tracks them to this location and for some reason they invite Tyler to join them, seemingly because of his supply of monkshood. Ghost then uses her knowledge of his illicit activities to make Brigitte think that Tyler has sexually abused her. Brigitte's response is to lock him outside, where he is quickly killed by the Beast, yet upon discovering that Ghost lied, and despite experiencing his manipulation for herself, she immediately feels remorse about his death. Still more disappointingly, although Brigitte eventually proves her mettle by fighting and killing the Beast, she ends the film locked in a basement by Ghost, who still manages to out-manoeuvre her. The sequel thus turns its hero into a victim whose fate is left unknown, yet whose earlier promise remains unfulfilled.

The runaway success of *Ginger Snaps* caused *Ginger Snaps: Unleashed* to be made simultaneously with *Ginger Snaps Back* (2004) – a prequel detailing the curse's origins in the 19th century which also severely detracts from the original, demonstrating how easily the lure of the profit motive can outweigh other considerations. As a culmination to the trilogy, *Ginger Snaps: Unleashed* may eschew outright populism, yet fails to take up the promise of its extraordinary lead and proves the difficulty of extending what should clearly have been an innovative one-off into an attempted franchise. Although it takes her further towards maturity by removing Brigitte from her family, and the relationship she had with her sister, the film also places her in a situation where she cannot experience any degree of freedom.

Many thematic parallels are sought with the first film, with lycanthropy again symbolising sexual identity and adolescence. However, the humour darkens to a discomfiting degree and former feminist impulses are lost. While Pamela represented a stronger parent than the girls' ineffectual father, female power is more at question in the sequel. Women may seemingly be in charge at the institute, including chief psychiatrist Alice (Janet Kidder), yet this notion is refuted at night when Tyler does his rounds. Far from being in charge of their sexuality, female inmates are powerless, and even the attempt to help them overcome their addictions is undermined by Tyler's illicit exchange of drugs for sex. Brigitte is accordingly placed in a situation where her burgeoning sexual identity cannot be experienced on her own terms, but is coercively traded instead. While Ginger called all the shots, Brigitte acquires a sexual partner she has not chosen, yet who she oddly feels some sympathy for nonetheless. Earlier in the film, when she agrees to have sex with Tyler in exchange for monkshood, Brigitte becomes aroused, yet as the wolf in her starts to kick in she forces Tyler away to avoid hurting him. That she is more motivated to protect him than herself reiterates the regressive nature of this film, with Brigitte prioritising the well-being of an unsavoury male for no good reason.

Molly Haskell's comments on her first screen idol, Margaret O'Brien, could equally describe Brigitte's earlier appeal, particularly in terms of her liminal status, stating that: 'She was independent but not alone . . . she had not entered the sexual arena or discovered the bondage of emotional dependency', inhabiting 'the interval of self-determination between childhood and womanhood'.[8] Lamentably, however, Brigitte does not retain this self-determination. Even after Ginger's death, and despite having left home, she is not free. As one commentator has argued: 'She is a destroyed person, both hollow and feral, empty and blank-faced . . . a rogue wanderer cut off from the rest of the world.'[9] Yet it is the fact that Brigitte chooses to align herself with the wrong people, misjudging and befriending Ghost seemingly as a means of replacing her lost sister, that is partly the cause of her downfall. While Sam offered a romantic interest who died to save her in the first film, the sequel provides a predatory male who is devoid of any redeeming qualities. That Brigitte seems to believe he might also serve as a helper, and feels guilt at her part in his destruction, seems unwarranted and naïve – even if this is intended to prove her continued humanity, and the troubling suggestion made is that an alliance with Tyler would have been preferable to Ghost. As in *The Craft*, and Sarah's posthumous affiliation with Chris, we are given to understand that Tyler may also have been 'basically a good guy underneath'.

As we have seen, female sexuality is a clear concern in the rites of passage narratives outlined in contemporary teen horror, yet if the slasher warns women about relations with dubious men, the films informing this chapter target pubescent females as a potentially dangerous force. Just as Nancy's desire for Chris acquires murderous overtones when occult powers give her the ability to exact vengeance for having spurned her, so Ginger proves to be equally threatening once hormonal lust and the 'curse' combine.

In many ways this anxiety recalls a similar idea treated in *The Cat People* (1942). In this classic psychological horror we are invited to sympathise with another estranged female figure, Irena (Simone Simon), a young Serbian immigrant who has been told that the women of her village are descended from 'cat people' and are cursed to return to their savage ways if sexually aroused or physically threatened. This has left Irena with a fear of sexual intimacy that causes problems with her American husband, Oliver (Kent Smith). While her fears seem psychological, the film reveals that there are numerous threats that surround her, including a female friend of her husband's, Alice (Jane Randolph), who has designs on him, and lascivious male psychiatrist, Dr Judd (Tom Conway). Irena's belief in the legend of the cat people may resemble a form of sexual repression designed to control females, yet it is ultimately shown to be true. Although we never see her in her panther state, the film alludes to this transformation in Irena's jealous pursuit of Alice and her violent defence against Judd's unethical advances. Her worst fears are realised upon causing Judd's death and she elects to kill herself by opening the panther's cage at the zoo, where she is destroyed. Her astonished husband, who had formerly believed her to be mentally ill, looks at her body and exclaims 'Irena never lied to us' – a realisation that tragically arrives too late.

Essentially the film is an interesting early variant of the werewolf myth, with a female at its centre who is misunderstood and mistreated by those around her. As Tony Williams puts it: 'Irena becomes a conveniently designated monster, a cat woman society may either destroy or incarcerate within a mental institution.'[10] Already estranged in terms of coming from a different culture, Irena is a lonely and vulnerable figure who ultimately punishes herself for succumbing to her 'true nature'. Afraid to recognise a Serbian 'sister' she meets on her wedding day, yet unable to be the wife her husband desires, she is unable to exist in the world that she has tried to make her new home. As Williams argues, 'lacking a sustaining female community, she masochistically inhabits a world of darkness, a psychological pit that threatens any single independent woman who resides within patriarchy'.[11]

Irena's legacy can be traced to horror's more recent female misfits, who similarly unlock a mysterious force within themselves, partly as a response to being unable, or unwilling, to fit into conventional society, and are punished accordingly. Yet while Irena eliminates herself out of remorse, despite her transformation having been fuelled by the monstrosity of those around her, Nancy and Ginger have to be bound over against their will. The sexual connotations are just as clear however, revealing untempered female power to be both formidable and unacceptable. Most importantly, just as Irena becomes the monster her society has warned about in a form of self-fulfilling prophecy, so Nancy and Ginger each invoke archetypal myths of the witch and werewolf; reiterating, and reinterpreting, a long cultural history.

James Twitchell observes the werewolf's link to witchcraft, noting that, despite its probable cause in terms of rabies infections during the 16th and 17th centuries, reports of lupine activity were frequently misunderstood by the church as a manifestation of the occult. This conflation is understandable, in his view, arguing that: 'after all, the whole ontological basis of witchcraft rested on the assumption that shape-changing is demonic subterfuge, and what other beast is so directly the result of such shifting than the folkloric werewolf?'[12] Both witch and werewolf trials were common in Europe during the 16th century, and Jack Zipes points out that not only were werewolves, like witches, thought to be accomplices of the devil, they also underwent a cultural transition from being highly regarded for their integration with nature (as midwives and 'wise women' were previously respected) to being condemned as dangerous undesirables.[13] Witches and werewolves became emblematic of society's need, with the advent of Christianity, to distance nature, find a convenient scapegoat for problems, and create social cohesion through fostering hatred. Women were frequently targeted and Zipes contends that 'in particular, the witch and werewolf crazes were aimed at regulating sexual practices and sex-roles for the benefit of male-dominated social orders'.[14]

What is remarkable about *The Craft* and *Ginger Snaps* is that female outsiders willingly embrace these castigated images as an alternative to existing norms, adopting them as a measure of dissatisfaction and refusal. Twitchell maintains that 'the werewolf is created out of a man who *wants* to be possessed ... the human about to become a werewolf consciously participates – at least initially – in the process'.[15] Although this is refuted by the many hapless men who are suddenly bitten by werewolves in such narratives, or women whose lupine nature is shown to be the product of a family curse, Ginger's demeanour suggests that wolfdom is a willing trade against conventional womanhood, just as the high-school misfits constituting Nancy's coven are happy to live up to their reputations as local pariahs in embracing the occult. However, the confidence and power these young women acquire is accompanied by a dangerous sexuality and other 'primitive' emotions, such as envy and anger, which seem to be exacerbated in female form. Just as witches were often accused of unbridled carnality, werewolf myths warn against reverting to animal instincts – a motif that acquires additional narrative currency in films where female adolescents are concerned.

Tony (Michael Landon), the surly teen protagonist of *I Was a Teenage Werewolf* (1957), becomes a monster when, thanks to the ill-advised meddling of a psychiatrist, his pubescent libido goes into overdrive and primitive instincts take over, altering both his attitude and appearance. Although his Bulgarian high-school janitor diagnoses the problem, the only resort seemingly left open to the police is to kill what has now become a beast. If the elimination of an ego is what makes Tony monstrous, unfettered rage and sexuality are still less acceptable in women. Like Nancy, Ginger is chiefly distinguished by anger, violence, and an apparent absence of morality, and just as Nancy goes too far in her witchery when she kills another human, Ginger must also be despatched when the wolf in her looms. Women who kill in the name of survival may be applauded in the slasher, but to kill for pleasure, or anger, is unacceptable. Twitchell contends that the werewolf has transformed into the sexually frustrated psychopath of slasher films,[16] a figure who, as we have seen, it is largely the task of an equally frustrated female to vanquish (albeit often temporarily). *Ginger Snaps* and *The Craft* provide interesting alternatives to the Final Girl in presenting females who also refuse a position of passivity, yet cannot be narratively approved.

As innovative as such figures are, there are necessary detractions to be made, not least because we are seemingly invited to celebrate female transgressions while also shrinking from their excesses. Nancy may be witty and powerful, yet the insane contorted expression shown in the film's last shot of her undermines this appeal. In a similar vein, although Ginger's attractiveness initially increases during her transformation, she enters the arena of the abject when her appearance is mistaken for a Halloween costume near the close of the film – incorporating as it does several teats, white hair, and a withered face – just as her morality undergoes an equivalent deterioration. However, if female viewers are warned against over-identifying with such figures, just as Susanna is warned against aligning herself too closely with Lisa, this does not mean that we necessarily follow suit. Indeed, there is much to admire in the self-possession displayed by these characters, and their unwillingness to comply with the rules by which conduct and morality tend to be governed. Even as they are punished, far from necessarily breathing a collective sigh of relief, we may equally sigh with disappointment at the measures taken to bring such misfits in line. After all, while Nancy is incarcerated for exceeding permissible boundaries, and Ginger is annihilated for much the same reason, Brigitte is also punished – seemingly because of her inability to seize the power in her grasp.

Writing in 1975, Catherine Clement suggests that it is possible to appropriate the mythic means of female abjection. Identifying the hysteric and witch as the two most prominent archetypes by which patriarchy has sought to castigate women, she argues that a degree of strength can be found in adopting, rather than rejecting, such characters. As she puts it: 'The heart of the story linking the figures of sorceress and hysteric lies in the subversive weight attributed to the return of the repressed, in the evaluation of power over the archaic, and in the Imaginary's power or lack of it over the Symbolic and the Real.'[17] Yet while Clement argues that such icons may be powerfully reconfigured, she also affirms that they are now 'old and worn out figures' who no longer exist.[18] As it has turned out, this is manifestly untrue. The hysteric has even been partially vindicated within psychological thrillers in which 'disturbed' female behaviour is found to have a legitimate (frequently patriarchal) cause, even if this is countered by persistent images of dangerous female psychotics. In a similar vein, although the witch has been significantly re-vamped in popular culture, this is not necessarily with progressive results.

Witchcraft has increasingly been presented as a comic fantasy in Hollywood films such as *The Witches of Eastwick* (1987) and *Practical Magic* (1998), approving supernatural powers when placed in a familial setting, yet with an overall message that it is best not to tamper with the occult. The recent film version of *Bewitched* (2005) reiterates this message, while television series such as *Sabrina The Teenage Witch* (1996–2003) and *Charmed* (1998–2006) domesticate their witches within familiar scenarios, showing them with relationship problems, struggling to bring up babies, and attempting to hold on to careers while battling against the forces of evil. Although ostensibly celebrating female power, and clearly aiming to appeal to a female audience, such texts carefully render their witches as commonplace as possible, with the idea of supernaturally empowered women played mainly for laughs.

The films evaluated in this chapter take this idea much more seriously, using the supernatural to invoke a dangerous female power which cannot tolerate kinship and is ultimately destructive. Nancy and Ginger become foils against which seemingly weaker counterparts prove their relative strength and virtue. Just as *The Craft*'s Sarah learns that she wants to live when faced with the enmity of her former friends, so *Ginger Snaps*' Brigitte learns the same lesson when her own sister turns against her. Significantly, however, although both heroic figures prove what they are capable of, they also deny it. Sarah discovers who her mother was yet opts to conceal her own power, while Brigitte seems unwilling to cross the line and explore her abilities after being infected by her sister. Both figures are approved as moral agents compared to the unruly Nancy and Ginger, yet the part they play in denouncing these women remains troubling, particularly given the relative sympathy given to lecherous men in their stead.

The relationship between female misfits, as touching and empowering as it is initially presented, is ultimately portrayed as destructive and damaging, with the promise of female kinship resolutely shattered by these films. If the slasher warns young women about men, these narratives expressly caution against trusting other women. Various sub-textual warnings occur, including the threat of sexually transmitted diseases found in each film, yet while boys are roguish, only after 'one thing', female anger is shown to be far more perilous. Nancy and Ginger share a hunger that cannot be sated, but their amorality and violence is deemed intolerable, and the bitter conflict between young women simplistically coded as 'good' or 'bad', divided by their differing values and, finally, their relations with boys remains highly questionable.

The most progressive element shared by these films is to powerfully illustrate the limits of female transgression. If the witch is symbolically used to represent a potentially dangerous female power in *The Craft*, the werewolf's positioning within a female psyche in *Ginger Snaps* interestingly updates *I Was a Teenage Werewolf* on gender lines, yet also corroborates Paul Wells' assertion that werewolf transformation can function as a 'metaphor of rebellion against oppression and conservatism'.[19] The Fitzgerald sisters were always outsiders in their small town, but rather than suggest that they will grow out of this they undergo a transition that makes their difference more manifest – realising, as well as satirising, horror's usual equation of rebellious females and monstrosity. It is no doubt due to *Ginger Snaps'* cult success that Wes Craven and Kevin Williamson reunited to explore the werewolf myth in *Cursed*. However, despite playing on similar coming-of-age themes, this shies away from taking any pleasure in wolfdom, and fails to challenge the conventions it parodies.[20]

Citing Marina Warner's suggestion that folk tales are responsible for 'articulating a complex feminine voice', Wells contends that a similar concern occurs in horror cinema.[21] However, while films such as *The Craft* and *Ginger Snaps* allow specific fears and desires to be voiced, a form of binding also ensues that may be undertaken by women yet works to legitimate an established patriarchal order nonetheless. That is not to say that such an order is not additionally challenged, as these texts clearly do more than set up a rogue female to be quashed, yet while female power is offered as a brief fantasy, it is also warned against, and invariably punished. This reveals continued caution regarding female transgression, particularly where men are seen to be threatened, reiterating the need to question whether it is, in fact, a 'complex feminine voice' they speak with, and to ask what complexities are identified therein.

Both films represent adolescence as a testing ground in which certain young women learn more about themselves and their capacities. They question the significance of relationships – romantic, familial, and among peer groups – and their impact on female subjectivity. Perhaps most significantly, in the best fairy tale tradition, they champion put-upon heroines as they make the transition to adulthood, gaining confidence and the will to live, yet also abandoning their misfit sisters after puberty brings rivalry and distrust. Neither Nancy nor Ginger, for all their narrative prominence, are heroic figures, adopting instead the role of a villainous threat which must be denounced. Supernatural abilities function as a key trope, yet Sarah and Brigitte aim to keep their witch and werewolf selves at bay, having been shown the consequences of doing otherwise by the women they eventually disarm and disown. Female kinship thus proves to be short-lived, and much more destructive than relations with boys, with any notion of female power shown to be dubious at best.

Familiar fairy tale elements can be seen in both the female rivalry presented and the magical transformations that occur, with elements from 'Cinderella' and 'Red Riding Hood' interestingly reworked. Yet in setting up an opposition between virtuous and villainous females, we also have a variation on the story the Grimms called 'Mother Holle', described in folkloric terms as 'The Kind and Unkind Girls'. This tale type functions on the premise that certain forms of female behaviour merit reward or punishment, with traits such as compassion, duty, and forbearance being explicitly valourised. Sarah and Brigitte accordingly prove their worth by resisting the powers that corrupt their counterparts, their 'unkind' rivals are punished, and the supernatural is ultimately shown to offer more heartache than happiness.

Given the examples we have seen of unhappy adolescent females and their brush with the occult, death or mental disintegration seems to be a foregone conclusion. Can any young women be shown to have supernatural powers without being corrupted by them? Can she retain her virtue and explore her sexuality at the same time? Can she foster friendships with other women that do not result in murderous hatred? A remarkable television series, *Buffy: The Vampire Slayer*, airing around the same time as *The Craft* and *Ginger Snaps* were released, would explicitly tackle such questions. Given the greater narrative time available to chart its heroine's development, *Buffy* allows us to examine the trials experienced by female leads in more depth. Those we have looked at so far have faced a familiar catalogue of problems in trying to survive parental conflicts and broken marriages; to negotiate the treacherous arena of female friendships, male admirers, and misunderstanding authority figures; and, above all, to retain a sense of individuality and integrity in the face of dissatisfactions and disgruntlements so often dismissed as 'growing pains'. The supernatural was increasingly used to symbolise the difficulties associated with adolescence in teen drama series in the 1990s, and *Buffy* interestingly combines werewolves, witches, demons, and a host of other 'monsters' – to which we might add the female Slayer at its helm – in exploring this theme. It is to this series, and the way in which female power (and rivalries) are reprised within it, that the next chapter shall turn.

5
Fighting Demons: Buffy, Faith, Willow, and the Forces of Good and Evil

> You need me to tow the line because you think you'll go over it, don't you B? You can't handle watching me go my own way, having a blast, because it tempts you.
> – Faith, 'Consequences', *Buffy: The Vampire Slayer*

> Buffy, I gotta tell you, I get it now! The Slayer thing isn't about the violence, it's about the power.
> – 'Evil' Willow, 'Two To Go', *Buffy: The Vampire Slayer*

So far this study has confined itself solely to films, yet the television series *Buffy: The Vampire Slayer* is considered also, chiefly because it unites many of the themes discussed regarding female identity and power in contemporary horror. Like the other texts evaluated it reprises *Carrie*'s theme of misfit outsiders, utilising the prom and graduation as key rites of passage in its heroine's progression towards adulthood. It also updates the Final Girl's negotiation of sexuality in the slasher, as well as the maternal role such figures have undertaken. In melding horror elements with the conventions of the teen angst drama the show can additionally be compared with *The Craft* and *Ginger Snaps*, similarly equating adolescence with supernatural transformation, while also placing females up against one another in another variation of 'The Kind and Unkind Girls'. Indeed, although *Buffy: The Vampire Slayer* embraces the supernatural as an empowering force, it reiterates the same warnings about the potential for corruption, particularly regarding the dangers of female rage, and sets out to test its hero accordingly.

Very much a coming-of-age narrative, the series follows main character, Buffy Summers (Sarah Michelle Gellar), as she learns to cope with various problems, yet far from simply charting the growing pains of a

disaffected teen and her friends, the series opts to explore their relationship with a dubious adult world set against the unlikely backdrop
of horror B-movies. Over the course of the series, Buffy comes to terms
with her appointed role as the Slayer – a female warrior given the task of
saving the world from evil. The self-consciousness that accompanies this
conceit is a key source of humour, and partially explains why *Buffy* has
attracted a wider market than the teen demographic it initially seemed
intended for, yet although the series is undoubtedly witty there is a
serious undertow that asks us to care for its protagonists, particularly
Buffy. One of the main topics investigated in this chapter is how this
character is asked to grow up and take responsibility, evaluating the way
in which Buffy's heroic qualities are contrasted against female villainy
in the show, particularly in terms of her two closest contemporaries,
best friend Willow and alter ego Faith.

The level of fantasy in the world presented is a mainstay of the action,
creating a wealth of possibilities. Various figures have special powers and
the conventional teen problems experienced by Buffy and her friends
are routinely disrupted by more immediate (frequently life-threatening)
dangers faced in the form of the monsters and demons that populate
the fictional location of Sunnydale, California – a district that houses a
bridge to the underworld known as the Hellmouth. That Buffy and her
mother relocate to Sunnydale at the start of the series is seemingly part
of a grand design intended for her to fulfil her destiny as the Slayer,
under the initial guidance of a 'Watcher' appointed to hone her fighting
skills, and aided by an important network of allies. Yet although she
is set up as a female warrior, Buffy eventually takes her mother's place
as the series draws to a close, underlining a motif assessed in previous
chapters, for in many ways the series plots the end of her innocence
and her eventual assumption of adulthood.

The series repeatedly places Buffy in danger, testing her strength and
skills, as much as her character, in formulating a heroic narrative. Traditional fairy tales are referenced, yet also challenged.[1] When Buffy goes to
a high-school prom ('Prophecy Girl') she wears a white 'Cinderella' dress
which is virtually ruined before she gets to her destination.[2] Another
episode ('Halloween') enchants a similar fairy tale dress while deriding
the old-fashioned femininity it is intended to connote, with Buffy losing
her ability to fight while wearing it. 'Red Riding Hood' is also frequently
drawn upon in the dangers she faces every day and her refusal to be
bound by convention, yet far from making her vulnerable, Buffy's curiosity is proven time and again to be a vital survival skill. 'Bluebeard'
crops up in 'Ted', when her mother's new boyfriend is revealed to have

killed several wives, while the episode 'Beauty and the Beasts' further exposes the realities of male aggression.

A brutal killing in Sunnydale woods sets the scene for the episode's exploration of male violence. Oz (Seth Green), a werewolf character who appeared frequently in the first season, becomes the prime suspect, along with reformed vampire, Angel (David Boreanaz), who is similarly not deemed responsible for his actions, having recently returned from Hell in an animalistic state. That the culprit is found to be an abusive boyfriend rams the message home – male aggression, far from being fantastical or supernatural, is an all too real danger.[3] Jenny Bavidge argues that the strongest theme in the series is 'the insistent protest against the violence done to real girls and women', going on to claim that Buffy's trials show 'that to be just a girl is often an epic task in itself'.[4] However, the series also avoids the standard 'female in peril' trope – a cliché that is decisively quashed from the very first instalment ('Welcome to the Hellmouth'), with male victims just as common as females. Furthermore, female villains are equally, if not more, prominent in the series, and often prove to be more ruthless than male counterparts. Indeed, while the series overtly champions a female Slayer equipped with a remarkable capacity to fight, other aggressive females are treated with much greater reserve.

The relationship between three of its female leads is particularly interesting in this respect, especially when a line is crossed between them. The close friendship between Buffy and best friend Willow (Alyson Hannigan) deteriorates when Willow transgresses her role as meek helper and is seen to abuse her magical abilities. Although her use of witchcraft initially empowers her, it is later equated with drug dependency, and when she is seen to lose moral control over such powers it becomes Buffy's mission to contain her.[5] 'Rogue Slayer' Faith (Eliza Dushku) provides another interesting counterpart, and is villainised along similar lines. Although she is the closest thing Buffy has to a peer in terms of her calling and abilities, Faith also goes over to the 'dark side' in terms of moral behaviour and her friendship with Buffy is severed accordingly, adding great drama to their ensuing antagonism. The series' focus on female experiences and relationships is particularly interesting, given the other texts we have looked at, as is the demarcation upheld in terms of approved female behaviour and its alternatives. In being shown to mature over seven seasons, Buffy makes the transition from establishing a closer relationship to her mother to eventually becoming a mother in her own right. She also learns to expect relatively little from men, while evincing greater distrust towards female friends. The chapter evaluates this relative antipathy, contrasting Buffy's heroism with the other gifted females portrayed.

As a cult television series *Buffy* has received a great deal of attention in fandom and academic analysis, accordingly proving that, despite being seemingly intended for teenagers, the series' appeal has been far broader. Indeed, one might question whether it is not only the intermeshing of horror, comedy, and teen drama that is instrumental in fostering such interest, but the fact that it provides such an appealing fantasy: one in which a young woman is given a remarkable ability to fight and charged with the responsibility of defending the world from demonic agents. It is testimony of the 'Buffy phenomenon' that similar series appeared almost simultaneously, such as *Charmed* (featuring three witchy sisters who similarly fight demonic forces) and *Sabrina The Teenage Witch* (in which the eponymous heroine also struggles to come to terms with her powers). In cinema also certain reverberations can be felt. *The Craft* was made shortly after *Buffy* began broadcasting, while a brief gothic revival followed in the form of *Van Helsing* (2004) and *Underworld* (2003), each of which feature vampire hunting offset with comic humour. In addition, perhaps responding to the show's appeal to a more mature female audience, older female characters with supernatural powers have since appeared in films such as *The Gift*, *What Lies Beneath*, and *The Ring* (which are discussed in the next chapter).

In terms of critical interest, several collections of essays have been published on the series, examining *Buffy* from a number of theoretical perspectives. The series lends itself to such analysis because of the richness of its writing and the challenges made to convention. Joss Whedon claims to have been motivated to create the show as a response to the tendency in slasher movies to kill off attractive blondes, wondering what might happen if she got to survive instead.[6] It is through making such a detour that the series carved out a niche for itself, for Buffy Summers is a born survivor, equipped with an innate prowess at defending herself (and a superhuman ability to heal), and although she is not immortal – having died twice in the series – her heroic status is clear.

The character derived from inauspicious beginnings however. In the original Whedon-scripted feature film, *Buffy: The Vampire Slayer* (1992), Buffy (Kristy Swanson) is a caricature dumb blonde, a *Clueless*-style cheerleader with an equally dumb jock boyfriend. The arrival of a Watcher called Merrick (Donald Sutherland) informs her about her destiny to be a Slayer ('The Chosen One'), who throughout history has been given the responsibility of keeping evil demons at bay. He also points out that teenage girls are selected for this task because they have a crucial ability to know when they are about to be attacked (leading to an amused retort from his charge that PMT is now an asset). Whedon thus upholds an essentialist notion of femininity, championing female intuition even as he exaggerates this quality, yet also instilling his heroine with a new-found confidence as she gradually accepts the role given to her. The film concludes with a prom that goes wrong, in time honoured fashion, and marks the scene of Buffy's transformation as she fights hordes of demons entering the school and dumps her boyfriend to boot. While there are trace elements of the factors that would cause the series to be such a sensation, including the humorous dig at uncomprehending adult authority as the principal walks around disciplining dead demons, the series would not only allow Whedon and his creative team further room to explore characters in greater depth, but to get much darker also.

The first season continues from the film's premise, yet shows its lead attempting to start her life over again in a new town. This Buffy Summers (now played by Gellar) is no longer part of the in-crowd. She has no clique, no boyfriend, and a previous record in 'slayage' has blotted her school record, partly prompting her mother's move to Sunnydale in the hope that this will enable her daughter to make a fresh start (the other factor being a recent divorce). The opportunity to turn over a new leaf proves redundant, however, as Day One at Sunnydale High provides a meeting with another Watcher, Rupert Giles (Anthony Stewart Head), who also serves as school librarian, and through whom she learns that the school library is positioned on the Hellmouth – a portal through which a variety of demons and other evil entities will routinely emerge. The opportunity to fit in, put her troubles behind her, and become a normal girl, which will be wistfully voiced throughout the series, thus falls at the very first hurdle. Yet Buffy is also defined by her seeming normality. Unlike the female misfits we have seen, she is, on the surface, unexceptional – an attractive blonde with a good range of trendy outfits, who is given the option early on of being a member of the school in-crowd largely because of her conventional good looks. Furthermore, she is anxious to prove herself in the same way as other American high-school girls: aiming to become a cheerleader and to be voted prom queen, buying endless clothes, and blowing her monthly allowance, as she puts it in typical Buffyspeak, on a 'cream rinse conditioner that's neither creamy or rinsey'. It is this normalcy (and wit) that makes her an endearing figure, and that offsets the more fantastical elements of each narrative. She may be the Slayer but she also regularly fights with her mother, is often vulnerable and insecure, and has a series of relationships that offer little more than heartbreak – all of which are sufficient cause to identify with her as a figure who, despite being placed in a heroic position, is also party to the foibles and problems of any other girl, perhaps more so, as Buffy seems to be made to endure specific trials as a test of her status.

In this vein, Whedon and the show's other writers appear to uphold many of the tenets laid out by Joseph Campbell in terms of heroic convention, which requires a hero to suffer to some degree, a phase referred to by Campbell as 'the road of trials'.[7] Buffy is assisted by supernatural means, including prophetic visions appearing in the form of dreams. As Campbell lyrically puts it: 'In our dreams the ageless perils, gargoyles, trials, secret helpers, and instructive figures are nightly still encountered; and in their forms we may see reflected not only the whole picture of our present case, but also the clue to what we must do to be saved.'[8] Buffy generally relies on Giles to interpret these dreams, with Willow assisting in more mystical matters, while her own role is largely determined by her superhuman strength. Campbell argues that the warrior hero's duty is to fight various tyrants in defence of humanity, arguing that 'many monsters remaining from primeval times still lurk in the outlying regions, and through malice or desperation these set themselves against the human community. They have to be cleared away ... The elementary deeds of the hero are those of the clearing field.'[9] Buffy is given a seemingly inexhaustible task, particularly given the Hellmouth's proximity and a host of other means available for demons to be conjured on Earth, and must balance being a regular schoolgirl in the day while her nights are spent patrolling graveyards to slay the undead. Like Psyche, she has the ability to move between both the ordinary world and the underworld, and can even joke about it. When a character commands her to 'go to hell', she retorts 'been there, done that' with a sarcasm that is born of actual experience ('Anne').

Much of Buffy's appeal is the degree to which she can endure suffering without being unduly phased, and a great deal of the show's humour derives from the additional gender twist in subverting expectations – such as when a terrified boy, having encountered a vampire, asks Buffy to walk him home – yet the series is also at pains to ensure that she remains properly 'feminine'. Part of this is shown in her reaction to life's adversities. Rarely does Buffy evince more than wry humour, even when clearly experiencing emotional pain, with anger and resentment virtually never surfacing. No matter how just the cause may seem, such as the sudden death of her mother, the hurtful relationships she experiences, and other traumatic events, she turns her pain inwards rather than outwards. This is in marked contrast to Willow, who succumbs to evil when her anger is ferociously unleashed in Season Six. It is also positively compared to the two other Slayers that appear in the series, each of whom is intended to replace the existing Slayer yet shown to be inadequate to this role, the first, Kendra (Bianca Lawson), having an apparent absence of emotion, while the second, Faith, has a dangerous and erratic excess.

According to Elyce Rae Helford, female anger is only deemed permissible when voiced by the 'white middle-class' Slayer, Buffy, as opposed to her black and working-class contemporaries, Kendra and Faith.[10] Kendra is called upon as the new Slayer when Buffy momentarily drowns in 'Prophecy Girl' before being revived by her friend, Xander (Nicholas Brendon). Speaking with a West Indian accent (although her exact origins are never specified), and represented as alien to American culture (even sneaking her way into the country), Kendra is the apparent antipathy of Buffy. Obediently complying with every command given by her Watcher, and seemingly denied any pleasure in life, she is presented as a relatively deprived figure who was taken from her family at a young age to be trained, and admits to owning only one set of clothes compared to Buffy's vast wardrobe. Their relationship begins with rivalry however, immediately having a face-off to establish who is the better fighter, and it is during this exchange that Kendra accuses Buffy of being too drawn by her emotions. Although Buffy replies that her emotions empower her, as we shall see, they also serve to detract from her role as Slayer. Nevertheless, Kendra is given the equivalent function of Mr Spock in *Star Trek* – the half-Vulcan alien who is similarly driven by logic and duty – and after swiftly assuming the role of a non-challenging sidekick she dies after only a few episodes.[11] It is her death in service, at the hands of evil female vampire Drusilla (Juliet Landau), that ushers forth her replacement, Faith.

Faith offers a very different alter ego to the series' lead, for where Kendra was compliant, Faith is confrontational. Buffy's sarcastic relationship with her Watcher and marks of individuality, such as attempting to have boyfriends, are relatively muted fare compared to the level of resistance offered by Faith, who admits to having 'a problem with authority figures'. This is explained, within the series rationale, by her background. No father is mentioned and, as she relates, her mother's alcoholism forced her to rely on herself from a young age – implying that she has had to grow up much sooner than her counterpart. Helford's reading of Faith as 'poor white trash' against Buffy's middle-class background is an interesting contention, for Faith is clearly intended as an example of what Buffy might have become without her mother's influence, perhaps even what might have happened to her if she had not returned to Sunnydale after Third Season episode, 'Anne', in which she briefly runs away and is forced to look after herself in the big city. (She is similarly anticipated in the tough loner version of Buffy seen in alternate universe episode 'The Wish' – without friends or family to 'balance' her.) Although Helford is on questionable ground in how she classifies socio-economic status, deeming Buffy to be middle-class due largely to the size of her wardrobe, and making an additionally problematic equation between Faith's ethical principles and her class position, it is an assessment that is corroborated within the series, which repeatedly notes Faith's relative economic disadvantage, and tougher life experiences, in order to explain her 'flaws'. In contrast to its hero, as Helford argues: 'Faith is a white girl depicted as lower in social class than Buffy. She is rebellious, sexual, and expresses her anger openly, often with relish.'[12]

The rivalry between Faith and Buffy is of particular interest because they have the potential to form such a formidable union. Faith provides Buffy with a peer who can truly understand her and the assertiveness needed to resist authoritarian efforts to undermine her. However, in the episode 'Bad Girls' she is deemed to be a negative influence, encouraging Buffy to cut classes and kill a nest of vampires for pleasure, even to steal with a 'want, take, have' philosophy. Faith steps over the line of acceptable conduct when she accidentally kills a human, causing a rift between them when, through a mixture of denial and derision, she refuses to show remorse. In the next episode ('Consequences'), she states that, as a Slayer, she is above the law, and by its end, after an attempt by the Watcher's Council to abduct and discipline her, she volunteers to work for the dark forces of Sunnydale.

Faith's development into a 'rogue slayer' is partly explained by her background. The absence of a positive female role model in her life is made clear. Her mother was a drunk, her first female Watcher was killed in front of her and her second, Gwendolyn Post (Serena Scott Thomas), betrays both her and the Council, thus seemingly encouraging her own likelihood to do the same. The male Watcher who is then assigned to her, Wesley Wyndham-Price (Alexis Denisof), arguably does still more damage with his heavy-handed attitude towards her rebellion, for as Mary Alice Money points out 'he is responsible for arranging the Council's kidnapping of Faith that, perhaps, pushes her over the line into conscious evil'.[13] Faith consequently provides an interesting contrast to Buffy, showing what she might have become without her supportive mother, dependable watcher, and close friendship network.[14] Indeed, it is seemingly her need for family of some kind that explains her relationship with the demonic figure known as Mayor Richard Wilkins III (Harry Groener), the 'man' in charge of evil forces infiltrating Sunnydale who she elects to work for in Season Three. He offers the closest thing she has to a parent, being affectionate and authoritative in equal part. Because some reasoning is thus given for her actions, Faith is presented as a complex figure who ironically reveals the limits of Buffy's relative virtue.

In many ways Faith is altogether more liberated, particularly in terms of her attitude to men, having sex to satisfy a physical rather than emotional need, and eschewing any relationships. She states that past experiences as a 'loser magnet' have influenced her decision to 'get mine and I'm gone' ('Revelations'), yet while it is motivated by a fear of being vulnerable, Faith's carefree attitude to sex makes her infinitely dangerous in moral terms. By contrast, although Buffy is continually hurt by her romantic endeavours – with such consistency, in fact, that a sense of masochism becomes evident – it is her attitude and demeanour that is approved within the narrative. Her first love, Angel, is an archetypal bad boy, a vampire with a sadistic history who reformed through being given a soul yet promptly loses it again when he and Buffy first make love on her seventeenth birthday – his moment of 'true happiness' causing the curse to be lifted. He then returns to monstrous form, viciously rejecting her while reverting to his evil ways, and although Willow succeeds in restoring his soul and making him 'good' again, the pair separate, knowing their love can never be fulfilled. A boy at college, Parker Abrams (Adam Kaufman), follows, yet breaks it off after sex with her, remarking that she is not the 'fun' girl she had seemed to be at school. In both cases she blames herself and questions what she did wrong. Her third love, Riley Finn (Marc Blucas), is seemingly more suitable; an assistant psychology lecturer at college who seems relatively normal yet turns out to be a covert member of the Initiative – a secret task-force aimed at capturing and reprogramming demons for military use. Clearly intimidated by her status as Slayer, and the fact that she is physically stronger than him, yet claiming that it is because she is emotionally distant, he also breaks their relationship off. The fact that he secretly allows vampires to feed off him reveals his low self-worth, yet these ego problems are seemingly eradicated when he re-appears in Season Six episode, 'As You Were', now married to a tough demon hunter. That Buffy must endure having to work alongside her in the episode, despite still having feelings for Riley, further underscores the emotional trials she is put through by Whedon and co, particularly where relationships are concerned.

As if to corroborate her masochistic streak in picking guys who are all wrong for her, Buffy's relationship in the last season is also the most perverse, falling for a character she has seemingly hated throughout the series, and who has expressed his desire to kill her on numerous occasions, another vampire, Spike (James Marsters). Their relationship takes a new turn in 'Smashed' when Spike, seemingly neutered by the Initiative with a brain chip that prevents him from physically hurting humans, learns that Buffy is the exception to this rule. In a dramatic twist intended to denote passion their subsequent fight transforms into sex. However, she feels guilt at their ensuing relationship and confesses to a fringe member of the gang, Tara (Amber Benson), that having sex with Spike is a form of self-loathing.[15] Her awareness of these motivations finally causes her to end their relationship, yet his response is one of obsession and resentment that culminates in an attempted rape. Curiously, and extremely problematically, he is forgiven for this and perceived, like *The Craft*'s Chris, as being motivated by love. Like Sarah, Buffy blames herself for having 'led him on' and romance underpins their relationship to the end, with Buffy continuing to defend Spike, even after friend and would-be lover, Robin Wood (DB Woodside) attempts to exact revenge for his mother's death, retaining her allegiance for reasons that extend beyond needing his fighting skills.[16] By remaining loyal to Spike, Buffy seemingly proves that she is above such traits as anger and vengeance, traits which are demonised in other female figures throughout the series, and although this causes everyone to question her judgement, her instincts are shown to be correct in the series finale 'Chosen' – when Spike becomes a martyr figure who helps destroy Sunnydale for the benefit of all. He is accordingly vindicated for the atrocities he has committed, as are Buffy's feelings towards him.

In contrast to such problematic relationships, Faith's nonchalant attitude to men seems far less destructive, yet when rivalry forms between herself and Buffy, Faith's 'want, take, have' philosophy extends to the men she has been involved with, and both Riley and Angel are used as a means of attacking her former friend. Faith is thus set up as a hate figure and in their ensuing acrimony Buffy becomes increasingly ruthless. When Faith shoots a poisoned arrow at Angel, and Buffy learns that only a Slayer's blood contains the antidote, she plans to feed Faith to him. Having been viciously beaten and stabbed by her, Faith is left in a deep coma, yet Buffy is not asked to show any remorse for this, proving to be much more forgiving when it comes to a vampire who has killed many more people, than a friend who has lost her way. A rupture thus becomes apparent in the show's moral code as love for Angel seemingly legitimates Buffy's desire to kill another human. As Mimi Marinucci points out: 'Though unsuccessful, Buffy's attempt to kill Faith violates the stricture against taking human life' – yet this violation is apparently excused because 'human beings with no remaining trace of humanity do not warrant the moral consideration that ordinary human beings deserve'.[17] However, traces of humanity are as evident in Faith as in virtually all the other characters in the series, and she is allowed both physical and spiritual recovery as the series gradually sets about rehabilitating her.

In 'This Year's Girl', she wakes from her coma to find the closest thing she had to a family dead, with Buffy having killed the Mayor.[18] All is not lost, however, as a magical amulet bestowed by him allows Faith to evade her would-be captors – the increasingly sinister Watchers Council – by swapping bodies with Buffy. Throughout the next episode, 'Who Are You?', Faith struts about in her enemy's guise, mocking Buffy's insistence on upholding prescribed moral laws by repeating the line: 'You can't do that, because it's wrong.' However, this attempt to usurp her enemy's life makes Faith increasingly unsettled. Buffy's mother unwittingly asserts to her 'daughter' that Faith must be 'horribly unhappy' and this view is confirmed in the events that follow. She sleeps with Buffy's boyfriend, Riley, yet when he declares his love she is clearly disturbed by such tenderness, reiterating the idea that Faith is a lost little girl who only ever wanted to be loved. The supposed freedoms she has enjoyed, including having sex without forming any attachments, are shown to be an evasion of what she really wants, and self-loathing is deemed to be her primary motivation. While she ends the episode by opting to do what is right, saving a church congregation from attack, she cannot resist fighting Buffy when she arrives at the scene, revealing in the process how much she hates her own self. As she effectively battles her self-image, Faith screams: 'You're nothing! Disgusting, murderous bitch! You're nothing. You're disgusting!' The body switch is reversed and Faith leaves town, lost and alone.

In a crossover episode ('Five by Five') of tie-in series, *Angel* (1999–2004), Faith attempts to provoke Angel into killing her in order to rid herself of the remorse the bodyswitch has seemingly stirred in her. In 'Sanctuary', Buffy travels to LA to confront Angel about protecting Faith, who she clearly wants dead, yet he is moved by a sense of kinship with Faith and orders Buffy to leave. Guilt and regret finally overwhelm Faith, and when Angel is arrested for harbouring her she hands herself in to the police in order to protect others from harm, as well as atone for her sins. As Helford states:

> Angel has committed far more and far greater atrocities than Faith in his hundreds of years on earth yet white man's anger is far more easily forgiven than a white woman's: Angel is a hero starring in his own series while Faith ends up mentally ill and imprisoned . . . she teaches us blatantly that girl's anger, when allowed full reign, is not only harmful to others, but entirely self-destructive.[19]

In this sense, Faith has an interesting counterpart in *The Craft*'s Nancy, who is similarly incarcerated because of the danger she poses. Both women bear some comparison because they are presented as equally lacking in self-control and moral compunction. Both come from poor backgrounds and have to exist without adequate parental support, yet while they are each seen to abuse their respective abilities in an attempt to ease their unhappiness this patently fails to work. Neither money nor magic can make Nancy feel good about herself, which is what leads her to hound Sarah, and while ostensibly enjoying the catharsis offered by violence, Faith finds that it cannot offer the release she craves, with Buffy serving as a continual reminder of opportunities she never had. Both women are possessed by an inner rage borne of their attendant frustrations and target female peers when jealousy forms a wedge between them, yet the explanation given in each scenario is that all they truly desire is to be loved. However, while Nancy is seemingly beyond any chance of redemption, bound by Sarah from causing harm and last seen strapped to a bed cackling dementedly to herself, Faith elects to confine herself, provoked by a conscience she can no longer deny.

Ironically, despite her flaws, Faith threatens to eclipse Buffy – The Chosen One – as the most interesting female character in the series. There is greater torment to her character, and consequently greater psychological complexity than her 'whitebread' predecessor, who seems destined to deliver perky one-liners whatever catastrophe might occur. By contrast, Faith is a remarkable depiction of the aberrant female, and as Helford notes, despite her anti-hero status, indeed, largely because of it, she 'challenges certain limits in representations of women's power'.[20] The series may have its share of female villains who are seen to abuse the power at their disposal and are despatched accordingly, including Drusilla (Juliet Landau), Darla (Julie Benz), and Glory (Clare Kramer), yet Faith survives, and although she is made to undergo a necessary redemption for her sins – in a Catholic gesture that is very much a Whedon trademark – she remains a creature of fascinating anomalies.[21]

Faith's astonishing self-possession is marked, even amidst the inner turmoil she faces. Unlike Buffy, she does not need the support group of friends, and, initially at least, says and does exactly what she pleases, providing the appeal of a female character who refuses to play by the rules. While Buffy continually has her heart broken, Faith feeds her sexual appetite when she feels like it; while Buffy befriends demons, witches, and werewolves, Faith seemingly has no need for anyone; and while Buffy begrudges her calling and craves to be a normal girl, Faith does her job with relish, indeed, in the series' eyes, too much so. Violence is an activity she clearly enjoys, yet innocent people are killed in the process, detracting from the pleasure afforded by her transgressions, necessitating a period of incarceration and the introspection this is intended to give her. For a character initially intended to have only half a dozen appearances in the show, the prominence given to her character reveals a reluctance to write her out as easily as some critics have assumed.

Season Four of *Angel* brings Faith out into the world once more. In 'Salvage', Wesley Wyndham-Price, the Watcher Faith once tortured in 'Five by Five' in order to goad Angel into killing her, now asks for her help. As he explains, with a creature known as 'the Beast' on the rampage in LA, and Angel's soul missing, the only person with sufficient strength and loyalty to Angel to help capture him is Faith (which interestingly ignores the supposed love of his life, Buffy). The ease with which Faith breaks out of the North California Women's Correctional Facility proves that her containment is self-governed. One kick at the glass, followed by a few non-fatal tussles with the guards and she is free, yet she appears increasingly convinced that she is back only to save Angel – viewing her likely death as inevitable. Badly beaten by the Beast at the end of the episode, a new fragility is also apparent. This is not the fearsome character we have previously seen, but someone whose humanity is painfully exposed.

The next episode ('Release') plots a showdown between herself and Angelus – the 'evil' alter ego by which Angel is known – in which he attempts to 'turn' her with a bite on the neck. However, because she has injected herself, at Wesley's suggestion, with the mystical drug, Orpheus, they pass out together. The final episode ('Orpheus') reveals their descent into a narcotic dream-world: Faith, Angel, and his evil alter-ego. Slipping into a coma due to the high dose of the drug within her, Faith is perilously close to death. Wesley provides a eulogy even before she is gone, stating 'she was brave and she died in battle' as if any chance of saving her is beyond consideration. Still more disconcertingly, she is shown to view her impending death with the same alacrity. Interior scenes of her mental activities show her repeatedly comment on her time being close, yet Angel is quick to dismiss her seeming readiness to die as they converse in their drug-induced hell, saying derisively of death that 'it's easier than redemption'. While their kinship is made evident in this psychological voyage together, his overweening piety is equally apparent, as the following exchange indicates:

Faith: It is my time.
Angel: Our time is never up, Faith. We pay for everything.

Propelled to fight to stay alive Faith eventually wakes from the effects of the deadly narcotic in time to save an inert Angel from being killed by his own son, Connor (Vincent Kartheiser). The episode concludes with the sense of a debt having been paid by Faith, not only in risking her life to save Angel, but in teaching his wayward son a lesson no one else could. In doing so she partially recovers her heroic status, while retaining the free spirit that makes her such an interesting character, and having said her goodbyes in typically aloof fashion, she leaves with Willow for Sunnydale and the events of Buffy's last season.

That Willow has also done some good in the episode by once again restoring Angel's soul effectively serves the same redemptive function: proving how far she has come since an obsession with magic, and revenge for her lover's death, first led her astray. 'I flayed a live human and almost destroyed the world' she tells Wesley in an effort to empathise with his own sense of guilt, yet the line is delivered in such a perky manner that it fails to convey any great qualms about past misdeeds. Willow's crime, like Faith's, is that she abused her powers, transgressing the moral line upheld in the series that humans cannot be killed, but on a narrative level it lies in threatening to upstage Buffy. The moral message is clear. If both women can learn to use their powers for good, and remain within permissible rules of conduct, they can join Buffy in fighting the ultimate fight – one the series has brought us to on numerous occasions: the end of the world – but they must also defer to her greater wisdom.

Why Buffy has never been tempted to err in the same way as Faith and Willow is apparently explained by her status as the 'true' Slayer. The only deed that causes her moral difficulty is her relationship with Spike, which emanates from an inexplicable self-loathing, and for which she is punished in his attempted rape. In all other respects, Buffy seems to know the distinction between right and wrong better than anyone. This is seemingly a quality given to her by her mother, helping to sustain her and propelling her to always do the right thing, even against her best interests.

The extent to which Buffy, Faith and Willow have each been shaped by their relationship with their mothers, as well as other older females in their lives, warrants some consideration. J.P. Williams uses Nancy Chodorow's analysis of mother–daughter relationships to compare Buffy's mother, Joyce Summers (Kristine Sutherland), Faith's Watcher, Gwendolyn Post (Serena Scott Thomas), and Willow's one-time mentor, computer teacher, and techno-pagan, Jenny Calendar (Robia LaMorte), viewing them all as poor role models and arguing that although Jenny is seemingly the most able to nurture her ward, her sudden death (caused in part by a sense of duty to her tribe) signals an inability to sustain female strength in maturity. As Williams puts it: 'Not even Jenny, a woman who speaks against patriarchy and envisions a new society that marries magic and technology, can escape the influence of the patriarchal order.'[22] All such characters allegedly fail as mentors and Williams additionally cites Joyce's initial denial of Buffy's true identity, the intellectualised neglect Sheila Rosenberg (Jordan Baker) offers daughter, Willow ('Gingerbread'), and the competitive relationship between Catherine Madison (Robin Riker) and daughter, Amy (Elizabeth Anne Allen) ('The Witch') as further examples of poor motherhood in which biological ties are less than ideal.

However, Joyce greatly improves as a mother when she learns to trust her instincts, as well as her daughter, and when Buffy struggles to come to terms with her new-found responsibilities following her sudden death in Season Six, Giles notably informs her: 'Your mother taught you all you need to know to be a human being.' Jenny Calendar's legacy, by this point in the series, is more questionable as Willow's interest in the occult, initiated by her former teacher, becomes destructive. While magic initially allows Willow to make the transition from shy school nerd to powerful witch, her eventual dependence on it is paralleled with drug abuse, causing girlfriend, Tara, to leave when she proves unable to abstain from casting a spell for even one week.[23] Nevertheless, despite abuses that include bringing Buffy back to life and effectively ripping her out of heaven (the psychological effects of which remain disappointingly unrealised), as well as putting Buffy's younger sister, Dawn (Michelle Trachtenberg), at risk when 'under the influence', Buffy forgives her friend and blames herself for not having noticed that she was 'drowning'.

Willow is thus given a reprieve that Faith is largely denied. Instead, Buffy's hatred of Faith is manifest – and can be explained not only because Faith betrayed her with Riley, or because she shuns the duty Buffy has undertaken, but because she makes her own insecurities manifest. Faith may be jealous of Buffy's life, yet this envy works both ways, as she reminds her, because Faith represents a level of freedom Buffy resents. In fact, Buffy is jealous the moment Faith first enters her life, simply because she gets on so well with both her friends and her mother. Buffy fears being replaced and resents her darker sister long before she ever went bad, and as the series develops any level of kinship or understanding becomes further undermined.

Just as the shallow Cordelia (Charisma Carpenter) represents what Buffy might have become without her calling, Faith reflects an outcast status she is keen to reject, a fact made all the more ironic because of Buffy's own experience of being a misunderstood teen with a bad reputation. An interesting early episode illustrates this when Buffy's mother becomes involved with a sinister new man ('Ted'). His attempts to discipline Buffy result in accidentally falling to his death and the police arrest her and read out her record. The various violent offences detailed make her sound like a highly disturbed and dangerous young woman. In fact, they make her sound very much like Faith. The crucial difference is Buffy's relationship with her mother, for while Joyce has, until this point, been too scatty and self-interested to offer adequate support to her daughter, she immediately realises the severity of the situation and lies to enable the charges to be dropped. Such instances show how easily Buffy could have become scapegoated, and perhaps made into a bitter outlaw like Faith, without a loving mother to defend her.

Willow's equivalent lack of a mother is notable. Shiela Rosenberg appears only once in the series yet leaves the impression of an emotionally distant academic lacking any attachment to her daughter. If Willow has inherited her mother's intelligence she is also psychologically burdened by the lack of interest taken in her. Former friend, Amy, continues this theme of poor maternal legacies by abusing witchcraft in the same way as her mother did before her. Writing before Joyce's character development, and affirming an absence of mature women in the series with whom to identify or confide in, Williams argues that: 'The Chosen One, and her friends, will have to invent their own ideal of womanhood, with few positive models to guide them', asserting that 'its ability to provide an alternative model of womanhood is perhaps the series' most intriguing cliff-hanger.'[24] In fact, the series ultimately avoids any such pursuit, placing Joyce as the role model whom Buffy is destined to follow, and otherwise displaying an avowed distrust of powerful women.

While this claim may seem to be at odds with a series that champions a young girl's heroism, it is nevertheless the case that Buffy's narrative position is only approved because she is non-threatening. Indeed, she is the average girl-next-door in every way but her fighting skills; assertive enough to say what she thinks but never to step outside the confines of permissible behaviour, always displacing any tension with humorous (frequently self-deprecating) dialogue, and open and honest to a frankly monotonous extent. Part of her attraction is that she is so ordinary and familiar – lamenting the purchase of hair products that do not fulfil their promises, wearing a range of trendy clothes, making bad choices in relationships – yet also treading a very narrow path regarding what is deemed 'right'. Few episodes portray her as a wayward teen, and any resistance towards her assumed destiny as Slayer is relatively short-lived. Following a near-death experience in Season Two opener, 'When She Was Bad', Buffy upsets her friends by riding roughshod over their feelings yet is soon remorseful and back to normal. In Season Three's opener, 'Anne', she exchanges her home for the horrors of city life yet returns to Sunnydale in the very next episode ('Dead Man's Party'), where her friends berate her for having run away. Denied the right to be selfish, even to the extent of trying to 'find' herself after a painful sacrifice, she must always put others first, thus proving herself as a model mother in the making.

She has ample lessons in what to avoid in undertaking this role. College provides her with a false mentor figure in Professor Maggie Walsh (Lindsay Crouse), a variation on Willow's academic mother, who turns out to be a villain in the mould of Dr Frankenstein, intent on creating cyborg soldiers made from circuitry, demons, and reclaimed corpses. Despite being an intelligent female in a position of power, Walsh is portrayed as a 'ball-breaker' whose inability to bend Buffy to her will makes her intent on destroying her instead: incarnating the ultimate bad mother. Tragically, Joyce's qualities are never appreciated before her untimely death, after which Buffy has to become a mother herself, taking responsibility for magically created kid sister, Dawn.

By this point in the series Buffy is at her most conventional, struggling to support her new household and be a good parent. She sacrifices herself to save Dawn ('The Gift') yet even after Willow's magic resurrects her, changing Buffy from a human into something Other – as Spike puts it, 'you came back wrong' – this does little to provide her with any renewed interest. Unlike Faith, whose life has consisted of living on the road and having to fend for herself, Buffy's life remains relatively comfortable, even after the loss of both parent figures (her father's disinterest having been confirmed in 'Family', when he goes on vacation with his secretary rather than spend time with the girls during Joyce's illness). The series evades plausibility in asking us to believe that Buffy's minimum wage job in a burger joint, or the school counsellor role she later takes at Sunnydale High, can keep the rather impressive roof over their heads – or that she can convince the authorities she is capable of the responsibilities of child care. Although she learns that certain adjustments have to be made, particularly when a vengeance demon hears Dawn complain about being left alone, making Buffy aware of her sister's needs and agree to stay home more ('Older and Far Away'), it would seem that all the sacrifices and strength of character she has acquired in being a Slayer have ultimately prepared her for the role of motherhood, like the Final Girls of the slasher film examined in Chapter 2. Indeed, the rather spurious invention of a sister, created through supernatural means yet accepted as flesh and blood, coincides with the somewhat hurried demise of her mother to deliver Buffy to this fate. Having proven her courage and virtue, she is given the responsibility of raising another young woman to adulthood, and one might wonder whether Williams' call for an alternative portrayal of womanhood is either met or evaded in this fate.

Buffy undertakes the role of self-sacrificing nurturer in not only proving herself willing to die for Dawn, but in finally being placed in charge of an entire group of young women in the series finale – potential Slayers gathered from around the world to be trained by her. Faith returns with Willow to help Buffy win her ultimate challenge and it is a testimony to her greater vitality and charisma (as much as Buffy's comparative arrogance) that Faith is elected leader in preference over her, thereby being legitimated as The Chosen One (and thus fulfilling Buffy's worst fears). Yet Faith's turn at the helm is short-lived, endangering the Potentials' lives still further, and it is Buffy who comes to the rescue.

The experience makes Faith aware of the difficulties that come with leadership, including being alone, which she had not anticipated when envying Buffy's life, easing their antagonism with a new level of understanding. As Faith states in reference to the status they have fought over: 'There's only supposed to be one. Maybe that's why we can never get along. We're not supposed to exist together.' Yet it is the anomaly of their co-existence that also provides the way to defeat their opponents: inspiring Buffy to further change the rules. The series ends with a nod to feminist intentions as Willow performs a spell that transfers Buffy and Faith's power to the adolescent Slayers-in-waiting. Reinstalled as leader, Buffy gives the speech:

> In every generation a Slayer is born – because a bunch of men who died thousands of years ago made up that rule. They were powerful men. This woman [indicating Willow] is more powerful than all of them combined. So I say we change the rule. From now on every girl in the world who might be a Slayer *will* be a Slayer, every girl who could have the power, *will* have the power... Slayers, every one of us. Are you ready to be strong?

The spell works, Willow's virtue remains intact, and Faith fights at Buffy's side, along with all the transformed Potentials, yet while the message is a well-intentioned hymn to girl power, it is also invariably compromised, with the series having gone out of its way to warn against female power being taken too far.

For all its willingness to redeem male demons, werewolves, and vampires, transgressive females tend to be despatched. Vampires, Drusilla and Darla, are both incinerated, Glory is annihilated, a female werewolf, Veruca (Paige Moss), who takes pride in her identity, is not permitted to exist, and the maniacal Maggie Walsh is killed by her own creation. Of the females who are redeemed we might ask at what cost? Willow may be rehabilitated yet her misdemeanours have smashed her confidence greatly – implying that she will never use magic again without Buffy's permission. As to Faith, the 'rogue' slayer who taught Buffy how to defy the oppressive authority of the Watchers Council and be true to herself, while she threatens the established order for the majority of the series she also undergoes a form of redemption that harnesses her powers for good, yet necessarily humbles her in the process. Her main purpose throughout has been as a mirror image to Buffy, showing what she might have become without a supportive mother, or the close friendship network Buffy frequently draws upon. Likened to a 'Spartan' by former Watcher, Gwendolyn Post, Faith is battle hardened and self-sufficient and therefore potentially dangerous, yet her unruly power is decisively reigned in, having stood as an example of what Buffy could have become, in another life, and testified to how unacceptable such an option is.

Like Willow, Faith's relationship with Buffy follows a path of resentment, rivalry, and hostility, yet the finale affirms the viability of female affinities as they work together for a common goal, intended to demonstrate how far they have each come. Over the course of the series viewers have witnessed Buffy transform into a mature young woman who eventually comes to terms with her destiny and assumes the responsibilities given to her. While she experiences the difficulties of a typical teenager in her parents' divorce and various failed romances, she admirably faces up to her duties as Slayer, yet it also remains perplexing that, despite possessing exceptional qualities, Buffy only wishes to be normal – a claim she repeats at several points in the series and which she achieves at its end by no longer having the weight of the world on her shoulders. Willow and Faith have each wished for much more over their narrative development, yet Willow is left with even less self-belief than she had at the beginning of the series, afraid of her powers and unsure of herself, while Faith is placed firmly in Buffy's shadow, a dismal hint at her further rehabilitation suggested in a potential relationship developing with Robin Wood.

By using their abilities to empower the Potentials, the series ultimately upholds a feminist idea of mutual strength and solidarity. Buffy, Faith, and Willow have all grown up in their own ways, tested their respective powers, endured their losses, and matured into capable and responsible women, yet it is Buffy who finally calls the shots and it is her wish for relative normalcy that is fulfilled. The series finale features the destruction of home and school (a la *Carrie*) as Sunnydale implodes, freeing them to make their way in the world, with the implication that they have all finished fighting their demons.

Whedon planned to create a spin-off series after *Buffy*, as he did with *Angel*, and among the mooted ideas he proposed a show that centred on Faith, in which she was intended to travel around America on a motorbike, sorting out problems as she went, her renegade status necessitating that she would always have to move on. The idea of a show focusing on Faith is testimony to the character's popularity, yet Dushku opted to make *Tru Calling* (2003–05) instead, a series about a psychic mortuary attendant who uncovers how murders occurred through contacting the dead.[25] Although the series proved to be short-lived it nevertheless makes an interesting link to the subject dealt with in the next chapter, which evaluates the investigative role played by women in recent horror who unveil a murder in their midst and avenge troubled spirits. While they are older than the largely adolescent characters seen in horror, these women are equally compelling in the abilities given to them, and their courage is heightened by their role as mothers, continuing a thematic thread noted throughout this study. As with *Buffy*'s finale, they also affirm the possibilities of female kinship and extend the notion of a rites of passage beyond adolescence, even if many of the same obstacles are encountered, as we shall see.

6
Demeter's Daughters: Wronged Girls and the Mother Avenger

> You never saw such a wild thing as my mother . . . behind her the breakers of the savage indifferent sea, like the witnesses of a furious justice.
>
> – 'The Bloody Chamber', Angela Carter

This chapter examines the maternal hero in horror, arguing that the investigative avenging role that has been undertaken in recent narratives is a significant development in the genre's treatment of mothers. As a heroic character, the mother avenger can be understood as an extension of the slasher's Final Girl – equipped with the resourcefulness and courage needed to defend herself against harm, as well as the compassion and intuitiveness required to unearth specific wrongs. Her emergence is notable, it is argued, because vengeful mothers have tended to be castigated in horror. We need only think of Mrs Voorhees (Betsy Palmer) in *Friday the 13th* (1980), whose grievance against the neglectful teenagers that allowed her son to drown at Crystal Lake summer camp sparks a murderous rampage, to find a legendary example of dangerous maternal excess. Reynold Humphries reads this character as a 'distorted' Final Girl, complying with Clover's coding of active heroines as 'phallic' in arguing that 'her initiative and activity have enabled her to avenge her son and, in so doing, she becomes masculine and therefore doubly guilty socially and ideologically'.[1] In his assessment, Mrs Voorhees is a castrating woman who is ultimately punished for displaying 'masculine' traits – being decapitated by another woman, Alice (Adrienne King), at the end of the film. But why should one woman be punished for gender transgression when the Final Girl is arguably guilty of the same 'crime' within this coda? After all, the slasher routinely usurps traditional gender roles in equipping its Final Girl with the skills necessary to survive, including Alice and her counterparts. Humphries demonstrates evident confusion in his assumptions, yet even in doing so he reminds us that vengeance has, alongside the notion of narrative agency and heroism, all too often been associated with masculinity. Only rare instances are allowed in horror cinema in which women are permitted revenge, and they demand greater analysis because of this.

A central argument throughout this book is that many horror narratives derive from much older stories, and the mother avenger film is no different, drawing as it does upon ancient mythology. Demeter was a goddess who challenged the king of the gods, Zeus himself, when he refused to intervene over her daughter Persephone's abduction by Hades. As goddess of fertility, she uses her power to blight the harvest and starve the mortals, thus forcing Zeus into action, and eventually recovers her lost girl. It is a story of female rage, and revolt, against male violence (the god of the underworld in this case), and male indifference (the formerly apathetic Zeus), as well as being a moving testament to maternal devotion. Demeter refuses to give up on her daughter, she refuses to submit to what remains a patriarchal order in Olympus, and uses what power she has to gain justice. The films we shall look at in this chapter present women at different stages of motherhood, who similarly find the power within themselves to stand up and make a difference. Although they do not work to save their own biological daughters, they defend girls who are similarly lost to Hades in the sense that they are all dead, recovering their lost bodies while also discovering something about themselves in the process.

The maternal avenger film centres on a murder investigation conducted by a female protagonist, aided and abetted by supernatural forces. In each of the films discussed, the lead female's status as a mother provides a sense of responsibility that motivates them to engage in a form of vengeance by proxy on behalf of younger women that have each been killed; utilising intelligence, integrity, and some degree of intuition in trying to achieve justice on the part of those who have been wronged. They may, it is argued, be considered to be Demeter's daughters in both the moral stand that they take and their maternal status – which seems to inform their actions. By placing older women at the forefront of their narratives, these films interestingly comment on the female characters assessed thus far, and the destinies that are largely approved for them.

In the films examined in this chapter, *What Lies Beneath* (2000), *The Gift* (2000), the US re-make of cult Japanese film *Ringu, The Ring* (2002), and its sequel *Ring Two* (2005), a mother is led by supernatural elements to expose the murder of a young woman. All lose the men in their lives, all have some involvement with the occult in focusing on the troubled spirit of a murdered girl, and all champion a mother's courage and compassion as they investigate the events surrounding each death and, in most cases, lay the victim's soul to rest. These films are regarded as important, not only because an older woman is focused upon, but because the maternal avenger provides a culmination of the themes we have looked at: placing narrative interest and moral responsibility with female figures; articulating the difficulties they experience; validating what are presented as explicitly 'female' skills in both understanding what has happened and overcoming the dangers faced; and indicating that independence and assertiveness can be achieved with maturity – as proven by the heroic role assumed by the women that lead each narrative.

In each of these films a multiple exploration is undertaken by its protagonist. The mother avenger is positioned as an investigator who, by uncovering the circumstances behind the death of a young woman, learns more about herself. Because of this investigative role these characters share an affinity with Clarice Starling (Jodie Foster) in *Silence of the Lambs* (1991). When repeatedly asked by her boss, Jack Crawford (Scott Glenn), to tell him what she 'sees' during their search for serial killer, 'Buffalo Bill' (Ted Levine), we are alerted to the fact that Starling has a particular aptitude for this work, seemingly by dint of her age and, more specifically, her gender. Indeed, it is the combination of these factors, as much as her training, that allows her to spot the glitter nail polish on a victim's body (and denote its significance), and which additionally urges her to look inside Frederica Bimmel's jewellery box when checking her room for clues. What lies beneath the pre-pubescent ballerina figure displayed on top, as Starling discovers, is evidence of a dawning sexuality represented by naked photographs of Frederica, which, together with her clothes-making apparatus, help to explain the killer's modus operandi. Although her relationship with Hannibal Lector (Anthony Hopkins) tends to be given greatest critical attention, Clarice relies on her best friend, Ardelia (Kasi Lemmons), to help decipher the killer's identity, and utilises her own intuitive skills to interpret the clues his victims have left behind, demonstrating a level of intelligence and courage that is shared by later female protagonists undertaking equivalent investigations.

Linda Williams' article 'When the Woman Looks' acquires additional meaning in respect of the female investigator in horror, for what all the films evaluated maintain is that when the woman looks she sees in a particular way, led partly by intuition, partly by intellect, and partly by some other mysterious force that is presented as supernatural. Neither is it simply the act of looking that, as Williams asserts, presents a 'potentially subversive recognition of the power and potency of non-phallic sexuality',[2] it is the host of female experiences that are drawn upon, the kinship established with female spirits, and the questions that are asked of patriarchy. Like Clarice, these female investigators are gifted with a particular 'sight', one that allows them to uncover specific secrets, as well as providing some insight into their own lives.

This is particularly evident in *What Lies Beneath*, in which Claire Spencer (Michelle Pfeiffer), a woman who seemingly has it all in terms of a loving marriage to husband Norman (Harrison Ford) and a beautiful home, starts to experience strange phenomena while home alone, and eventually discovers that she is being haunted by her husband's murdered lover. Claire's experiences initially seem to be the product of an overactive imagination, seemingly triggered by the fact that her daughter, Caitlin (Katharine Towne), has left home to attend college, prompting a level of anxiety now that her only child has moved out and her role as mother is no longer central – a rationale she describes as going through 'an empty nest syndrome'. However, as the film probes deeper into Claire's behaviour it also explores her marriage more closely and reveals it to be a sham. *What Lies Beneath* proves that rites of passage are not limited to puberty but can occur at any stage of a person's life, including middle age. In fact, while Claire initially seems like a woman with too much time on her hands, whose apparent frustration with being a trophy wife has led to 'neurotic' behaviour in order to get attention, we learn by the end of the film that this is not the case. What lies beneath the façade of a crumbling marriage she has tried in vain to preserve turns out to be a murderous secret that she eventually uncovers by piecing specific clues together.[3]

That curiosity leads her to discover her husband's true nature has obvious shades of 'Bluebeard', yet while the heroine of this tale is newly married, Claire's long marriage to Norman suggests that she has been in a constant state of denial. By the end of the film, having acquired a degree of self-knowledge, she effectively regains control over her life. Significantly, it is a rival for her husband's affection, a young female student he had an affair with, who will provide the catalyst for this change, her spirit contacting Claire after her death, and even saving her from her husband's murderous intent.

The departure of Claire's daughter for college is an event she claims to look forward to at the start of the film. As she says to her husband: 'I get my life back. Some time for myself. Some time for us.' Norman makes it clear that it is the latter option he has anticipated. Alone together, the couple's relationship seems intimate and loving, even competing with their amorous new neighbours to see who can make the most noise. However, a growing sense of unease develops as odd events occur around the house when Claire is alone. An electrical fault shocks her, the front door keeps opening, the stereo turns on by itself, and a framed photograph of herself with Norman being awarded the Du Pont chair in Genetics repeatedly falls and breaks, seemingly of its own accord. Yet it is the bathroom where odd things happen the most, and water becomes a crucial element in the supernatural activity to follow (as it will in the other films discussed). Claire begins to see visions of a young woman in her bathtub and reflected in the lake their house backs onto, prompting her husband to recommend a psychiatrist. The man appointed, in contrast to the majority of cinema shrinks, is refreshingly sympathetic and level-headed, advising her to examine for herself what she thinks the problem might be.

Despite the film's supernatural theme, Claire's subsequent investigation could be read as a search for her lost self, as much as an actual figure that has entered her life. This possibility is hinted at in several ways, most notably when her psychiatrist asks what the woman she sees looks like and Claire replies 'me'. As we eventually discover, their similarities extend beyond surface appearance. Both women were gifted, yet had promising careers cut short, and the man responsible, in each case, is Norman. Claire's gradual realisation of who this woman was and what happened to her serves as the equivalent of an epiphany in which she can no longer deny who her husband is and what he is capable of. It allows her to see her marriage clearly for the first time and forces her to take control. However, it is a long journey before Claire is prepared to see things as they are, and the narrative is peppered with false clues that deliberately lead us astray.

From the outset, despite their seeming intimacy, Claire is presented as an immature figure who is very much in her husband's shadow. Scared of being left alone in the house after strange events begin to occur, she even goes to Norman's research lab one night, leading him to ask she is punishing him for prioritising his work. The question suggests a level of guilt and draws us further into their past. We learn that he is an ambitious research scientist endeavouring to escape his father's esteemed reputation, and that she was a former cellist who forsook any ambitions of her own after their marriage. The re-discovery of her Juilliard tee-shirt in Caitlin's bedroom is a forgotten part of herself that fills her with nostalgia, indicating an early talent and ambition that never fully developed. As we later find out, Norman met her shortly after her first husband died, when she was playing in concerts with a young baby in tow. In his view of their marriage, his arrival was a welcome intervention, in hers, it effectively put a stop to her life as she attempted to become the perfect wife he wanted: 'I gave up everything! My life. My music.' However, she only admits this fact when she realises that Norman had an affair, being forced to do so by the spirit haunting her. The repressed memory parallels her repressed feelings of frustration with her life, which significantly only emerge when Caitlin leaves home.

Claire's daughter is only seen briefly at the beginning of the film yet serves as an important figure in their relationship, one Norman initially seems to resent yet later professes more disturbing feelings towards. If he begins the film seeming anxious for his step-daughter to leave so that he can have his wife to himself, this later becomes transmuted into discomfiting hints of sexual interest. He finally makes this evident when he attempts to kill his wife in the film's climax, suggesting that she may serve as Claire's replacement by saying: 'Maybe your "tragic suicide" will help push Caitlin and I closer together. You know every time I look at her I see you.' As we learn by this point, the fact that he has already been involved with a young woman who resembles Claire – a relationship he defends because she made him feel good about himself – indicates Norman's reluctance to mature, or to accept that his wife is ageing. While Claire has shown herself to be in emotional denial about certain events in her life, Norman displays intense jealousy about his father's reputation and an inflated ego that has led to his interest in younger women. What lies beneath their marriage, as the narrative unfolds, are a host of insecurities and resentments.

When Norman asks if Claire is punishing him for neglecting her she retorts: 'This isn't about you. It's about me.' However, as events transpire, the matter at hand is clearly about them both, as her 'haunting' will illuminate. The fact that she crashed her car a year earlier, for seemingly no reason, suggests that she had an 'episode', while the increasing anxiety focused on her neighbour, Mary Feur (Miranda Otto), reiterates the idea that Claire is a 'neurotic'. Convinced that she has been murdered by her husband, Claire attempts to contact Mary via a ouija board, inviting 'kooky' best friend Jody (Diane Scarwid) over to help. However, the rite is aborted when Jody fails to take it seriously and, seemingly confirming that Claire is merely suffering from an overactive imagination, Mary appears, alive, soon afterwards. Apologising for the concern she has caused, she tells Claire that she regularly leaves her husband yet always returns, seemingly out of dependence. 'You must think I'm pathetic' she laments, but Claire understands all too easily.

Her fears for Mary turn out to be both a classic means of transference and a portent of things to come. It is her own husband who turns out to be a murderer and her own life, both literal and symbolic, that is at risk. Having solved this 'disappearance', the narrative pushes her to look elsewhere for the woman in her visions. When the photo of Norman's award ceremony breaks for a second time, Claire looks more closely at the newspaper cutting and sees the story of a missing girl on the other side, a girl who resembles her 'ghost' and whose name, Madison Elizabeth Frank (Amber Valletta), curiously provokes anger from her husband. The journalist reporting the case describes Madison as 'a real live wire' whose disappearance was not treated seriously by the police, while the girl's mother, all alone now, proudly informs Claire how gifted her daughter was, winning a full scholarship to Princeton. Madison's physical resemblance to Claire is proven by the photograph in her bedroom, underscoring the extent to which she is an image of her younger self, talented and beautiful, yet ultimately forsaken.

The connection between the two women increases as Claire's investigation continues. Inspired by a book on the occult given to her by Jody, seemingly as a joke, she ties a lock of Madison's hair to her thumb. This allows the dead girl's spirit within her and forces her to suddenly remember finding Madison and her husband in bed together the year previously – solving the mystery of why she crashed her car. Norman confesses that he had an affair with his former student, yet blames Claire's devotion to Caitlin for making him feel left out ('You gave it all to her!') revealing himself for the demanding egotist that he is. Claire leaves, staying with Jody, yet promptly returns when Norman fakes a near-fatal accident the next day. Blaming herself for reawakening Madison's presence in their marriage, Claire reveals deep levels of denial, and perhaps an unwillingness to dispense with the comfortable life from which she has to be continually nudged. Like Mary Feur, she seemingly lacks the will for independence and needs to be pushed further.

When she finally uncovers a box in the lake, and finds Madison's necklace inside, Claire realises that her former rival is not missing but dead. Madison haunts her because her fate demands to be known and avenged. Norman yields further denials however. His story is that Madison confronted him at the Du Pont ceremony and killed herself in the house a week later, leading him to hide her body in the lake. In response to his plea for forgiveness, Claire is unequivocal, stating: 'That girl must be brought up.' But Norman is anxious to preserve his name, even at the cost of his marriage, and finally confesses what really happened as a prelude to doing away with his wife. He tells her Madison threatened to expose their affair after he broke the relationship off, prompting him to strangle her in the bath and dump her body. Intending to kill his wife in the same way as his lover, Norman administers a product of his all-consuming research – a drug that elicits temporary paralysis.

Things look bleak for Claire as the water rises in the bath during a tense set-piece, yet the dead girl's necklace offers a form of protection in her hour of need. Madison appears as a corpse in her stead, shocking Norman into banging his head and falling unconscious, buying Claire enough time to save herself from drowning. Her spirit intervenes again when Norman subsequently attempts to crash Claire's car as she tries to escape, and together both women engineer his destruction. As the car falls from a bridge into the sea, Claire pleads with her husband 'I beg you, think of Caitlin', yet any attempt to reach him is clearly futile. The ghost of Madison arrives instead to free her from the underwater wreck, tearing the pendant from her neck and discarding it in the water while ensuring that Norman drowns, meting out the very fate he gave her.

A seemingly loving husband thus becomes exposed as a murderous monster and Claire ends the film by helping justice to be administered. Having devoted herself to being a loyal wife and mother, she is finally able to see what lies beneath their seemingly happy marriage. Where she was weak and dependent on her husband, she gains the strength and assertiveness required to be responsible for herself. As she affirmed at the beginning of the film: 'I get my life back', yet this is not made possible by her daughter's absence, as she had thought, but by her husband's. The film closes with a misty scene in a graveyard, reminiscent of the nightmare finale in *Carrie*, showing Claire paying her respects to the woman who may have wrecked her marriage, yet also saved her, equipping her with the resources to begin her life again.

The Gift also centres on a mother who is given the responsibility of uncovering a murder in her midst, and again it is an apparent rival that haunts the protagonist, warning against another man who is not what he seems. Filled with warmth, generosity of spirit, and remarkable strength of character, Annie Wilson (Cate Blanchett) is a figure of importance in the small southern town where the story is set. Acting as an unofficial social worker, she uses her 'gift' – an abstract psychic ability – to offer advice and understanding to the community's troubled residents, using their donations to help support her children after her husband's sudden death. An element of the supernatural is evident not only in Annie's abilities, which prompt some to term her a witch, but in the particularly strong visions she begins to have of a young woman's body floating in water, a figure she eventually helps to identify and locate.

Jessica King (Katie Holmes) is the spoilt young daughter of the local tycoon, whose engagement to schoolteacher, Wayne Collins (Greg Kinnear), a pleasant and good-natured man, seems to stand in the way of Annie's attraction towards him. Yet Jessica is presented as being extremely promiscuous, having had affairs with several men in town, as well as a somewhat shady relationship with her father, leading to her eventual murder by a jealous and aggrieved Collins. Although another man is falsely accused of killing her, Annie's visions help to unlock the mystery of what really happened to Jessica, consequently uncovering Collins' true nature. Although he seemed to offer a sympathetic and understanding new father figure for her children, and was obviously attracted to her, Collins' fear at being discovered by Annie soon endangers her life. Just as Norman displays his utter ruthlessness in not only covering up one murder but subsequently attempting to kill the woman he claims to love, Wayne similarly proves his duplicity when he is in danger of being found out. Equally, just as Madison's haunting of Claire serves as a warning about her husband, Jessica's drowned body reappears to Annie not only so that the truth will be known, and the right man convicted, but in order to help her see what lies beneath the seemingly innocent and gentle exterior of the man she is becoming involved with.

Another strand of this southern Gothic tale lies with Buddy Cole (Giovanni Ribisi), whose devotion to Annie is clear and whose own tragic circumstances further underscore the notion that what lies beneath family life, within this narrative at least, is anything but normal. Buddy has a mysterious psychological block that prompts sudden outbursts of rage and violence. Eventually, he remembers that he was sexually abused by his father as a boy and attempts to exact revenge by setting him on fire. A still more shocking revelation occurs when Buddy accuses his mother of knowing about the abuse, leaving a suggestion of appalling maternal neglect. Buddy is locked up in the local mental hospital after his attack, yet appears when Annie needs him most, knocking Collins out at the remote lakeside where he attempts to kill Annie in the same way as his former fiancee. How Buddy knows that she will be at this location is a mystery that becomes pronounced in the events that follow. Having helped bring Collins to justice, Buddy delivers an erstwhile commendation to Annie, declaring his love for her and stating: 'You're the soul of this town, Miss Wilson, and you just need to keep doing what you're doing.' She enters the police station alone, only to be informed that Buddy's intervention with Collins could not have occurred, as he killed himself earlier that evening in the hospital. This obviously throws into question who she spoke to in her car only moments earlier, and how she managed to overpower Collins single-handedly. At precisely the point where Buddy seems at his most psychologically balanced, with some suggestion that, given a chance to recover from his abuse, there might even be a chance of a relationship forming between himself and Annie, we are left with the idea that he was simply a ghost. However, the towelling bib he returns to her serves as tangible proof that they did meet again somehow, and that he did indeed save her from harm. By the film's end, Annie is left on her own once again to look after her young family, yet with the comforting idea that she not only has her 'gift', but someone to watch over her also.

Like Claire, Annie learns something about herself in the course of her investigation, and the theme of repression is evident. Just as it is suggested that Claire buried her memory of the affair as a means of denial, and in much the same manner as Buddy is haunted by repressed memories of what happened to him as a boy, so Annie learns that she must come to terms with her grief for her husband, and allow her children to do the same. Earlier in the film her oldest boy asks why they do not visit his father's grave, and although she is dismissive of this at the time, clearly too hurt to listen to what he is saying, the last scene ends precisely with this image around the gravestone, indicating some hope for this family's recovery.

Many liberties are taken in the narrative's use of the supernatural. Annie's 'gift' is sufficiently respected to have some credence in a court of law, which seems patently unbelievable, yet in standing up to attorneys to ensure that justice is done, she also shows that Buddy's words about her role in the community are true. Over the course of the narrative she endures the terror of being attacked by both a wife beater, Donnie Barksdale (Keanu Reeves), who she initially thinks is guilty of Jessica's murder, and the real killer, seemingly mild-mannered Wayne Collins, yet survives these rigours with her family intact and a belief in herself confirmed.

The last film to be assessed also features a maternal heroine, yet the woman responsible for investigating the murder mystery at the heart of *The Ring* is not led by visions or intuition, but by her instincts as a journalist working for the Seattle Correspondent. Rachel Keller (Naomi Watts) is further distinguished by the fact that she is a single parent from the outset. In fact, her career is presented as her main focus – with the inference made that she is a poor mother figure who fails to attend to her son's needs, repeatedly arriving late to pick Aiden (David Dorfman) up from school and generally leaving him to look after himself. Significantly, it is not herself but her son who serves as a conduit for the troubled spirit of the film – a dead girl he draws pictures of, who is eventually revealed to be Samara Morgan (Daveigh Chase). Other characters become linked to her spirit by watching a video, and dying 7 days later. Rachel's involvement in this mystery begins when her niece dies of a heart attack at the age of 16. Quickly ascertaining from her friends that a video is deemed responsible, and discovering that 3 others died exactly 7 days after seeing it, she resolves to find out more, and sees the 'cursed' video for herself.[4]

A host of disturbing images are found on the tape, including a scene that seems lifted straight out of 'Snow White', showing a woman combing her long dark hair in front of an oval mirror. Following these visual clues Rachel discovers a twisted tale of child abuse, superstition, and the paranormal. She learns that a horse-breeding couple living in Moesko Island in the Pacific Northwest became subject to ill fortune after adopting Samara as a young child. The mother, Anna Morgan (Shannon Cochrane), revealed as the figure in the mirror, became tormented by visions she attributed to her daughter, and other misfortunes occurred on the island, leading first to committing Samara to an asylum, then imprisoning her high up in a stable (with obvious echoes of 'Rapunzel'). After the horses killed themselves, Anna finally locked her in a deep well, its ring of light being the last thing she saw before her death.

Unlike the murders in *What Lies Beneath* and *The Gift*, this story is less easy to resolve, for although Samara's fate seems unspeakably cruel, particularly as it occurs at the hands of her adoptive mother, there is an indication that the child was not truly human. This is made more explicit in the original Japanese version, *Ringu* (1998), in which we are informed that the mother conceived her daughter, Sadako (Rie Inou), with an evil sea spirit, while *Ringu 2* (1999) goes so far as to claim that Sadako survived 18 years inside the well – clearly an impossible feat for any human.[5] *The Ring* asserts that she only survived for 7 days – the same time that is given to those she curses – yet her fate remains deeply unsettling nonetheless, particularly as her unfocused desire for vengeance implies that everyone is at risk.

Rachel initially blames the adoptive parents for mistreating their daughter and consequently understands that she has neglected her own child. Indeed, she is motivated to find out what happened to Samara not only through her job, and her niece's sudden death, but in order to save Aiden after he accidentally watches the cursed video. By unearthing what happened to Samara, and becoming angry on her behalf, Rachel finally proves herself to be a good mother. The scene of her lovingly cradling Samara's corpse upon its discovery in the well is an incredible image of maternal affection, vindicating Rachel's previous shortcomings. However, her heroism is seriously questioned by the film's ending, alongside horror's usual conventions about assuaging troubled souls, as the recovery and burial of Samara's body does not lay her to rest.

The fact that Aiden's father, Noah (Martin Henderson), assists Rachel in her investigation suggests that a romance might be rekindled between them as they work to protect their son. Having discovered Samara's body together, and learning the sad circumstances behind her death, the sense is given that this family might even reunite. This is not to be however. Unlike *What Lies Beneath* and *The Gift*, which both neatly conclude with comforting scenes at a graveyard, no such resolution is allowed in *The Ring*. At Samara's funeral, an agitated Aiden tells his parents that Samara does not want to be at rest and, in the most celebrated scene of the film, Noah is subsequently attacked by Samara when she appears on his television set and enters his living room. In dying of fright, like many of her previous victims, any chance of a reconciliation between himself and Rachel is thus (quite literally) killed off.

Rachel realises that what has spared her from a similar fate is the fact that she has made a copy of the video, and the film ends with an odd pact being made with Samara's spirit. Rachel helps Aiden make another copy, telling him that this will keep him safe. Spreading the curse as widely as possible appears to be Samara's aim, and the consequences are considered unimportant compared to saving her son.[6] When Aiden asks, 'What will happen to the person who sees it?' his mother has no reply, leaving her moral position in the film seriously at issue, for while she has learnt to put her son first this is conducted at the apparent expense of everyone's safety, with the video functioning as a high-tech chain-letter that forces complicity with everyone it comes into contact with. Discovering Samara's body, and the story behind her death, has not provided any solution to her anger, which is seemingly implacable, and, as in *Poltergeist* (1982), television serves as the conduit between an unhappy spirit world and ordinary existence, potentially threatening us all.[7]

If Rachel has learnt, over the course of the narrative, that children need to be heard, she finally takes this idea too far, for Samara seemingly wishes to extend herself in the world simply to destroy people. A video Noah obtains of Samara as a young girl in a mental hospital is particularly disturbing because, when asked if she will stop hurting people, she too gives no response. Instead, she asks for her mother, declaring 'I love my mummy' with such earnestness that she cannot seem totally evil (an idea the sequel would corroborate). Samara's relationship with her 'father' is much more obscure. As Richard Morgan (Brian Cox) states to Rachel, by way of explanation for the bad luck that befell his family: 'My wife was never meant to have a child' – and it is this idea of nature having been tampered with that lends the film its haunting quality. Recalling Snow White's tragic mother, who wished for a child with hair as black as ebony and skin as white as snow, Anna Morgan goes to extreme lengths in her effort to have a child and is seemingly punished for this, alongside her unnatural prodigy. Horror has often utilised the idea of the 'evil child', yet why Samara wishes to hurt people, even as a young girl, remains unknown, although a degree of blame is clearly fixed on her surrounding environment.

In the course of Rachel's investigation she learns that the island community where Samara was raised is characterised by small-minded superstition and secrecy. As the local doctor states, bearing the stigma of a handicapped child who Samara is irrationally blamed for: 'When one of us has a problem we all have a problem.' The suggestion made is that they have all conspired to evict her from their lives, accusing her of misfortunes in the same way that 'witches' of old were used as scapegoats for all manner of tragedies. Resembling a modern-day changeling, there are traces of *Carrie* not only in Samara's telekinetic abilities, but the way in which she is brutally rejected, even by a woman who was desperate to have her. As Anna Morgan says prior to pushing Samara into the well: 'All I ever wanted was you' – and it is the fact that she could do this to a child she had yearned for that astonishes, as much as the fear this girl provokes. Whether Samara was 'born evil' or gifted with powers that are misunderstood and eventually misused remains open to question, yet it is notable that while *Ring Two* (2005) redeems her motives as simply wanting a 'mummy', and fixing on Rachel to be this figure, she is ultimately 'killed' by her also.

Despite moving to rural Oregon in order to devote more time to Aiden, Rachel discovers that her role as a mother is still being tested when Samara's unhappy spirit resurfaces in their lives and again threatens her son. Clearly, copying the video was no solution and, rather than aid Samara, she learns that, to be free of her, she must prevent her from doing further harm. Having met Samara's real mother, Evelyn (Sissy Spacek), and seeing her own reflection in Anna Morgan's oval mirror, Rachel is destined to repeat the same fate as these women, having to prove herself as a 'good mother' by showing a willingness to sacrifice Samara. Any sympathy for this girl is finally transmuted into an acknow-ledged need to contain her, and having re-entered the well, which is now a dream-space rather than a geographical location, Rachel closes the lid to lock Samara back inside, ignoring her cries by retorting: 'I'm not your fucking mummy!' After severing her ties to her and symbolic-ally throwing herself from the cliff (in the same way that Anna Morgan committed suicide), Aiden's voice calls Rachel back to reality and the small-town life where they are presumably free to continue their lives in peace.

As in the first film, which resists the impulse of re-uniting its estranged family, the suggested father figure proffered in sympathetic colleague, Max (Simon Bourke), also dies at Samara's hands, presenting the film's final image of the family still resolutely without a father. Instead, we are left with a sense of equanimity between mother and son, with Aiden's relative aloofness seen as preferable to Samara's needy affection. Although Rachel began the film trying to bake pies and asking her son to call her 'mummy' in an attempt to emulate the cosy domestic ideal with which motherhood tends to be judged, by the end she is happy to accept him as he is, having learnt yet another lesson in maternal responsibility.

In contrast to *What Lies Beneath* and *The Gift*, it is not male violence that is critiqued by the *Ring* films, but a mysterious female malevol-ence, and the idea of maternal vengeance becomes more complicated as a result. While Rachel felt anger towards Anna Morgan's seemingly inexplicable act in the first film, she is placed in the same position by its sequel, and forced to emulate it. The troubled spirits of Madison and Jessica may attain peace via their female accomplices, yet Rachel is unable to secure peace for Samara's unhappy soul, with contain-ment being the best she can achieve. Having looked more closely at her actions, she refuses to bear the loss of further lives, and realises that her son will always be threatened while Samara is free.

In all three films, mothers have to follow specific clues and face the truth of what has occurred. All probe beneath surface appearances, all lose the men in their lives, all experience occult phenomena, and all demonstrate an admirable degree of courage. *What Lies Beneath* provides its lead with the chance to begin her life again, having exposed the husband who largely dominated her life for what he is. Significantly, her voyage of self-discovery is only made possible once her daughter has left home, giving her the space to see what is really going on in her marriage. *The Gift* also shows that all is not as it seems when the town thug is accused of murdering a young woman and a psychic exposes a seemingly mild-mannered teacher to be the real culprit. Just as Claire realises that there is more to be afraid of than being alone, Annie learns an equivalent lesson in being warned against a dangerous attraction to Collins; uncovering the murderous intent beneath his ostensible decency and education, she realises that her dead husband's shoes cannot be filled so easily.

The *Ring* films cannot settle their problems with equal ease. What the protagonist learns, in this case, is that being a good mother is fraught with complexity. Like the Final Girls who eventually become single mothers, Rachel is tough, resourceful, and courageous, and similarly vindicated in her ability to take care of her child after accusations of neglect, and even physical abuse, are disproved. Just as Claire and Annie each learn valuable lessons, so Rachel has to mature also. We are told that she and Noah were very young when they had Aiden, and their relationship did not work out – according to Rachel – because of his immaturity. Both parents grow up in trying to protect their son, yet only Rachel survives, finally assuming sole responsibility for Aiden's welfare.

Female independence is writ large for these women. Claire's first husband died tragically young, much like Annie's, and it is notable that Noah shares the same destiny. Although he provides valuable assistance in discovering Samara, she kills him anyway. This is puzzling as Noah's job in film-making would seem to make him ideally equipped to continue Samara's quest of spreading the curse. Indeed, the fact that Samara's adoptive father has so much video equipment at home suggests that he was her accomplice before she decided to enlist Rachel. He kills himself shortly after complaining to Rachel of horrible visions inside his head, apparently provoked by Samara to electrocute himself in the bath (the means Norman uses to fake his 'accident' in *What Lies Beneath*). Father figures are relatively unimportant it seems, and *Ring Two* reveals that Samara spares Rachel not simply as a means of disseminating the curse, but to fulfil her dreams of having a mummy. It is a dream Rachel refuses, however, as Aiden's life would clearly be at risk in doing so.

Our feelings for Samara remain highly ambivalent. Although she is far younger than Madison or Jessica, and meets with a similarly cruel end, she surpasses victim status – largely because she is a great deal more powerful than either woman and does not simply avenge her murderers, as these wronged girls do, but uses technology to transmit herself to any victim of her choosing. Like a modern Medusa, simply gazing upon her leads to insanity or death, yet although she is seemingly omnipotent, and angry as hell, a vulnerable little girl resides beneath her fearful exterior, one whose love and trust are finally used against her.

Although Rachel's initial complicity in the curse promotes a troubling self-interest, placing herself and her son before the well-being of everyone else, the fact that she eventually puts things right by eliminating Samara from the world is in some ways equally unsettling, for while she proves herself as a good mother by protecting Aiden, the compassion she once had for this child is swiftly jettisoned. Indeed, it is both ironic and sad that the spooky girl at the centre of the *Ring* films desires so ardently to be loved and is rejected by every mother she is given. Samara chooses Rachel to be her new mother because, as she puts it: 'She went looking for me and found me. That's why I love her.' Yet Rachel despatches her to the same well from which she formerly retrieved her body, leaving Samara cursed to remain a misfit who will never attain peace, and who is cast instead as an ominous spectre of female anger.

In probing beneath conventional assumptions about family, marriage, and motherhood, these films attest to the fact that rites of passage lie beyond the stage between puberty and adulthood generally explored in folklore and popular culture. Although they confirm that becoming a mother is the primary approved role for women, they rewrite this figure with admirable strength, resolve, and dignity. Horror narratives frequently test a female character's virtue, alongside her ability to undertake the responsibilities of motherhood, yet these texts provide more than a reactionary paean to the traditional family. Claire and Annie each realise that they are capable of independence, while Rachel learns to balance her career with being a good mother. There is also an interesting confirmation of female kinship where it is least expected, with younger women, formerly depicted as rivals, proving to be vital allies, while supposed friendships with other women are interestingly called into question.

Although *What Lies Beneath* ends with Claire having been liberated from an unhappy marriage, whether she will remain friends with Jody is uncertain. In discovering the truth about her husband, Claire learns that her supposed best friend knew about his affair and covered it up, arguing that, because Norman seemed so desperate at the thought of losing her, she thought it best not to say anything. Claire says little in response, yet the admission is another form of betrayal. Not only has her husband deceived her, so has her friend. Despite crowing about her divorce settlement, and the sports car she got out of it, Jody is clearly male-identified, and betrays her best friend by withholding the truth from her – an act that may have been intended for Claire's benefit, yet ultimately serves her husband instead. Significantly, it is not the two of them together that we see in the film's finale, but Claire, alone, tending Madison's grave. Ironically, the woman who once slept with her husband becomes her closest ally. As to the other prominent female in the film, the neighbour Claire feared had been killed by her husband, Mary presents another image of what Claire herself might have become if the 'haunting' had not forced her to face the truth. Humphries asserts that 'the woman neighbour who suffers from hysteria is already overwhelmed by precisely the life of suffocation and death that now awaits the heroine. Each woman in the film sees herself in another woman, with no possibility of escape.'[8] This is too pessimistic a conclusion to draw however, as the ending suggests that freedom is indeed possible, away from the stifling confines of a damaging relationship. While Claire's neighbour repeatedly takes flight from her marriage, only to return because she is unable to imagine anything else, Claire manages to find a new life for herself, with more owed to her former rival than her former friend.

In *The Gift*, Annie is similarly betrayed by a female friend; a battered wife, Valerie Barksdale (Hilary Swank), who she has repeatedly sought to help and who similarly offers a hollow apology after letting her down. Another apparent friend, Linda (Kim Dickens) seems solely interested in getting her hooked up with a man and displays a similar level of immaturity and male-centredness as Jody. As with *What Lies Beneath*, it is another unlikely source that provides true friendship: Wayne Collins' fiancee, Jessica King. Although unsympathetically portrayed when alive, dismissing Annie with bitchy contempt, she returns in death to warn her about falling for a man who is concealing his real nature.

Refreshingly, a sense of female kinship overcomes rivalry when women unite to right specific wrongs. The spiritual guidance offered to Claire and Annie can be seen to update the dead mother's folkloric function of overseeing female offspring, yet these roles are reversed generationally, with younger women passing their wisdom to older counterparts. As Cristina Bacchilega argues, in the tale-type known as 'Rescue by the Sister', murdered women often warn and advise the heroine against meeting the same fate.[9] An inverted initiation similarly occurs in both *What Lies Beneath* and *The Gift*, with female spirits warning against undue loyalty and disavowing romantic inclinations in order to enable the heroine to survive.

By contrast, the relationship between Rachel and Samara is more problematic. In agreeing to perpetuate the curse, Rachel may be motivated to protect her son yet ceases to be a moral agent, even as she seemingly behaves like a good mother, while her actions in the sequel, despite stemming from similar motivations, remain troubling because Samara's goal is no longer vengeance, but love. As Rachel intuits: 'All she wants is a mummy and she'll keep coming until she finds one.' However, taking care of Samara seems to be too much of a task for any woman, particularly one with an existing child. By framing her as an abusive parent, and aiming to take Aiden's place, Samara pushes Rachel to reject her. Her biological mother, Evelyn, institutionalised since trying to kill her as a baby, yet curiously dubbed 'a patron saint' for women who have problems with their kids, advises Rachel with a corny admonishment: 'Be a good mother. Listen to your baby.'[10] However, good motherhood, in this instance, means finishing the job Evelyn started, and returning Samara to her watery grave.

Revisiting the same territory as *Wes Craven's New Nightmare* and *Halloween H20*, in which single mothers are ultimately exonerated from charges of abuse, *Ring Two* ultimately questions what being a good mother entails. It is a question all the films in this chapter take seriously, with each protagonist being tested in terms of her sanity, her reputation, and her character, ultimately proving herself at the end of each narrative by perceiving the truth of a situation, ridding her community of danger, and overcoming the threat of death, consequently achieving heroic status.

The development of the maternal avenger film is seemingly indicative of contemporary horror aiming to address a female audience, not least in providing assertive women struggling with unhappy marriages and family responsibilities. This suggests that the genre's audience is wider than generally acknowledged, and that the genre itself is undergoing continued innovation. Even as horror has gone mainstream, it has re-invented itself in ways that merit renewed analysis. The Final Girl may be a cliché, yet she has grown up in maternal variations, acquired greater levels of responsibility, and proved herself to be far more than Clover's androgyne, emerging instead as a genuinely heroic female, even if she is by no means ideal.

Admittedly, the maternal avenger film could easily be criticised for leaving each of the women with an idealised dead partner for romantic company. Claire's first husband (clearly missed) is likely to be remembered still more fondly after Norman's death; Annie is finally able to grieve over her own husband – knowing that he cannot be replaced; while Rachel will always have the memory of Noah's transformation into a supportive partner and caring father just before he died. Left with these ideals to treasure, the sense is given that these woman are likely to remain alone, aside from their children, fulfilling the abstinence promoted by the Final Girl.

Like the other narratives we have looked at, a contradictory message is offered in terms of approved gender roles. Although new levels of insight and independence are acquired by female characters, clear limitations are imposed in moral terms. Both Madison and Jessica pay a fatal price for engaging in sexual relations with married men, and while the ghostly vengeance they wield is narratively approved this is largely because of the 'good' woman that serves as mediator. While motherhood is validated above any other ambition or career choice, the way in which it is depicted both reflects social changes and questions them. The prominence of the single mother provides a more realistic reflection of existing family structures, including the level of scrutiny such characters endure, yet these narratives are also at pains to preserve the memory of an idealised irreplaceable man in protagonists' lives, seemingly in order to retain a vestige of patriarchal affiliations. Cultural expectations of women are made manifest. Claire may be free to live her life again after Norman's death, yet her denial of very real problems in their marriage, and a life devoted to homemaking, remains at issue, as does the fact that she only attains freedom when her role as mother no longer defines her. Annie may be as courageous as she is caring – particularly in challenging the many aggressive men she encounters – yet she is chiefly defined as a nurturer, the very role Rachel struggles so hard to accommodate. That Rachel is the only one of the three with any kind of career is equally interesting, as is the fact that she is asked to modify her lifestyle in order to better accommodate the needs of her son, yet despite the clear sense of conservatism present, these characters all battle with the demands of motherhood in various ways, prove that they are up to the responsibilities given to them, and remain admirable. They also indicate a refreshing departure from the tendency to concentrate horror solely on adolescent protagonists, acknowledging that older characters are equally, if not more, interesting, with a host of trials and obstacles met in later life than is generally acknowledged among the screenplays we see today.

Paul Wells, rueful of the shape contemporary horror has taken, argues that it reiterates a sense in which 'the world is rife with futility in the absence of any morals, values or traditions'.[11] It is a contention the films we have looked at thoroughly oppose, with a strong sense of morality governing the genre's depiction of female characters. This is particularly evident in the avenging mother cycle, which (along with the slasher) provides a rare instance where female anger is approved. Such films may be seen to exemplify a 'return of the repressed': acknowledging that maternal power need not be feared as a devouring or disempowering force – as psychoanalytic interpretations suggest – but serves to protect, to preserve a sense of morality, and to win out in the fight against evil. These narratives demonstrate a progressive willingness to view the world from a female perspective and to champion the embattled women at their helm. Most importantly, examples of female maturity are given that do not simply retreat into either the demonic or domestic, but show older women capable of looking out for both themselves and others, refusing to be subjugated, and exercising a power that may involve the supernatural yet is also very apparent in the real world, women we may aspire to become.

As I argued in the introduction to this chapter, just as the other texts we have looked at draw upon established tales, the maternal avenger is affiliated to the myth of Demeter and Persephone and its testament to female kinship and maternal devotion. Persephone's removal to the underworld may be equated with death, yet Demeter does everything in her power to regain her. Although she only wins a partial victory when it is decreed that Persephone must continue to live in the under-world for half the year (over which time nothing would grow on earth), the myth is remarkable because, in place of the jealous Hera – who serves as the original wicked stepmother in punishing her husband's 'illegitimate' children – or other envious goddesses portrayed in Greek mythology, we are given a mother whose love for her daughter promotes a righteous rage and the ability to challenge the authority of Zeus himself.[12] Mothers may not save actual biological daughters in the films discussed, yet the connection between Claire and Madison, and between Annie and Jessica, intones a similar sense of female camaraderie that has proven to be very rare, with mother–daughter relationships, both symbolic and biological, often being strongly questioned in horror.

If Claire and Annie can be viewed as Demeter's daughters, then Rachel provides an interesting contrast. She realises that it is a desire for a 'mummy' that motivates Samara, yet is not prepared to take this role, particularly given the level of control her would-be daughter is capable of exercising. Although Samara states that she will take care of Rachel, echoing the role that she has unfairly placed upon Aiden over the years in having to think like an adult, what is obviously needed is for her to grow up herself, take responsibility, and expel this female spirit from their lives – demonstrating an equivalent degree of ruthlessness as Demeter herself for the sake of her own child.

Persephone's annual return to her mother has traditionally symbol-ised hope that spring would return after each winter (thereby ensuring that humanity would survive), and, contrary to Wells' speculation that contemporary horror presents a world 'rife with futility', the mothers we have seen provide a similar sense of hope concerning the possibilities of renewal and recovery – their brush with death having ultimately invig-orated their lives in the way of all rites of passage. However, it is just as well to remember that Demeter is at her most fearful when she is driven nearly insane with grief and almost eliminates the human race until her wish is granted, for while the maternal avenger heroically continues her legacy, this sense of a potentially destructive female power has also informed horror's more cautious treatment of supernatural women, all of whom have an equal claim as Demeter's daughters.[13]

Despite noted levels of containment, contemporary horror has clearly approved greater agency for women, allowing specific transgressions, within specific confines. The genre has provided a space in which female characters have been permitted to be 'bad', and even if they are almost uniformly punished, conventional representations of 'femin-inity' are often questioned in the process. The rules that were so accur-ately parodied in *Scream* are changing. Sex does not necessarily equal death, and mothers are not to blame for every misfortune. Sidney may lose her virginity to a psychopath, yet she keeps her head, and while she concludes the trilogy with treasured ideals of her mother forever tarnished, she also becomes a woman in her own right who learns to put the past behind her, dismissing Roman's attempt to blame their mother for his problems and telling him to accept responsibility for his own actions. Horror has a long history of blaming mothers, and few instances of championing them. When it does so it may be all too easy to suspect sinister motives, such as urging women that staying at home is their best chance of fulfilment, but of course this flies in the face of practically every fairy tale and horror story we know. The tales we grew up with linger on, and the modifications they undergo in cinema update the same warnings – and the attendant sense of hope also: advising us that life is tough, that there are perils everywhere, but ultimately that we can make it.

Conclusion

> Once upon a time... once... and once again Beauties slept
> in their woods, waiting for princes to come and wake them
> up. In their beds, in their glass coffins, in their childhood
> forests... Beautiful but passive, hence desirable: all mystery
> emanates from them.
>
> – Helen Cixous, *The Newly Born Woman*

As this analysis has shown, horror narratives resemble fairy tales in their
mutual reflection (albeit exaggerated) of common adolescent experiences,
including the numerous dysfunctional families portrayed, and the initiation characters undergo in approaching adulthood. Questions of female
identity and maturation have taken precedence in this study, evaluating
how protagonists are asked to accept parental disappointment and overcome rivalries as they grow up, while romantic relations are shown to
be less than perfect. As we have seen, far from waiting for the arrival of
a prince, horror's heroines must learn to fend for themselves. Although
the passive model of femininity, cited above, has commonly been associated with the fairy tale, contemporary horror openly confronts this idea
by featuring assertive women who are required to take action. Indeed,
the urge towards independence has become ever more explicit. The
slasher's Final Girl, having realised that she cannot rely on anyone else for
protection, demonstrates a remarkable capacity for survival, while older
counterparts fight off mortal threats and protect their children virtually
single-handedly in the maternal avenger film. Even if protagonists are
fortunate enough to find themselves a good man, they promptly lose
them, while life continues to bring hardships and perils they must invariably face alone. Sometimes the peril in question even turns out to be
a man who is closest to them, as in *Scream* and *What Lies Beneath*, films

that reiterate the murderous spouse of 'Bluebeard' yet do not provide a convenient set of brothers waiting to despatch the foe, but force imperilled females to do so instead. The pleasure to be had from such narratives is that they rewrite familiar motifs but dare to give women the upper hand.

In updating and altering numerous themes from fairy tale tradition, horror can be seen to continue a process that has been going on for centuries. In fact, both narrative forms have undergone perpetual revision, reflecting and responding to the climate in which they are produced, changing audience tastes, and the various inclinations of their 'tellers'. Fairy tale scholars have shown how socio-historical factors influenced the way in which stories changed from their oral origins and became ascribed with didactic moralising value. Arguing that folk tales were initially devised as adult entertainment, Maria Tatar reminds us of the bawdy, coarse, and often very grisly elements that were removed when they were later adapted for the burgeoning children's literature market, 'changes that divested the tales of their earthy humour, burlesque twists, and bawdy turns of phrase to make room for moral instruction and spiritual guidance',[1] designed, in her view, to serve patriarchy. Marina Warner has similarly explored the oral version of such tales, yet pays particular attention to the way in which they enabled women to communicate to one another, with attendant warnings offered therein. As she puts it:

> fairy tales exchange knowledge between an older voice of experience and a younger audience, they present pictures of perils and possibilities that lie ahead, they use terror to set limits on choice and offer consolation to the wronged, they draw social outlines around boys and girls, fathers and mothers, the rich and the poor.[2]

Providing an image of early storytelling conducted over household duties (rather than in a bourgeois child's bedroom or aristocratic salon), Warner argues that these tales were not devised simply to pass the time, or even to indoctrinate their listeners into the ways of domesticity, but allowed a rare opportunity for women to share their experiences.

Nevertheless, while Warner affirms the predominance of female taletellers, she is also keen to point out that female characters and relations were not idealised. Noting that they frequently set out to warn as much about women as they did men, Warner outlines the historical reasons why relations between women were often very strained, and points out that female rivalry has a long and global history, with versions of 'Cinderella' having been told a thousand years ago.[3] As

Angela Carter states with typical acuteness: 'When women tell stories they do not always feel impelled to make themselves heroines and are also perfectly capable of telling tales that are downright unsisterly in their attitudes'.[4] As we have seen, female rivalry is often foregrounded in horror, yet should not merely be seen as a patriarchal means of dividing women, but a partial acknowledgement instead of how 'unsisterly' we can be – and how lamentable this situation is. When Carter published a selection of fairy tales collected from around the world she described her intentions as 'wanting to demonstrate the extraordinary richness and diversity of responses to the same common predicament – being alive – and the richness and diversity with which femininity, in practice, is represented in "unofficial" culture: its strategies, its plots, its hard work'.[5] A similar intention has prompted this book, particularly in evaluating what options are allowed for female characters in their negotiation of 'femininity'. Tatar lists what she terms as the 'seven deadly sins' of womanhood outlined in fairy tales as pride, disobedience, curiosity, stubbornness, infidelity, gluttony, and sloth; noting that stories which reward female cunning, wilfulness, and disobedience were rarely selected for publication.[6] However, just as Carter has helped to disseminate such neglected tales from 'unofficial' culture, horror narratives can be seen to perform an equivalent task: celebrating female cunning as a heroic quality and often inciting disobedience as a necessary survival skill. This suggests that a strain of feminism is at work in the genre, and although it is not without serious limitations, it remains notable, particularly given the pessimistic conclusions that have increasingly been drawn.

As the horror film has undergone a process of refinement over the last few decades a number of critics have denounced what they see as a dilution of its earlier promise. Carol Clover is suspicious of this 'gentrification' because she claims that the rougher, more dangerous output of its marginal years allowed the genre to tackle gender politics in a much more open and adventurous manner than is now possible. What she terms as 'kinky creativity' has accordingly been exchanged, in her view, with 'dominant fiction in its dominant forms'.[7] Yet, despite such reservations, the fact remains that while fairy tales underwent changes that largely corroborated patriarchal concerns during the 19th century, with any signs of female capability taking a back seat to the heroic males that entered texts, contemporary horror – the genre that has so often been castigated for marginalising and exploiting women – has ironically provided some of the most powerful images of female self-sufficiency. Far from ignoring the difficulties faced by women caught in the predicament, as Carter put it, of being alive, the examples evaluated here have even questioned existing social relations. For all the criticisms that might be made about its greater commerciality, horror is able to capitalise on its still quite marginal status and openly derivative nature to question and test existing assumptions, including responding to criticism.[8] Women have increasingly taken centre stage within the genre, and although clear misgivings continue to be voiced about powerful females, the differing ways in which they are represented nevertheless deserves attention.

A crucial enquiry has been to question why such narrative prominence has been given to female protagonists within horror, and to ask how gender roles and expectations have changed, if at all. Tatar has explained the relative predominance of heroines in fairy tales by stating that stories of female initiation and obedience reflected the pedagogical intent of 19th century literature to 'promote a safe docility' in women.[9] We might question whether the same rationale governs the increasing number of feisty females that have populated horror, each of whom is asked to deal with all manner of perils on their path to maturity. Forming the contemporary equivalent of cautionary tales, horror has warned against the dangers of both deceitful men and treacherous females, seeming to reflect an equivalent cynicism regarding romantic relations and the possibilities of 'sisterhood'. However, it has also questioned a number of assumptions concerning female identity and expectations, with 'docility' and its domestic ramifications being heavily targeted.

The rites of passage outlined in horror offer a curious inversion of the tales we heard as children. Marriage is no longer conceived as the epitome of female fulfilment – if it ever was – and romance is seen to be a misguided ambition at best, often deluding, if not explicitly endangering, female protagonists. Families, although always represented as sites of turmoil and conflict, run the gamut from unnatural, sometimes even cannibalistic, unions to more prosaic images of parental neglect, reiterating the need for the child's separation as adulthood is reached, yet also serving as an ominous image of their likely destiny. Even motherhood does not necessarily bring fulfilment and pleasure, but stress, frustration, terror, and sacrifice. If the fairy tale has long been considered a source of comfort that invariably ends with protagonists living 'happily ever after', horror cinema presents its flip side, reworking similar contents to suit an adult audience with a greater appetite for exploring the unsettling – and a greater propensity to question particular institutions and ideas. Horror allows a critical space from which to look at life from unusual perspectives, arguably providing the same opportunities as the early unregulated version of folk tales that were designed to entertain and instruct, but also to inspire listeners.

Nevertheless, while there is much to celebrate in the texts evaluated, they are invariably undermined by a number of factors – including the various female figures that do not make it to adulthood, who die (or are otherwise disarmed in some way) as a consequence of their transgressions, most of whom are explicitly figured as a threat to patriarchy. Although the genre questions traditional gender roles in presenting women who are active, assertive, and, occasionally, aggressive – even offering sympathy towards such figures at times – it also confirms and concretises certain ideas. Morality and virtue are still claimed as necessary markers of female good character, a compulsory heterosexuality seems to be in operation, and a woman's maternal identity is stressed over any other aim or occupation.

The result is a mixed message, but a fascinating one also in reflecting the evident conflicts making themselves felt in popular culture, conflicts concerning not only what is appropriate in terms of 'feminine' behaviour, but the possibility of alternatives. The supernatural in these updated coming-of-age tales does not take the form of a glass slipper or magic dress but symbolises instead a source of strength, power, intuition, and enlightenment that characters variously experience. Tatar has noted the troubling 'consistency with which women are punished with death, threats of murder, and cruel physical abuse' in the fairy tale[10] – a tendency for which horror cinema has been equally condemned, yet while the evils of unbridled male sexuality were sublimated during the folk tale's transition to print, the questioning of male rage and sexual inadequacy remains prominent in horror, with female characters often made responsible for doing so. Far from castigating women who 'begin breaking all the rules in the book of feminine behaviour by taking steps in the direction of acquiring knowledge and power',[11] as Tatar states of the fairy tale, contemporary horror infers that unless women exercise caution and curiosity, and take steps towards self-sufficiency, they will perish.

In the examples we have looked at, maturity implies a rejection of certain patriarchal myths. Not only is the father's role as an authority figure questioned, but the idea of an idyllic love match is also put to task. These narratives can accordingly be seen to extend a mode of questioning that was largely suppressed as folk tales were altered for print, showing an equal propensity to portray men in a negative light. However, while the attempt to acknowledge male violence is laudable, it has also produced ambivalent results. Most problematically, in many of the texts we have seen would-be rapists are pardoned by their victims. Sexual predators in *The Craft* and *Ginger Snaps: Unleashed*, as well as the lovelorn Spike in *Buffy: The Vampire Slayer*, may ultimately die yet are also forgiven, thereby lessening, and even potentially trivialising, the intended crime, while female characters are uncomfortably tested according to the loyalty they offer them.[12] Any challenge made to patriarchy by the feminist inroads taken is thus carefully distanced from 'man-hating'. This can only be seen as an indication that the gains once secured in terms of condemning sexual violence do not remain inviolate, but must continually be fought, particularly as one of the unhappy consequences of 'postfeminist' attitudes is that it is hipper to take these gains for granted than campaign for their extension. By the same token, and equally problematic, is that while female audiences are given protagonists who defy convention, and thus offer an encouraging glimpse of possible alternatives, these characters' lives are frequently curtailed, alongside their new-found powers, when certain boundaries are crossed.

In her analysis of fairy tales, having assessed their origins and discerned their provocative qualities, Marina Warner concludes that they 'offer a way of putting questions, of testing the structure, as well as guaranteeing its safety'.[13] The examples appraised in contemporary horror also ask certain questions about roles and expectations surrounding women, playing on a host of fears and desires, and appearing to reflect key societal changes in providing female characters who are both assertive and independent. Although the same virtues are largely championed as in heroines of old, with moral responsibility wedded to a capacity for nurturing, the fairy tale's discernible legacy can also arguably be credited for the prominence horror has given to females, and the courage they exhibit. If young women are often placed in a heroic role, in which particular strengths and abilities are tested, this is not only the result of the 20th century's feminist movement, but complies with the original intentions of many stories. As Warner has argued, oral folk tales were far removed from the sanitised parables that later resulted, with a cautionary attitude to the vicissitudes of life, particularly where men are concerned, apparent many centuries ago, when these tales were largely the domain of women. Contemporary horror can be seen to draw upon this legacy, perhaps in acknowledgement of the growing number of women attracted to the genre, as much as an increasing female presence in production itself. Indeed, the fact that both pubescent characters and older female figures have featured in recent narratives suggests more than a bald attempt to appeal to the teen market, but a deliberate exploration of the myths we have grown up with and their perceived relevance to the modern world.

In placing females in peril, horror unveils its own wolves as metaphors of predatory males. Young women are advised to exercise continued vigilance in their relations with men, while older counterparts also discover a new sense of identity (and strength) through battling various Bluebeards. Beyond the insipid examples of Cinderella and Sleeping Beauty that have tended to be conflated with the fairy tale's represent-ation of women (and the celebration of heterosexual romance housed therein), horror has displayed a cautionary attitude towards romance and focused on active female protagonists in the mould of Red Riding Hood.[14] Indeed, as Zipes points out, in the original oral version she 'shrewdly outwits the wolf and saves herself. No help from granny, hunter or father', leading him to conclude that 'the folk tale was not just a warning tale, but also a celebration of a young girl's coming of age'.[15] Contemporary horror marks the female passage to adulthood with the same mixture of caution and celebration. Some characters prove them-selves as virtuous heroes, such as the *Scream* trilogy's surviving female, Sidney Prescott, who abandons her life as a recluse in the woods when she comes out of hiding and slays her murderous half-brother. Others embrace 'monstrous' transformations, such as the female lead of *Ginger Snaps*, who opts for savagery over civilisation and kills indiscriminately. That Ginger does not survive indicates the extent to which such narrat-ives, as innovative and challenging as they often are, also retain specific conventions – including a sense of morality as an essential trait for approved females.

While conspicuously absent in other genres, mothers are a key arche-type in horror. Although usually depicted as a flawed role model – including the two examples that fail *Carrie*'s eponymous heroine, or an idealised spirit – such as is presented in *The Craft*, mothers have also become main protagonists in their own right, and heroic ones at that, proving to have equal amounts of courage and compassion in such films as *The Gift*. Not all female characters may graduate to this destiny yet motherhood remains the sole occupation to which women are asked to aspire, and the trials they are given form a testing ground to see if they are up to the duties required of them. Various perils abound, the path to adulthood is strewn with danger, and not every protagonist survives, yet in many ways it is the ones that fail the initiations that are the most interesting.

Although I have likened female-centred horror to rites of passage tales, I have been particularly interested in the ruptures that are exposed in the journey to womanhood. Exceptional young women distinguish them-selves from the norm not only in terms of the narrative agency they are granted, but in their values and behaviour also. Occupying a liminal stage between childhood and adulthood, they try to balance their own sense of identity against the various competing demands made of them. Coming-of-age necessitates a jettisoning of innocence and the need to grow up and take responsibility, yet not all the figures evaluated have been willing to do so. Some have their lives decisively cut short, seeming to self-destruct in a fit of rage like Rumpelstiltskin (as occurs with Carrie and her half-sister, Rachael), or they are otherwise disciplined by other females. However, this does not foreclose against our ability to potentially identify with such figures, or even celebrate them. As Christine Gledhill has argued, 'meaning is neither imposed nor passively imbibed, but arises out of a struggle or negotiation between competing frames of reference, motivation and experience'.[16] After all, as female viewers we have always had to take our pleasures where we can, sometimes necessitating a gymnastic ability to identify with improbable objects of affection, and horror's allure lies chiefly in the fact that it has offered such dramatic female images to choose from.

Vera Dika hits upon horror's key link with fairy tales in assessing what she terms as the 'stalker cycle', arguing that 'by representing adolescents in situations depicting their imminent social passage from a world of childhood into adulthood...they also dramatise a young person's coming to knowledge of a world that threatens violence and evil'.[17] Such acknowledgement includes an awareness that parental figures can no longer be relied upon and that boyfriends are just as likely to let you down as supposed friends, influencing a corresponding need to be responsible for oneself, sometimes even demanding a willingness to engage in violence in the name of self-preservation. That girls are asked to abandon the usual notions of feminine passivity is a radical departure – even if this is still only approved within specific limits. Fairy tales have commonly been understood as valourising virtue and villainising any demonstration of vanity, greed, and heartlessness displayed by women. While horror similarly demands that a specific morality is upheld by female characters, it approves the need to be strong, self-sufficient, capable, and resilient. Forbearance and devotion are dispensed with in these modern fables, and although romantic inclinations persist, men are far from idealised. Precedents set in the oral tradition of these tales have thus interestingly resurfaced in recent years, and we might well ask why.

Arguing that there are 'cracks in the pedestal' of Hollywood's conventional treatment of gender, Philip Green claims that the impact made by the feminist cultural revolution of the 1970s can still be seen in certain representations, contending that 'women as unsocialised outcast heroes; women in quest of dangerous secrets; women pursuing vengeance; women engaged in physical combat; women as killers – all are tokens of our fragmented reality'.[18] Significantly, all such figures have appeared in contemporary horror, taking advantage of the genre's greater capacity for experimentation by offering a wider choice of characterisations than is usually available for women.

The figures examined here are transgressive in the sense of not fitting into the parameters of femininity generally presented as the norm, yet, as we have seen, these texts are far from unproblematic. Independence and sexual assertiveness are still regarded with mistrust, and aligned with a dangerous sense of immorality. *The Craft*'s Nancy, *Buffy*'s Faith, and *Ginger Snaps*' Ginger are each deemed monstrous, and punished accordingly, when a moral line is crossed in killing humans – revealing the extent to which a double standard continues to exist in this area. While horror is filled with celebrated male figures who repeatedly and mercilessly kill (much to the audience's delight), it is difficult to conceive the same possibilities for women, with gendered expectations allowing less narrative room for manoeuvre. Try imagining a female Freddy Krueger, Michael Myers, or Jason Voorhees and the point is readily made. A villain we love to hate that is also female seems anathema still, and while the likes of Samara may prove this contention wrong it seems unlikely that this strange little girl will have the same longevity. What is acceptable (and even amusing) in seemingly invincible male psychopaths is clearly insupportable in a female character, and the reasons behind this are likely to be found in the maternal ideal that persists in defining women as carers, requiring them to be positioned as moral agents. To fail this criteria usually merits punishment of some kind. While 'good' girls survive their looser counterparts in the slasher, and indicate – by their relative virtue, responsibility, and maturity – their future potential as mothers in the making, a similar duality can be seen in the witch and werewolf narratives set out in *The Craft* and *Ginger Snaps*, with the more 'moral' females of each text, Sarah and Brigitte, made responsible for disciplining their unruly peers when they are seen to abuse their new powers. The maternal avenger film may allow greater scope for female kinship, particularly in turning former rivals into allies, yet the ghostly guides presented in *The Gift* and *What Lies Beneath* have also met with a premature death – in true slasher fashion – due to prior sexual misconduct, aiding and enlightening the films' heroes via their own tragic example. Their deaths may be avenged, and dangerous men punished, yet the avenger also learns an equivalent lesson – to trust in herself over any man and accept sexual abstinence – much like the Final Girl she has developed from.

Although horror allows a vital testing of parameters, specific ideals are clearly maintained. Even *Buffy: The Vampire Slayer*, a series frequently hailed as postmodern and praised by fans and critics alike for innovations such as the silent 'Hush' and celebrated musical episode, 'Once More With Feeling', upholds certain conventions by approving specific examples of femininity while castigating others. Buffy is indisputably the hero, Willow and Faith more prone to folly, and, in accordance with the moral code outlined in this study, Buffy's capacity as a nurturer, following in her mother's footsteps in looking after younger sister Dawn, is used to confirm her heroic status. The 'safety' of established codes such as a maternal ideal is thus guaranteed, albeit modified, and aspirations regarding permissible female behaviour changed very little.

What remains encouraging, however, is that horror still offers a place in which female characters are foregrounded and in which the audience's assumptions, not to mention those of critics, are sometimes contested. Women can survive murderous attackers and thus confound the misconception that they are simply victims in horror; they can engage in sexual relations without necessarily being punished; and they can be heroic – while still showing themselves to be more than 'phallic' figures designed for male identification. Their ability to behave unethically may prove to be more problematic, suggesting continued anxiety about the potential dangers of female power, yet in terms of comparative cultural representations such unruliness may be precisely what is most pleasurable for a female audience, particularly one that has been neglected for so long.

Writing with regard to the 'unruly woman' in comedy, and the disruptive capacity she holds, Kathleen Rowe describes this figure as 'vulnerable to ridicule and trivialization' but also 'vaguely demonic or threatening'.[19] Horror ups the ante on this latter quality, allowing us to not only perceive the ways in which women have been deemed fearful within patriarchal culture, but to potentially reclaim the power to unsettle. As Rowe argues, 'women must be willing to offend and be offensive, to look beyond the doomed suffering women of melodrama and the evil ones of film noir'.[20] The femme fatale is an interesting example of the aberrant female that has been celebrated by critics such as Janey Place, who argues that this figure can be reclaimed by female audiences for her power and agency, rather than her eventual fate.[21] The same strategy might be applied in evaluating the misfit sisters assembled in horror, because women again assume narrative prominence – and a particular degree of freedom also. While film noir typically sets its 'spider women' against virtuous female characters, Jeanine Basinger has sought to argue that a potential site of liberation is offered to female audiences through temporary identification with the 'bad girl', even suggesting that this allows a means to engage with a version of 'female radicalism'.[22] The 'bad girl' of horror may offer a similar means of engagement for female viewers, even if she is narratively positioned as threatening.

Karen Hollinger has contended that, where women are fictionally set against one another, any 'subversive pleasure' elicited effectively works as a 'safety valve', one that fails to override the preferred meaning of such texts and their narrative insistence that 'what women need is to form alliances with men and to beware of the dangers inherent in attachments to members of their own sex'.[23] This is a pessimistic conclusion to draw, yet it remains the case that while mistrust towards men is all too evident in the narratives assessed, female rivalries also figure largely, with alliances between women often short-circuited through jealousy and betrayal. This is not always the case however. Carrie may face the enmity of Chris Hargensen and her cronies yet has the sympathies of both Miss Collins and Sue Snell; Sarah may feel betrayed by her 'coven' yet discovers a sense of kinship with her dead mother that fills her with new-found confidence; Faith may play every dirty trick in the book against Buffy, including attempting to sleep with virtually every man she is close to, yet the two eventually join forces in an attempted hymn to feminism; and the maternal avenger film, despite admitting the realities of rivalry and conflict between women, also supports the need to work together to right specific wrongs.

Neither is it the ostensible 'good' girl that necessarily attracts our attention, for just as Warner has argued that the wicked stepmother in Disney's *Snow White* is far more powerful than the insipid heroines we are offered, so it is the more petulant, angry, and outspoken females presented in teen horror that arguably figure strongest in our memories and imaginations. Just because the likes of Nancy and Ginger and Faith are invariably quelled for their excesses does not mean that audiences necessarily approve when this occurs, and we may even sneer at these methods of containment as much as applaud them.

Among the characteristics Rowe uses to define the unruly woman she cites the importance of liminality, thresholds, borders, and margins, 'rendering her above all a figure of ambivalence'.[24] This recalls Kristeva's understanding of the abject as that which does not respect borders, yet seeks to champion this quality rather than use it to confirm misogynistic thinking. Adolescence provides a key area of interest because it is a site of uncertainty and transformation, a testing-ground for characters in which boundaries are re-evaluated in the attempt to re-orient oneself in the adult world.

In Robin Wood's analysis of 'teenpics' – light-hearted coming-of-age narratives that appeared in the late 1990s – he concludes that 'women are generally subordinated to men', with plots that remain 'resolutely male centred'.[25] Could it be that the not so separate development of teen relationships and graduation themes in horror, and the greater interest given to female characters and experiences, is a means of balancing this tendency? The flip side to comedies like *Road Trip* (2000) and *American Pie* (1999) – in which boys get all the attention and girls generally function as one-dimensional sex objects – are much darker parables of puberty and self-discovery, presenting disquieting images of poor parenting, failed relationships, and broken ideals. If manhood is humorously achieved in the teen pic through good-natured brawling, boozing, having sex, madcap travels, and making it back to campus by morning, then teen horror provides an altogether more unsettling view of the relative pain and frustrations of womanhood, giving us figures like Carrie, bathed in blood, eyes unblinking, unleashing her fury when her prom queen dreams are mercilessly dashed; or Nancy's desperate wish to have everything made better again – her own rage presented as an equivalent response to the numerous abuses she has already experienced in her comparatively young life; or Ginger's refusal to lie back and relax during her first sexual encounter, and her exultant transformation beyond womanhood itself; or, still more alluringly, Faith's sexy swagger, both before and after her character's 'redemption', punctuating her refusal to tow the line. We may feel for Carrie when she is so cruelly excluded by her peers, just as we may feel for these other characters as they are variously reprimanded for their transgressions, yet these are twisted rites of passage tales in which belonging and acceptance were never really the point. These misfit sisters can never fit in, how could they, when they exist to demonstrate the narrow confines by which womanhood continues to be approved?

We have looked at women for whom normalcy is eventually granted, as well as characters who fail to conform – and often fail to survive also, and the parameters of acceptable behaviour are amply demonstrated therein. Approved womanhood clearly necessitates exhibiting approved qualities, and while an unparalleled degree of freedom is made available in the assertiveness and abilities granted to females in horror, this is always tempered with the need to prove what can best be described as 'virtue'. Nevertheless, what remains of interest is the level of sympathy extended towards certain characters and their plights, not necessarily in terms of pity exactly, but in understanding the difficulties they are facing. The focus given to females cannot be seen apart from the socio-cultural conditions in which these texts were produced. As Clover has asserted, the fact that woman-headed households have become more prominent since the 1970s must partly explain the greater ability film-makers have granted audiences in accepting female figures taking the narrative lead in the genre,[26] yet we might ask to what extent female liberation, the changing shape of the family, and a growing female presence in the workplace have also influenced the apparent reserve exhibited towards ideas of female empowerment.

Horror has reflected a certain trepidation about shifting gender rela-tions and the family has frequently been used to question these develop-ments: detailing divorce, broken homes, and strained marital relations as the seeming result of feminism. One consequence of this has been the number of lone mothers featured, many of whom either smother their offspring or seemingly ignore their needs. The significance of female-headed families in teen horror bears particularly close scrutiny as the mother's ability to function as a suitable role model for adolescent daughters is severely tested.

A case in point is *The Exorcist* (1973), in which Tony Williams disin-geniously blames the mother Chris (Ellen Burstyn) for her daughter's 'possession', arguing that it is because Regan (Linda Blair) overhears Chris's animosity towards her ex-husband (contradicting assurances that she still loves him) that she dramatically transforms into a monster.[27] In fact, what the narrative implies is that Regan does not want to mature, to accept her parent's divorce, or, more significantly, to have to share her mother with her job, her new lover, and her surrounding friends. It is by forfeiting her career, and instating male religious figures in place of the absent father at home, that Chris finally helps to 'cure' her daughter, leading Paul Wells to contend that 'arguably the film is merely a parental fantasy in which a deeply troubled adolescent is coerced through a period of rebellion into maturity, reinforcing patri-archal authority along the way'.[28] However, this seems more specifically to be a *paternal* fantasy, as the mother is asked to abandon any other identity by devoting herself entirely to her daughter while the father neatly avoids having to prove himself, yet retains his status nonetheless.

In a similar vein, the films discussed frequently question mothers while paternal responsibilities take a back seat. *Carrie* presents its female-headed household as dysfunctional and damaging, condemning Mrs White – long since abandoned by her husband – for her unremitting abuse of her daughter. Nancy may be deeply disappointed by her dad in *Nightmare on Elm Street*, yet the film appears to be more critical of her mother's drinking, abruptly killing her off in the denouement. *Scream's* Sidney may have a loving father, yet it is her mother's death that has traumatised her, and only by discovering that she was imperfect is she able to finish grieving for her. *The Craft* is more even-handed, featuring examples of both maternal neglect and protection – which can be seen to variously result in Nancy's murderous wrath and Sarah's relative 'morality' – yet while Nancy imitates her mother's greatest failing by similarly prioritising a man over any other consideration, as her obsession with Chris indicates, Sarah opts to abandon the power her mother bequeaths her. *Ginger Snaps* confronts many of the clichés of its predecessors. Taking issue with the idea that mothers are always to blame for their offspring's misdemeanours, it provides a supportive nurturing maternal figure who clearly wants to help her girls, even if they evince little more than embarrassment towards her. An evident pattern of absent fathers and (frequently) errant mothers re-occurs in such texts, reiterating the need for daughters to mature and become women in their own right (if permitted to do so).

Nevertheless, as horror has grown up, its attitude to mothers has become increasingly positive, even granting them heroic status, as we have seen. While the single mother may continue to provoke some element of doubt, she has also been sympathetically drawn in recent narratives, and confirmed as an important and capable presence. By *Buffy: The Vampire Slayer* the father is absent from the beginning yet our protagonist, initially hurt by his neglect, soon learns to live without him. The strained relationship with her mother grows stronger as Buffy matures and ultimately assumes her role – a development which suggests that, even when a young woman can break all the rules by acquiring preternatural strength and taking on the traditional male role of heroic protector, she is still required to prove herself as a carer, and thus as good mother material. Joyce must die, it seems, for her daughter to mature, returning us once again to the idealised dead mother motif of fairy tale tradition.

I began this book by citing *Star Wars* as an exemplary male rite of passage tale in which women are highly marginalised. Princess Leia even goes so far as to say in awe to her twin brother that he has a power she could never know in *Return of the Jedi* (1983), humbly acknowledging that she lacks the same birthright, simply by dint of her gender. In the conclusion to the prequel trilogy, *Revenge of the Sith* (2005), their mother, Padme (Natalie Portman), is disempowered still further by dying in childbirth. Padme's short life is marked by royal duty, romance, and a tragic demise; undergoing a transition from an adventurous young girl to conscientious senator and finally a maternal martyr whose most noble act is to survive long enough to bring the proverbial New Hope, Luke Skywalker, into the world. While she has proven to be as feisty as the daughter she will never know, her heroism is chiefly distinguished by being a mother – one who is pointedly not allowed to survive. Like the death of Sarah Connor in *Terminator 3*, Padme is seemingly killed off lest she eclipse the heroic role that fate has decreed for her son, proving the difficulties that persist in granting female characters prominence – particularly when it is a male coming-of-age that is clearly of chief concern.

The films examined here make an interesting contrast to such tendencies because it is the female experience that is evaluated and because an unprecedented degree of power is tasted (and tested) by protagonists. Motherhood figures as a crucial, albeit complex, arena, yet maternal sacrifice remains the most potent form of female heroism imaginable. The likes of *Wes Craven's New Nightmare*, *Halloween H20*, *Ring* and *Ring Two* all feature mothers who must battle to prove their sanity and be willing to sacrifice themselves for their children in the ultimate test of their virtue. Although these characters triumph – and survive – the US remake of the Japanese film, *Dark Water* (2005), takes this tendency to a disturbing level: contending that, as its heroine's mental health is fragile, custody of her daughter, and, indeed, her own life, must be sacrificed. Replete with folk tale references, including the dead mother as spiritual guide, the film also demonstrates the contrary position that contemporary horror has often taken with respect to female characters, invoking our sympathies for an embattled young woman while scrutinising her as a potentially threatening figure.

Dahlia (Jennifer Connelly) attempts to re-build her life with her young daughter after an acrimonious divorce from her husband, Kyle (Douglas Scott). He questions her sanity in order to gain custody of their daughter Cecilia (Ariel Gade), using his knowledge of the 'issues' she continues to be burdened with from an unhappy childhood in order to undermine her case. He makes his feelings known at one of the hearings, shouting: 'Be honest with yourself. You can't raise Ceci alone. You can't handle it! Just be honest with yourself.' Although she tries her damndest to prove him wrong, events conspire against her. Economic hardship forces her to choose a run-down apartment that happens to house the product of another dysfunctional family – a female spectre, about the same age as her daughter, who haunts the building and seems, at times, to be a manifestation of Dahlia's neurosis. In portraying the move to this haunted apartment, the film functions like a revamped Gothic thriller: Dahlia enters a mysterious menacing dwelling and begins to suspect her husband of plotting to drive her insane in order to gain the upper hand in the custody battle. Although these suspicions are disproved when she finds out more about the occupants of the apartment above, the narrative nevertheless indicates how beleaguered Dahlia's position is as a woman trying to raise her daughter alone.

Her strike for independence as a single mother is thwarted by various male figures, including her hostile ex-husband; the deceitful property manager, Mr Murray (John C. Reilly); and the neglectful caretaker, Mr Veck (Pete Postelthwaite); as well as the vague yet disturbing sexual threat that emanates from two teenage tearaways also living in the building. Only her lawyer, Jeff Platzer (Tim Roth), offers a positive male figure to turn to, having been recommended by a female friend, Mary, who we only ever hear on the telephone. Through Jeff's help Dahlia discovers that Ceci's new imaginary friend was, in fact, a little girl who lived in the apartment upstairs and died of neglect, drowning in the water tower when her estranged parents failed to take care of her. Natasha's story makes Dahlia realise the tragic consequences of parental rivalry and failure to communicate, forcing her to question what is best for her daughter.

After conceding an end to hostilities with Kyle, the rain that has permeated every frame of the film abruptly stops. However, this is a false dawn, in the *Ring* mode, with another supernatural little girl intent on keeping her new 'mother' by threatening to replace her real child. Unable to physically stop her from trying to drown Ceci, Dahlia offers to trade her own life for her daughter, affirming to Natasha: 'I'll be your mother. Forever.' In contrast to Rachel's angry response to Samara in *Ring Two*, shouting 'I'm not your fucking mummy!' after locking her would-be daughter back in the well, concession is the only option available to Dahlia.

The sacrifice has added poignancy because it is implied that she will now have a daughter that no one can take away from her. The fact that the same actress (Perla Haney-Jardine) is used to play both Natasha and flashback images of a young Dahlia makes their symbolic parallel clear, for as Ceci has observed, both are 'lost' because both suffered maternal neglect and abandonment. Indeed, Natasha's story so resembles Dahlia's, right down to each having a drunken mother, that she seems to symbolise the threat that she herself poses to Ceci.

Once again, fathers luck out in this scenario. Although Natasha was 'lost' by the neglect of both parents, it is a mother she specifically craves. More disturbingly, while Dahlia allegedly experienced physical abuse from her father as a child, she is haunted solely by her mother's drunken resentment, suffering from nightmares that Ceci states only resumed when 'daddy left', and which she complains are upsetting to her. Kyle may be a loathsome figure who, despite having abandoned his family for another woman, seems savagely resentful of Dahlia's presence in Ceci's life, yet his demand for total custody is ultimately upheld. By electing to die in her daughter's stead Dahlia saves her life, yet also, by implication, her daughter's mental health, breaking the cycle that her continued existence and influence might supposedly exert.

Although Dahlia shows herself to be a devoted and loving mother, the character profile drawn up by her husband's lawyers is that of a delusional woman who is manifesting similar problems in their daughter – a view that is corroborated by the school recommending a psychiatrist for Ceci after witnessing her repeatedly talking to an 'imaginary' friend. Interesting resonances of *Curse of the Cat People* (1944) manifest themselves, for while the discovery of Natasha's body reveals that neither Dahlia nor Cecilia is delusional, their ability to detect her supernatural presence is similarly misread by others as disturbed behaviour, with Dahlia – like Irena – perceived as a negative influence who must be eradicated.

Although Dahlia capitulates to her husband's demands in agreeing to move closer to him, she effectively sacrifices everything by the end of the film. Kyle assumes custody over a daughter he apparently had no interest in before the marriage break-up, while Dahlia watches over her in spirit form. The closing shots show her appear in the elevator, as Natasha's spirit had before her, braiding her daughter's hair in a gesture of maternal protection. In vowing to always be there for her, she returns us to the benediction given in early folk tales by dead mothers who remain as a nurturing presence in their children's lives. Ceci leaves the apartment for the last time with her father, clearly comforted by the encounter, seemingly released from any damage caused by her parents' conflict, and safe from the psychological harm that her misfit mother might otherwise inflict.

If the other films we have looked at indicate a sense of caution around female independence, and specifically single mothers, *Dark Water* makes this concern explicit. Dahlia's past, coupled with the traumatic end to her marriage and difficult living conditions, threatens to consume her, and thus her daughter also. (In their favourite game Dahlia enacts the traditional part of an ogress in pretending to cover her 'muffin' with jam and gobble her up – yet while Ceci squeals with delight at this the psychological implications are clearly frowned upon.) Although she has already indicated proof of good motherhood by such actions as taking a menial job because the hours coincide with her daughter's schooling, it is ultimately proven by eliminating herself from a troubled existence.[29] Unlike the other single mothers we have seen, Dahlia is seemingly ill-equipped to survive in such a hostile world. Jeff, the infinitely under-standing lawyer, may be likened to a 'prince' but cannot genuinely make things any better. Dahlia's emotionally abusive mother has effectively cursed her and only her own selfless gesture will put things right. Like 'Rapunzel' – the last story she reads to her daughter – this is a tale where the mother is forced to relinquish her daughter, yet its bittersweet ending problematically celebrates the tragedy of a brave, loving, and much wronged woman, even as it romanticises her fate.

Fear of losing one's child, or of being a bad mother, strike at the heart of maternal anxieties explored in horror: a fact that might explain why adolescent girls are so thoroughly tested in the genre, and why many do not survive – obviously failing the criteria by which women seem to be invariably judged. *Dark Water* emblematises the odd logic of many horror narratives in portraying the very real difficulties faced by a woman, including her husband's betrayal and continued torment, only to blame the damage done long ago by her mother, finally asking the victim herself to make amends. While men do not escape criticism in the genre, it is focused most strongly on women, particularly mothers that fail their daughters, returning us, once again, to fairy tale territory. Dahlia is no less a misfit than her younger counterparts, and no less valiant than the maternal avenger, but at heart it is suggested that she remains a troubled young girl, never quite making it to adulthood in this thwarted coming-of-age scenario.

If horror charts the difficulties involved in growing up female, then it also suggests that the horrors of adolescence may never truly be over-come: that life in the adult world is just as prone to rivalries, hostile communities, and treacherous men, warning against unrealistic myths of living 'happily ever after', as the many 'twisted' Cinderella tales attest.

Wes Craven once stated, in deciding how best to end *A Nightmare on Elm Street*, that 'the ghost of *Carrie* haunts us all'. What he meant by this potent remark is that it was virtually impossible for film-makers to avoid emulating De Palma's shock conclusion to the film, in which Carrie's hand famously rises from her grave in Sue Snell's last gasp night-mare. The remark can be interpreted in another way however, implying that film-makers are equally compelled to return to the same thematic territory: charting a female misfit's attempt to escape her troubled background and become accepted. That Carrie does not succeed is not a failing in her, but in a world in which she cannot fit. As Bettelheim has remarked of Goldilocks: 'She is and remains an outsider who never becomes an insider . . . and has no place to go.'[30] This is true of the many misfit protagonists that have followed Carrie: while some eventually gain acceptance, others stay resolutely on the outside, and are arguably more interesting because of this.

At the outset of this study I contended that the rites of passage that are discernible in horror have an affiliation with the function Warner observes in her analysis of folklore, warning female audiences about a host of likely obstacles they must face in their journey towards adulthood. Among the themes discussed we might list the following insights: that life is far from easy – and even potentially dangerous; that you have to be tough and courageous to survive – without losing a vital sense of responsibility; that you cannot rely on anyone else – with other women being just as likely to betray you as men; that you must remain true to yourself – while balancing the needs of others; and that as women we are capable of almost anything – yet also of losing everything we have.

Fairy tales originated as a means of both entertaining and instructing listeners, providing characters for audiences to identify with and, in some cases, aspire towards, yet also those we are invited to reject. Horror is essentially no different, yet the genre often invites siding with the underdog, and this is not necessarily the 'good girl'. As Warner has argued: 'Fears trace a map of society's values; we need fear to know who we are and what we do not want to be'.[31] A trait that is unanimously rejected among the females presented in horror is a willingness to be victims. Protagonists are taught the importance of self-reliance in attempting to triumph over various perils, including death itself. The world is far from idyllic, and terrors exist in many guises, including certain capacities within ourselves. Yet the women portrayed in horror are not simply a product of male anxieties about female castration (as Creed has argued), and while we are invited to see things from a female point of view, this is not necessarily a means for male viewers to experience masochistic pleasure (as Clover claims), but potentially more positive: making audiences aware of the specific anxieties women are faced with as they attempt to negotiate the difficult terrain of adulthood. The sexual prudence nurtured in the slasher, far from functioning as a controlling device, may equally serve as a sobering antidote to romantic myths, warning women against making dangerous alliances simply to be accepted. Although rape is problematically treated, as has been discussed, neither are men exclusively villainous, with positive male figures offering crucial support and often sacrificing themselves to help the heroine survive. Such developments possess many progressive elements, yet it remains difficult to conclude whether contemporary horror reveals actual changes in our cultural expectations or playful variations on the same entrenched ideas. Are we more open to strong females in the wake of feminism, or does the residue of distrust evident in these narratives negate this? Certainly, motherhood remains the ultimate destiny for women, with any notion of a career hardly even considered, which seems somewhat regressive in the 21st century, yet the fact that motherhood is also shown to be loaded with difficulties suggests that horror is trying to explode a maternal ideal in the same way as a romantic one. The texts evaluated seem to confirm a difficult journey ahead for younger female audiences, yet they also reveal the mechanisms by which women are critically evaluated. Ultimately, although narratively approved figures are clearly placed in opposition to women who seemingly misuse their power, we know better than to take sides. The ambiguities present are recoverable spaces, providing textual openings by which to reinterpret meanings and debate possibilities – which is, after all, what the stories we circulate have always sought to achieve.

Notes

Preface

1. Cristina Bacchilega, *Postmodern Fairy Tales: Gender and Narrative Strategies* (Philadelphia: University of Pennsylvania Press, 1997), p. 68.
2. Catherine Orenstein, 'Dances with Wolves: Little Red Riding Hood's Long Walk in the Woods', available online at http://www.msmagazine.com/summer2004/danceswithwolves.asp, p. 5. The tale's socio-cultural transition and its contemporary revisions are further elaborated in Orenstein's book *Little Red Riding Hood Uncloaked: Sex, Morality and the Evolution of a Fairy Tale* (New York: Basic Books, 2002).

Introduction

1. Catherine Clement, *The Newly Born Woman* (written with Helene Cixous, first published in 1975 as *La Jeune Nee*, repr. London: IB Tauris, 1996, trans. Betsy Wing), p. 6.
2. Isabel Cristina Pinedo, *Recreational Terror: Women and the Pleasures of Horror Film Viewing* (Albany: State University of New York Press, 1997), p. 70.
3. See Linda Williams' article 'When the Woman Looks', *The Dread of Difference: Gender and the Horror Film*, ed. Barry Keith Grant (University of Texas Press, 1996).
4. Brigid Cherry, 'Refusing to Refuse to Look: Female Viewers of the Horror Film', *Horror: The Film Reader*, ed. Mark Jancovich (London: Routledge, 2002), pp. 172–74.
5. Ibid., p. 176.
6. Pinedo, *Recreational Terror*, p. 69.
7. Although the female equivalent of *Stand By Me* exists in the form of *Then and Now* (Lesli Linka Glatter, 1995), the film simply substitutes identical female figures for the male characters in Reiner's film, yet notably exchanges the narrative task from the discovery of a dead body to the investigation of a suspected murder, even involving a séance in a graveyard in order to 'feminise' the subject matter.
8. Laura Mulvey, 'Visual Pleasure and Narrative Cinema', *Screen* 16, no. 3 (Autumn 1975), pp. 6–18.
9. Elizabeth Wanning Harries, *Twice Upon a Time: Women Writers and the History of the Fairy Tale* (New Jersey: Princeton University Press, 2001), p. 104.
10. Ibid., p. 101.
11. Carol Clover, *Men, Women and Chainsaws: Gender in the Horror Film* (London: BFI Press, 1992), p. 12.
12. Robin Wood, *Hollywood From Vietnam to Reagan and Beyond* (New York: Columbia University Press, 2003), p. 70.

13. James B. Twitchell, *Dreadful Pleasures: An Anatomy of Modern Horror* (New York: Oxford University Press, 1985), p. 7.
14. Ibid., p. 66.
15. Clover, *Men, Women and Chainsaws*, pp. 10, 19.
16. Ibid., p. 17.
17. Twitchell, p. 66.
18. Bruno Bettelheim, *The Uses of Enchantment: The Meaning and Importance of Fairytales* (London: Penguin Books, 1976, repr., 1991), p. 12.
19. Sibylle Birkhauser-Oeri, *The Mother: Archetypal Image in Fairy Tales* (1977, Toronto: Inner City Books, 1988), p. 9.
20. Maria Tatar, *Off With Their Heads!: Fairy Tales and the Culture of Childhood* (New Jersey: Princeton University Press, 1992), p. 46.
21. Marina Warner, *From the Beast to the Blonde: On Fairy Tales and Their Tellers* (London: Vintage, 1995), p. 33.
22. Ibid., *From the Beast to the Blonde*, pp. 24, 297.
23. Ibid., pp. 318, 351.
24. Barbara Creed, *The Monstrous Feminine: Film, Feminism, Psychoanalysis* (London: Routledge, 1993), p. 3.
25. Clover, *Men, Women and Chainsaws*, p. 18.
26. Ibid., p. 231.
27. Pinedo, *Recreational Terror*, p. 4.
28. Ibid., pp. 70, 95.
29. Stephen King, quoted by Clover, *Men, Women and Chainsaws*, p. 3.
30. Clover, *Men, Women and Chainsaws*, pp. 3, 6.
31. Warner, *From the Beast to the Blonde*, p. xvi.
32. Vera Dika, *Games of Terror: Halloween, Friday the 13th and the Films of the Stalker Cycle* (New Jersey: Associated University Press, 1990), p. 87.
33. Warner, *From the Beast to the Blonde*, p. 195.
34. Pinedo, *Recreational Terror*, p. 39.
35. Tatar, *Off With Their Heads!*, p. 39.
36. See Alison Lurie's introduction to *Clever Gretchen and Other Forgotten Folktales* (New York: Thomas Y Crowell, 1980, pp. xi–xiii).
37. Birkhauser-Oeri, *The Mother*, pp. 18–19.
38. Tatar, *Off With Their Heads!*, pp. 226, 228.
39. Ibid., p. 230.
40. E. Ann Kaplan, *Women and Film: Both Sides of the Camera* (London: Routledge, 1983), p. 201.
41. George Beahm also describes *Carrie* as 'The Catcher in the Rye with a supernatural element', yet unlike Salinger's teenage protagonist, Holden Caulfield, who recognises and rejects the 'phoniness' of the adult world while opting out of school, Carrie's tragedy is her naive wish to be accepted by the very world that rejects her. *The Stephen King Story* (London: Warner Books, 1994), p. 78.

1   Telling tales: Fairy tales and female rites of passage narratives

1. Twitchell, *Dreadful Pleasures*, p. 7.
2. Twitchell's view that horror cinema is essentially conservative is shared by Tony Williams who claims that while films of the 1970s were critical

of the family, the 1980s was an 'era pathologically affirming conservative family values' ('Trying to Survive on the Darker Side: 1980s Family Horror', *The Dread of Difference*, p. 165), while Christopher Sharret agrees that the majority of horror films in this decade were a reactionary defence of family values and patriarchy ('The Horror Film in Neo-Conservative Culture', *The Dread of Difference*, p. 253).

3. Bettelheim, *The Uses of Enchantment*, p. 73.
4. Not only were women the principal tale-tellers in the home, as Marina Warner has pointed out, they were also responsible for spreading stories to a wider audience. Maria Tatar asserts that while the Grimms used sources of mixed gender for their collection of tales, most were attributed to female informants, including Dorothea Viehmann, Jeanette Hassenpflug, and Dorothea Wild. *The Hard Facts of the Grimms' Fairy Tales* (orig pubd 1987, 2nd edn, Princeton University Press, 2003), p. 25. In addition, while Charles Perrault remains well known for writing tales in 17th century France, a number of women were also engaged in this role, as Marina Warner and Elizabeth Wanning Harries have sought to remind us.
5. Warner, *From the Beast to the Blonde*, p. xix.
6. The pain inflicted on Andersen's female characters is as curious as their redemption. See, for example, 'The Little Mermaid' and 'The Red Shoes', in which young girls are mutilated prior to being allowed into heaven.
7. This aversion to mature females has been attributed to Andersen's homosexuality, as much as his religious beliefs, and a recent biography argues that promiscuous female relatives led to this antipathy, citing Andersen himself stating that girls older than 12 made him 'shudder'. See *Hans Christian Andersen: A New Life* by Jens Andersen (trans. Tiina Nunnally, Overlook Duckworth Press, 2005).
8. Joseph Campbell, *The Hero With a Thousand Faces* (New York: Pantheon Books Inc., 1949), p. 10.
9. Warner, *From the Beast to the Blonde*, p. 17.
10. Wanning Harris, *Twice Upon a Time*, p. 17.
11. Jack Zipes, *The Brothers Grimm: From Enchanted Forests to the Modern World* (London: Routledge, 1988), p. 23.
12. Ibid., p. 24.
13. Ibid.
14. Tatar, *Off With Their Heads!*, p. 96.
15. Tatar, *The Hard Facts*, pp. 29–30.
16. Zipes, *The Brothers Grimm*, p. 149.
17. Tatar, *The Hard Facts*, pp. 4–9.
18. Zipes, *The Brothers Grimm*, p. 151.
19. In Tatar's view 'the facts of life seemed to have been more disturbing to the Grimms than the harsh realities of life' – causing them to remove sexual content more readily than instances of cruelty and violence. *The Hard Facts*, p. 11.
20. Zipes, *The Brothers Grimm*, pp. 24–5.
21. Ibid., p. 25.
22. Warner, *From the Beast to the Blonde*, p. 207.
23. Bettelheim, *The Uses of Enchantment*, p. 73.
24. Tatar, *Off With Their Heads!*, p. 141.
25. Ibid., p. 146.

26. Warner, *From the Beast to the Blonde*, p. 244.
27. In the version Tatar alludes to Red Riding Hood and her Granny survive by boiling sausage on the fire and thus enticing the wolf down the chimney and boiling him alive, while the Grimm's appended finale has him drown outside in a trough filled with sausage water. However, in other versions of 'Red Riding Hood' the heroine participates in such activities as unwittingly eating her grandmother's body and even engaging in sexual relations with the wolf, demonstrating the variations that have occurred around the story. *The Hard Facts*, pp. xvi, 23. For a chronological account of the tale's transition, see Jack Zipes' (ed.), *The Trials and Tribulations of Little Red Riding Hood* (London: Routledge, 2nd edn 1993).
28. Zipes, *The Trials and Tribulations of Little Red Riding Hood*, pp. 24, 26.
29. Tatar, *The Hard Facts*, p. 47.
30. Zipes, *The Brothers Grimm*, p. 149.
31. Clover, *Men, Women and Chainsaws*, p. 12.
32. Pinedo, *Recreational Terror*, p. 76.
33. Tatar, *The Hard Facts*, p. xix.
34. Warner, *From the Beast to the Blonde*, p. 213.
35. Bettelheim, *The Uses of Enchantment*, p. 245.
36. The origins of fairy godmothers and maternal spirits are instructive. In his analysis of ancient myths, Campbell has noted that supernatural aid would often come from a crone who presents an amulet or some other form of assistance (*The Hero With a Thousand Faces*, p. 69) and points out that her precursors are the protecting goddesses found in Greek myth (p. 71). This protection is usually given to a male hero by a female deity, yet we should not forget the importance of Demeter – who forced Zeus's intervention in her daughter Persephone's abduction by Hades. The relevance of the myth, and its role as a primary example of the mother-avenger, will be discussed in Chapter 6.
37. Zipes, *The Brothers Grimm*, pp. 137–8, 141.
38. Ibid., p. 142.
39. Cristina Bacchilega, *Postmodern Fairy Tales*, p. 56.
40. Campbell, *The Hero With a Thousand Faces*, p. 79.
41. The villainous Mirror Queen (Monica Bellucci) is preserved intact in *The Brothers Grimm* (2005) and accordingly blamed for corrupting men and murdering young girls in a film that plays with everything except negative female archetypes.
42. Zipes, *The Brothers Grimm*, p. 64.
43. See Creed's *Monstrous-Feminine*, especially Chapter 6 'Woman as Witch', which explores this theme in some depth, pp. 73–83.
44. Lyndal Roper, *Witch Craze: Terror and Fantasy in Baroque Germany* (Yale University Press, 2004).
45. Clover, *Men, Women and Chainsaws*, p. 113.
46. Wood, *From Hollywood to Reagan and Beyond*, p. 179.
47. Cherry, 'Refusing to Refuse to Look', p. 173.
48. Per Schelde, *Androids, Humanoids and Other Science Fiction Monsters: Science and Soul in Science Fiction Films* (New York University Press, 1993), pp. 6–7.
49. Campbell, *The Hero With a Thousand Faces*, p. 38.

50. Zipes, *The Brothers Grimm*, p. 26.
51. Warner, *From the Beast to the Blonde*, p. 415.
52. Ibid., p. 417.
53. Campbell, *The Hero With a Thousand Faces*, p. 11.
54. Ibid, p. 381.
55. Paul Wells, *The Horror Genre*, p. 35.
56. Ibid., p. 35.
57. Campbell, *The Hero With a Thousand Faces*, pp. 19, 20.
58. Ibid., p. 383.
59. Ibid., p. 385.

2   Sex and the Final Girl: Surviving the slasher

1. Adam Rockoff, *Going to Pieces: The Rise and Fall of the Slasher Film, 1978–1986* (North Carolina: McFarland & Company Inc., 2002), p. 14.
2. Reynold Humphries, *The American Horror Film: An Introduction* (Edinburgh: Edinburgh University Press, 2002), p. 140.
3. Rockoff, *Going to Pieces*, p. 14.
4. Ibid., p. 15. The two examples used where the 'good' girl turns out to be the killer are *Happy Birthday to Me* (1981) and *Sleepaway Camp* (1983).
5. Rockoff, *Going to Pieces*, p. 182.
6. Kim Newman, *Nightmare Movies: A Critical Guide to Contemporary Horror Films* (New York: Harmony Books, 1988), p. 157. Although Newman was enthusiastic about *Scream*, as his *Sight and Sound* review testifies, the summary remains accurate.
7. Clover, *Men, Women and Chainsaws*, p. 51.
8. Ibid., pp. 6–7, 23.
9. Isabel Cristina Pinedo contends that 'transgressive pleasures' are afforded by horror's violent women and that this is a primary source of their appeal to the female audience. *Recreational Terror*, p. 68. However, Brigid Cherry's study of female horror fans places an interest in violence firmly in the minority. 'Refusing to Refuse to Look', p. 173.
10. Clover, *Men, Women and Chainsaws*, pp. 3, 62–3, 231.
11. Ibid., p. 30.
12. Creed, *The Monstrous Feminine*, p. 142.
13. According to Hitchcock, 'Blondes make the best victims. They're like virgin snow that shows up the bloody footprints.' Barry Norman, 'Hitchcock's Birds', *Daily Mail*, Wednesday April 27th, 2005, p. 15.
14. See Tania Modleski's, *The Women Who Knew Too Much: Hitchcock and Feminist Theory*, which assesses how female spectators might reclaim his films within a feminist rationale.
15. Clover, *Men, Women and Chainsaws*, p. 39.
16. The casting of Janet Leigh's daughter as the hero adds an interesting dimension to *Halloween*. John Carpenter briefly unites Leigh and Curtis in *The Fog* (1979), with Curtis playing, by contrast, a sexually liberated drifter, while *Halloween H20* (1998) affords a wonderful moment when Leigh dispenses some 'maternal advice' to her real-life daughter on surviving the slasher.

17. Clover cites John Carpenter in forming this view, who responded to the criticism that *Halloween* punished female sexuality by pointing to the fact that Laurie's saving grace is the fact that she is 'the most sexually frustrated. She's the one that killed him. Not because she's a virgin, but because all that repressed energy starts coming out . . . She and the killer have a certain link: sexual repression'. Quoted in *Men, Women and Chainsaws*, p. 49.
18. Clover, *Men, Women and Chainsaws*, p. 36.
19. Tony Williams attempts to infer that Michael is the victim of childhood abuse but offers no evidence for this claim. *Hearths of Darkness: The Family in the American Horror Film* (New Jersey: Associated University Press, 1996), p. 220. Reynold Humphries elects to blame the first sister he kills (at 6) for having 'forgotten about him for other matters', thereby constituting the 'sister-as-mother abandoning the son for another'. *The American Horror Film*, p. 141.
20. Clover, *Men, Women and Chainsaws*, p. 38.
21. Ibid., p. 49.
22. Ibid., p. 50.
23. Ibid., pp. 60, 64.
24. Wes Craven, quoted by Adam Rockoff, *Going to Pieces*, pp. 152–3.
25. Humphries, *The American Horror Film*, p. 151.
26. Ibid., p. 160.
27. Craven in interview at the Toronto Film Festival, quoted by Tony Williams in *Hearths of Darkness*, p. 130.
28. Clover, *Men, Women and Chainsaws*, p. 38, fn. 22.
29. For further discussion of the debate James Bulger's death provoked, see *Ill Effects: The Media Violence Debate*, eds Martin Barker and Julian Petley (London: Routledge, 1997).
30. Jeremy Sconce, 'Spectacles of Death: Identification, Reflexivity, and Contemporary Horror', *Film Theory Goes to the Movies*, eds Jim Collins, Hilary Radner and Ava Preacher Collins (London: Routledge, 1993), p. 113.
31. Sconce, 'Spectacles of Death', p. 113.
32. Dika, *Games of Terror*, p. 136.
33. Molly Haskell, *From Reverence to Rape: The Treatment of Women in the Movies* (University of Chicago Press, 2nd edn, 1987), pp. 398–9.
34. Both *The Ring* and *The Gift* feature single mothers who similarly demonstrate the strength and resilience associated with the Final Girl, and are discussed in greater detail in Chapter 6.
35. Warner, *From the Beast to the Blonde*, p. xix.

3   Maternal monsters and motherly mentors: Failed initiations in *Carrie* and *Carrie II*

1. E. Ann Kaplan, *Women and Film: Both Sides of the Camera* (London: Routledge, 1983), p. 201.
2. George Beahm, *The Stephen King Story* (London: Warner Books, 1992), p. 78.
3. Tanya Krzywinska, *A Skin for Dancing In: Possession, Witchcraft and Voodoo in Film* (Trowbridge: Flicks Books, 2000), p. 136 .

4. Julia Kristeva, *Powers of Horror*, 1982, p. 4, quoted in Creed's *The Monstrous-Feminine*, p. 8.
5. Creed, *The Monstrous Feminine*, p. 10.
6. Ibid., p. 12.
7. Lucy Fischer, *Cinematernity: Film, Motherhood, Genre* (New Jersey: Princeton University Press, 1996), p. 30.
8. Stephen King has claimed that he first conceived *Carrie* as a symbol of women's liberation and the fear generated by the possibilities of a 'future of female equality' (as quoted in *Men, Women and Chainsaws*, p. 3), yet he also claims, in the same quote, that the story would appeal to any victim of school bullying, regardless of gender, who might identify with Carrie's plight. The second comment would seem to contradict the first, making the tale one of potential identification based not on gender, but mutual experience.
9. Dika, *Games of Terror*, p. 17.
10. Serafina Kent Bathrick, 'Ragtime: The Horror of Growing Up Female', *Jump Cut*, p. 9, part 14, 1977.
11. Shelley Stamp Lindsay, 'Horror, Femininity and Carrie's Monstrous Puberty', in Barry Keith Grant (ed.), *The Dread of Difference: Gender and the Horror Film* (Austin: University of Texas Press, 1996), pp. 285, 288, 289.
12. Humphries, *The American Horror Film*, p. 95.
13. Ibid., p. 95.
14. Stephen King, *Carrie* (London: New English Library, 1974), p. 132.
15. Tommy's jealousy towards Miss Collins implies that any intimacy between women must be sexual. This is matched by the equally bizarre incestuous connotations that Creed reads into the relationship between Carrie and her mother, arguing that 'Carrie's stabbing suggests a sexual assault by the mother', p. 82. The fact that Creed makes an equivalent claim about the relationship between Regan and her mother in *The Exorcist* seems equally absurd and unsanctioned.
16. *The Witches of Eastwick*'s Felicia seems almost a direct parody of Margaret White and is punished for her gossip-mongering with a spell that causes her to vomit cherry pips profusely. In *Edward Scissorhands*, although almost everyone eventually turns on Edward (Johnny Depp), it is the local Christian nut, Esmeralda, who is most vicious in her hostility towards him, and she is suitably lampooned as the nasty side of small-town morality. Still more reminiscent of Mrs White is the mother, Mrs Lisbon (Kathleen Turner), in *The Virgin Suicides* (1999), who is similarly presented as a religious zealot and ultimately held responsible for her daughters' deaths. The homecoming ball depicted in the film is almost a carbon copy of the prom in *Carrie*, with glitter and stars and a still harsher refutation of romance for the Lisbon girls.
17. Williams, *Hearths of Darkness*, p. 240. The fact that Amy Irving and Priscilla Pointer are a real-life mother and daughter adds interesting resonances to this on-screen relationship.
18. The female Goth has enjoyed a notable revival in recent horror cinema. *The Craft*'s foursome wear the designated garb of social misfits in their black clothes, crucifix jewelery, and heavy make-up, with the most 'unstable' of the four, Nancy, also wearing the most outlandish clothes. Buffy (Sarah

Michelle Gellar), by contrast, avoids such a 'uniform', and dresses much like any other high-school teenager, as opposed to the 'rock chick' clothes and heavy make-up favoured by her 'darker' alter-ego, Faith (Eliza Dushku). *The Hole* (2001) plays on the image of the depressed psychologically unhinged Goth for all it is worth in the character Liz (Thora Birch), who is shown to be unstable in the extreme, her obsessive love for fellow student Mike (Desmond Haughton) leading her to murder. Unlike *The Craft II*'s black-clad Rachael, who is redeemed by love, Liz exemplifies the misfit who is seemingly driven insane with passion, and stops at nothing to achieve her desire. *The Virgin Suicides* (1999) overtly romanticises the gothic tragedy of five sisters who kill themselves one summer, their obsession with death seeming to have stemmed from their heavily religious upbringing, while *Ginger Snaps* (2000) continues the theme of death-obsessed teens in its two misfit sisters who make a pact to have left home by 16 or to die together, an obsession that puberty exacerbates in full force. Ginger, like Carrie, is an outsider at school – although this is more elected in her case – and exemplifies the degree to which female rage is shown to be a monstrously destructive force, yet her transformation also provides a newfound confidence and allure that quickly attracts the interest of boys, adopting a glamorous Goth look, akin to that of the four girls in *The Craft*, as she makes her slow motion entrance through the school corridors in a sexy outfit complete with grey streaks in her hair. As with the other female Goths cited, she is also invariably punished.
19. Clover, *Men, Women and Chainsaws*, p. 23.
20. Bathrick, 'Ragtime', p. 10.

4   Misfit sisters: Female kinship and rivalry in *The Craft* and *Ginger Snaps*

1. Haskell, *From Reverence to Rape*, pp. 370–1.
2. *The Craft*'s denouement confirms the danger of powerful females and the difficulties of 'sisterhood', just as the short story, 'When I was a Witch', by Charlotte Perkins Gilman curtails the possibility of female emancipation – a wish that abruptly ends the angry narrator's supernatural powers.
3. This moral message refutes the claim made by one critic who argues that '*The Craft* refuses to put its maverick quartet back on the straight and narrow – they remain committed outsiders, treated with sympathy and considerable indulgence.' Chris Savage King, review of *The Craft* in *Sight and Sound*, reprinted in *Science Fiction/Horror: A Sight and Sound Reader*, ed. Kim Newman (London: BFI Publishing, 2002), p. 196.
4. Linda Ruth Williams, 'Blood Sisters', *Science Fiction/Horror: A Sight and Sound Reader*, ed. Kim Newman (BFI Press, 2002), p. 193.
5. Pamela was originally intended to prove her maternal loyalty still further. In a deleted scene of the collector's edition DVD of *Ginger Snaps*, when the police arrive at the Halloween party looking for Ginger, Pamela tells them that she killed Trina and is duly arrested.
6. Quoted by Paul Wells, *The Horror Genre*, p. 39.

7. As a further revision of 'Red Riding Hood', in the prequel, *Ginger Snaps Back*, a 19th century Ginger kills the grandmother figure, while Brigitte's ancestor kills the kindly hunter so that her sister may live, thereby continuing the curse.

8. Haskell, *From Reverence to Rape*, p. xii.

9. Internet Movie Data Base discussion board for *Ginger Snaps: Unleashed*.

10. Williams, *Hearths of Darkness*, p. 52.

11. Ibid., p. 54.

12. Twitchell, *Dreadful Pleasures*, p. 210.

13. See Zipes, *The Trials and Tribulations of Little Red Riding Hood*.

14. Ibid., p. 71.

15. Twitchell, *Dreadful Pleasures*, p. 208.

16. Ibid., p. 257.

17. Catherine Clement and Helene Cixous, *The Newly Born Woman* (first published in 1975 as *La Jeune Nee*, repr. London: IB Tauris, 1996, trans. Betsy Wing), p. 9.

18. Ibid., p. 56.

19. Wells specifically refers to Spanish werewolf film *The Werewolf's Shadow* (Leon Klimovsky, 1970), yet the remark is equally pertinent to the *Ginger Snaps* films, *The Horror Genre*, p. 71.

20. In fact, the sole character that exults in being a werewolf is vilified as a ball-breaking bitch for whom no sympathy is offered, despite having contracted the curse through unprotected sex, the underlying AIDS metaphor being used with astonishingly tasteless results.

21. Wells, *The Horror Genre*, p. 37.

5 Fighting demons: Buffy, Faith, Willow, and the forces of good and evil

1. For a more detailed discussion of this theme, see Sarah E. Skwire's 'Whose Side Are You On Anyway?: Children, Adults and the Use of Fairy Tales in *Buffy*' in *Fighting the Forces: What's at Stake in Buffy the Vampire Slayer?* eds Wilcox and Lavery (Lanham, MD: Rowman & Littlefield, 2002).

2. That her mother notices Buffy eyeing the dress and buys it for her, as well as urging her to go by herself to the prom as 'the wrong someone' invited her, is a crucial character development that positions Joyce as a wise maternal benefactor. 'Snow White' is additionally referenced, and subverted, when Buffy loses her life later in the episode and is revived with a 'kiss' by the same 'wrong someone', her heartbroken yet ever loyal friend Xander (Nicholas Brendon), who performs CPR.

3. Detracting somewhat from this conclusion is the fact that his dead girlfriend is finally blamed for wanting him to be more macho, leading him to experiment with a 'potion' that increases his threat, as much as his attraction, to her.

4. Jenny Bavidge, 'Chosen Ones: Reading the Contemporary Teen Heroine', *Teen TV: Genre, Consumption and Identity* (London: BFI Publishing, 2004), p. 50.

5. In fact, Buffy's strength proves insufficient to defeat Willow, with Xander's defiant testimony of love finally evoking the human buried within her ('Grave').

6. As reported in Kathleen Tracy's *The Girl's Got Bite: The Unofficial Guide to Buffy's World* (Los Angeles: Renaissance, 1998), p. 41.

7. Campbell, *The Hero With a Thousand Faces*, p. 97.

8. Ibid., p. 101.

9. Ibid., pp. 337–8.

10. Elyce Rae Helford, 'My Emotions Give Me Power: The Containment of Girl's Anger in *Buffy*', *Fighting the Forces: What's at Stake in Buffy the Vampire Slayer?*, eds Rhonda V. Wilcox and David Lavery (Rowman & Littlefield Publishers Inc., 2002), p. 21.

11. For a closer analysis of the racial ramifications of this figure, see Lynne Edwards' 'Slaying in Black and White: Kendra as Tragic Mulatta in *Buffy*', *Fighting the Forces*, pp. 85–97.

12. Helford, 'My Emotions Give Me Power', p. 21.

13. Mary Alice Money, 'The Undemonization of Supporting Characters in *Buffy*', *Fighting the Forces*, p. 104.

14. Roz Kaveney notes the importance Whedon attributes to Joyce Summers in the series as intensely personal, having based her on his own mother – including her cause of death – and hailing her as 'one of the great unsung presences of his show'. Kaveney, *Reading the Vampire Slayer: An Unofficial Critical Companion to Buffy and Angel* (London: IB Tauris, 2002), p. 33.

15. Thomas Hibbs reads sex with Spike as sadomasochistic, quoting Buffy's admission that she has 'been in love with the pain' ('Wrecked') and further arguing that her relationships with men have 'always been tinged with elements of sadomasochism'. 'Buffy the Vampire Slayer as Feminist Noir', p. 57. Conversely, Mimi Marinucci views Buffy as the dominant partner, linking this to Faith's admission of feeling aroused after slaying, arguing that 'the violent nature of her relationship with Spike suggests that Buffy is similarly aroused by her own aggression, particularly when she feels disengaged from humanity'. 'Feminism and the Ethics of Violence: Why Buffy Kicks Ass', p. 73. Both articles appear in *Buffy the Vampire Slayer and Philosophy: Fear and Trembling in Sunnydale*, ed. by James B. South (Illinois: Open Court/Carus Press, 2003). In my view, Faith is more sexually liberated because she does not experience the same sense of guilt and shame that so clearly affects Buffy in acting on her desires, even if the series tries to suggest that all she wants is to be loved.

16. The fact that Robin's mother was also a Slayer further underwrites Buffy's greater loyalty to the bad boys she is attracted to than fellow women – a loyalty that is subsequently used to justify the resulting distrust her former friends, male and female alike, later exhibit towards her. As former vengeance demon, Anya says in relation to Spike, having witnessed for herself the way Buffy overlooks his many transgressions: 'A whole new set of rules apply when it comes to Spike. It's like he can do no wrong.'

17. Marinucci, 'Feminism and the Ethics of Violence', p. 65.

18. In one of the most complex and moving scenes of the entire series, Faith provides a vital clue in the Mayor's defeat ('Graduation Day, part 2'), mentally contacting Buffy while in a coma to hint at his human weakness. Why she

does this is never explained, particularly given their animosity and the pain she clearly experiences when she eventually awakes to find he is dead, yet the gesture, and her lack of recrimination, testifies to a depth of character that renders Buffy shallow by comparison. Although it is Buffy's dreams the series tends to prioritise, Faith also has prophetic dreams and is far more perceptive in waking life than her counterpart. Another shared dream in which they make Buffy's bed together offers a similarly touching example of the sisterly relationship that is both hinted at yet refused between them, reiterating the sibling nature of their rivalry, the domesticity Faith envies, and the life her former friend has literally attempted to take from her – a dream that notably culminates in Buffy stabbing her again. For further discussion of Faith's dreams, see Donald Keller's 'Spirit Guides and Shadow Selves: From the Dream Life of Buffy (and Faith)', *Fighting the Forces: What's at Stake in Buffy the Vampire Slayer?*, pp. 165–77.

19. Helford, 'My Emotions Give Me Power', p. 33.
20. Ibid., p. 21.
21. Although Whedon claims to be an 'atheist', as he acknowledges in a web-site post to fans, 'the fact is the Christian mythos has a powerful fascination to me, and it bleeds into my storytelling'. The Bronze VIP Posting Board Archives, www.cise.ufl.edu, 15th December, 1998.
22. J.P. Williams, 'Choosing Your Own Mother: Mother/Daughter Conflicts in Buffy', *Fighting the Forces: What's at Stake in Buffy the Vampire Slayer?*, p. 71.
23. Tara's relationship with Willow, like that of later female lover, Kennedy (Iyari Limon), can be seen to provide the love her mother negated, with both women bestowing a grounding nurturing influence that encourages her self-belief.
24. Williams, 'Choosing Your Own Mother', p. 71.
25. Dushku has also appeared in the feature film *Wrong Turn* (2003), playing a similarly self-sufficient female character who struggles to stay alive in unknown woods, while Gellar has also found further work in horror films such as *I Know What You Did Last Summer* (1997), *Scream 2* (1997), and *The Grudge* (2004), notably playing victims of violence in all three, as well as two *Scooby Doo* films!

6 Demeter's daughters: Wronged girls and the mother avenger

1. Humphries, *The American Horror Film*, p. 152.
2. Linda Williams, 'When the Woman Looks', *Horror: The Film Reader*, ed. Mark Jancovich (London: Routledge, 2002), p. 65.
3. In many ways the film is a revised version of the 'woman's Gothic' of the 1940s in which a female character 'discovers that she has unwittingly stepped into a dire situation by marrying a man whom she comes to suspect may be a villain', as well as continuing what Sabrina Barton terms as the 'woman's psycho-thriller' emerging in the late 1980s and 1990s in which a female's suspicions are confirmed and her point of view validated 'when she sees through the lie of masculine masquerade'. Barton, 'Your Self Storage: Female Investigation and Male Performativity in

the Woman's Psychothriller', *The Film Cultures Reader*, ed. Graeme Turner (London: Routledge, 2002), pp. 320–1.

4. Watching the cursed video may be seen as the equivalent of entering the bloody chamber in 'Bluebeard', with Samara inviting this curiosity even as she punishes it.

5. According to Hideo Nakata the idea of the well stems from a Japanese folk tale in which a maid who is held responsible for a missing plate throws herself down a well, her spirit returning as a voice that continuously counts plates. By adapting the tale to a family situation, and making the mother responsible for the girl's death, a still more horrific scenario unfolds.

6. In a scene later deleted from the theatrical release, Rachel deliberately gives the video to a child murderer at the end of the film, thereby collaborating with Samara in an act of justified vengeance. It was replaced with the curse seeming troublingly random in its choice of victims.

7. The *Ringu* universe may borrow from such conspicuous Western influences as *Carrie* and *Poltergeist* yet also contains specifically Japanese elements, including a pronounced fear of water – and women! Various Japanese horror films concern restless female spirits (with a very similar appearance), including *Ju-on* (Takashi Shimuzu, 2003) and its American re-make, *The Grudge* (Takashi Shimuzu, 2004). These also involve a curse created by the spirit of someone who dies angry, and whose desire for revenge is seemingly implacable, yet they are still more dissolute in their denouements, for while Samara/Sadako saves those she wants to help her perpetuate the curse, Shimuzu's films do not allow even a glimmer of hope for any human who comes into contact with their evil female spirit.

8. Humphries, *The American Horror Film*, p. 193.

9. Examples cited by Cristina Bacchilega in which dead women warn heroines about murderous men include the Breton legend 'Comorre' and Italian tale 'Il Diavolo', *Postmodern Fairy Tales*, p. 179.

10. According to Evelyn, Samara told her to drown her as a baby, yet the fact that she never slept disturbingly suggests that she tried to do so out of frustration. Rachel, by contrast, is falsely diagnosed as having Munchausen by Proxy – accused of hurting her own son in order to get attention.

11. Wells, *The Horror Genre*, p. 96.

12. If Hera is a likely ancestor of the fairy tale's wicked step-mother then Zeus, as Persephone's father, may be equated with numerous accounts of paternal failure, particularly as he encouraged Hades to take her as his bride, which resembles 'Beauty and the Beast' and other tales of forced matrimony.

13. Persephone's status as goddess of the underworld also links her to Hecate, goddess of magic, ghosts, and witchcraft, who is also an important mythic archetype for horror's supernaturally empowered female protagonists. As Hecate also resides in the underworld, and has some control over the fertility of the Earth, she interestingly combines Persephone with her mother's powers.

Conclusion

1. Tatar, *Off With Their Heads!*, p. 8.
2. Warner, *From the Beast to the Blonde*, p. 21.

3. Ibid., p. 203.
4. Angela Carter, Introduction to *The Virago Book of Fairy Tales* (London: Virago, 1990), p. xiii.
5. Ibid., p. xiv.
6. Tatar, *Off With Their Heads!*, p. 114.
7. Clover, *Men, Women and Chainsaws*, pp. 20, 236.
8. Clover notes that today's film-makers are not only familiar with Freud and film theory, but that some have even made adjustments to their films after reading her essay on the slasher 'Her Body, Himself.' *Men, Women and Chainsaws*, p. 232.
9. Tatar, *Off With Their Heads!*, p. 96.
10. Ibid., p. 117.
11. Ibid., p. 119.
12. Perhaps the most heinous example of this tendency to forgive rape occurs in *Cherry Falls* (2000) in which the near-incestuous relationship between father and daughter culminates in her covering up the crime he committed in his youth – the rape, with three accomplices, of a small-town misfit who is very reminiscent of Carrie White. Ironically, he becomes an overprotective policeman who is eventually killed by the resulting child of this appalling assault, yet his good name is preserved by a conspiracy of silence agreed between mother and daughter.
13. Warner, *From the Beast to the Blonde*, p. 411.
14. In fact, these tales initially conveyed a cautionary attitude towards men also. In numerous versions of Cinderella across Asia, Africa, and Europe the heroine flees from an 'unnatural' father who wishes to marry her (Bettelheim, *The Uses of Enchantment*, p. 245), while Sleeping Beauty was originally raped by a male intruder as she lay in a coma.
15. Zipes, *The Trials and Tribulations of Little Red Riding Hood*, pp. 23, 24.
16. Christine Gledhill, 'Pleasurable Negotiations', from *Female Spectators: Looking at Film and Television*, ed. Dierdre Pribram (London: Verso, 1988), p. 68.
17. Dika, *Games of Terror*, p. 129.
18. Philip Green, *Cracks in the Pedestal: Ideology and Gender in Hollywood* (University of Massachusetts Press, 1998), p. 211.
19. Kathleen Rowe, *The Unruly Woman: Gender and the Genres of Laughter* (University of Texas Press, 1995), p. 3.
20. Ibid., p. 8.
21. See Place's article, 'Women in Film Noir' in Ann Kaplan's eponymous collection (London: BFI, 1998).
22. Jeanine Basinger, *A Woman's View: How Hollywood Spoke to Women 1930–60* (New York: Knopf, 1993), p. 105, cited by Karen Hollinger, *In the Company of Women: Contemporary Female Friendship Films* (University of Minnesota Press, 1998), fn 16, p. 32.
23. Karen Hollinger, *In the Company of Women*, p. 229.
24. Rowe, *The Unruly Woman*, p. 31.
25. Wood, *Hollywood and Reagan and Beyond*, pp. 312, 320.
26. Clover, *Men, Women and Chainsaws*, p. 231.
27. Tony Williams, *Hearths of Darkness*, pp. 112–3.
28. Wells, *The Horror Genre*, p. 86.

29. As Dahlia has trouble remembering how much medication to take during her 'lost weekend', her death is explicable as an overdose.
30. Bettelheim, *The Uses of Enchantment*, p. 218.
31. Marina Warner, *No Go the Bogeyman: Scaring, Lulling and Making Mock* (London: Vintage, 2000), p. 387.

Bibliography

Andersen, Jens, *Hans Christian Andersen: A New Life* (trans. Tiina Nunnally, London: Overlook Duckworth Press, 2005).

Bacchilega, Cristina, *Postmodern Fairy Tales: Gender and Narrative Strategies* (Philadelphia: University of Pennsylvania Press, 1997).

Barton, Sabrina, 'Your Self Storage: Female Investigation and Male Performativity in the Woman's Psychothriller', *The Film Cultures Reader*, ed. Graeme Turner (London: Routledge, 2002).

Bathrick, Serafina Kent, 'Ragtime: The Horror of Growing Up Female', *Jump Cut*, part 14, 1977, pp. 9–10.

Bavidge, Jenny, 'Chosen Ones: Reading the Contemporary Teen Heroine', *Teen TV: Genre, Consumption and Identity* (London: BFI Publishing, 2004).

Beahm, George, *The Stephen King Story* (London: Warner Books, 1994).

Bettelheim, Bruno, *The Uses of Enchantment: The Meaning and Importance of Fairytales* (London: Penguin Books, 1976, repr. 1991).

Birkhauser-Oeri, Sybille, *The Mother: Archetypal Image in Fairy Tales* (1977, Toronto: Inner City Books, 1988).

Campbell, Joseph, *The Hero With a Thousand Faces* (New York: Pantheon Books, 1949).

Carroll, Noel, *The Philosophy of Horror; or, Paradoxes of the Heart* (London: Routledge, 1990).

Carter, Angela, *The Bloody Chamber and Other Tales*, orig. 1979 (Middlesex: Penguin, 1981).

—— (ed.), *The Virago Book of Fairy Tales* (London: Virago, 1990).

Cherry, Brigid, 'Refusing to Refuse to Look: Female Viewers of the Horror Film', *Horror: The Film Reader*, ed. Mark Jancovich (London: Routledge, 2002).

Cixous, Helene and Catherine Clement, *The Newly Born Woman* (first published in 1975 as *La Jeune Nee*, repr. London: IB Tauris, 1996, trans. Betsy Wing).

Clover, Carol, 'Her body, himself: Gender in the slasher film' 1987, reprinted in *Dreadful Pleasures: Gender and the Horror Film*, ed. Barry Keith Grant (Austin: University of Texas Press, 1996).

——, *Men, Women, and Chainsaws: Gender in the Horror Film* (London: BFI Press, 1992).

Creed, Barbara, 'Horror and the Monstrous-Feminine: An Imaginary Abjection', *Screen*, vol. 27, no. 1, 1986.

——, *The Monstrous Feminine: Film, Feminism, Psychoanalysis* (London: Routledge, 1993).

Dika, Vera, *Games of Terror: Halloween, Friday the 13th and the Films of the Stalker Cycle* (New Jersey: Associated University Press, 1990).

Edwards, Lynne, 'Slaying in Black and White: Kendra as Tragic Mulatta in *Buffy*', *Fighting the Forces: What's at Stake in Buffy the Vampire Slayer?*, eds Rhonda V. Wilcox and David Lavery (Lanham, MD: Rowman & Littlefield Publishers Inc., 2002).

Fischer, Lucy, *Cinematernity: Film, Motherhood, Genre* (New Jersey: Princeton University Press, 1996).

Freeland, Cynthia A., *The Naked and the Undead: Evil and the Appeal of Horror* (Boulder, CO: Westview Press, 2000).

Friday, Nancy, *My Mother, My Self* (Glasgow: Fontana, 1979).

Grant, Barry K. (ed.), *The Dread of Difference: Gender and the Horror Film* (Austin: University of Texas Press, 1996).

Green, Philip, *Cracks in the Pedestal: Ideology and Gender in Hollywood* (Amherst: University of Massachusetts Press, 1998).

Halberstam, Judith, *Skin Shows: Gothic Horror and the Technology of Monsters* (London: Duke University Press, 1995).

Harries, Elizabeth Wanning, *Twice Upon a Time: Women Writers and the History of the Fairy Tale* (New Jersey: Princeton University Press, 2001).

Haskell, Molly, *From Reverence to Rape: The Treatment of Women in the Movies* (Chicago: University of Chicago Press, 2nd edn, 1987).

Helford, Elyce Rae, 'My Emotions Give Me Power: The Containment of Girl's Anger in *Buffy*', *Fighting the Forces: What's at Stake in Buffy the Vampire Slayer?*, eds Rhonda V. Wilcox and David Lavery (Lanham, MD: Rowman & Littlefield Publishers Inc., 2002).

Hibbs, Thomas, 'Buffy the Vampire Slayer as Feminist Noir', *Buffy the Vampire Slayer and Philosophy: Fear and Trembling in Sunnydale*, ed. James B. South (Illinois: Open Court/Carus Publishing, 2003).

Hollinger, Karen, *In the Company of Women: Contemporary Female Friendship Films* (Minneapolis: University of Minnesota Press, 1998).

Humphries, Reynold, *The American Horror Film: An Introduction* (Edinburgh: Edinburgh University Press, 2002).

Jancovich, Mark (ed.), *Horror: The Film Reader* (London: Routledge, 2002).

Kaplan, E. Ann, *Woman and Film: Both Sides of the Camera* (London: Routledge, 1983).

Kaveney, Roz (ed.), *Reading the Vampire Slayer: An Unofficial Critical Companion to Buffy and Angel* (London: IB Tauris, 2002).

Keller, Donald, 'Spirit Guides and Shadow Selves: From the Dream Life of Buffy (and Faith)', *Fighting the Forces: What's at Stake in Buffy the Vampire Slayer?*, eds Rhonda V. Wilcox and David Lavery (Lanham, MD: Rowman & Littlefield Publishers Inc., 2002).

King, Stephen, *Carrie* (London: New English Library Ltd., 1974).

Kristeva, Julia, *Powers of Horror: An Essay on Abjection*, trans. Leon S. Roudiez (New York: Columbia University Press, 1982).

Krzywinska, Tanya, *A Skin for Dancing In: Possession, Witchcraft and Voodoo in Film* (Trowbridge: Flicks Books, 2000).

——, 'Demon Daddies: Gender, Ecstasy and Terror in the Possession Film', *The Horror Film Reader*, Alain Silver and James Ursini (eds) (New York: Limelight, 2000).

——, 'Hubble-Bubble, Herbs and Grimoires: Magic, Manichaenism, and Witchcraft in Buffy', *Fighting the Forces: What's at Stake in Buffy the Vampire Slayer?*, eds Wilcox and Lavery (Lanham, MD: Rowman & Littlefield, 2002).

Little, Tracey, 'High School is Hell: Metaphor Made Literal in *Buffy The Vampire Slayer*', *Buffy The Vampire Slayer and Philosophy: Fear and Trembling in Sunnydale*, ed. James B. South (Illinois: Open Court/Carus Publishing, 2003).

Marinucci, Mimi, 'Feminism and the Ethics of Violence: Why Buffy Kicks Ass', *Buffy The Vampire Slayer and Philosophy: Fear and Trembling in Sunnydale*, ed. James B. South (Illinois: Open Court/Carus Publishing, 2003).

Modleski, Tania, 'The Terror of Pleasure: The Contemporary Horror Film and Postmodern Theory', *The Film Cultures Reader*, ed. Graeme Turner (London: Routledge, 2002).

——, *The Women Who Knew Too Much: Hitchcock and Feminist Theory* (London: Methuen, 1988).

Money, Mary Alice, 'The Undemonization of Supporting Characters in *Buffy*', *Fighting the Forces: What's at Stake in Buffy the Vampire Slayer?*, eds Rhonda V. Wilcox and David Lavery (Lanham, MD: Rowman & Littlefield Publishers Inc., 2002).

Mulvey, Laura, 'Visual Pleasure and Narrative Cinema', *Screen*, vol. 16, no. 3 (Autumn 1975).

Newman, Kim, *Nightmare Movies: A Critical Guide to Contemporary Horror Films* (New York: Harmony Books, 1988).

——(ed.), *Science Fiction/Horror: A Sight and Sound Reader* (London: BFI Publishing, 2002).

Perkins Gilman, Charlotte, 'When I was a Witch' in *The Yellow Wallpaper and Other Stories* (London: Penguin Classics, 1995).

Pinedo, Isabel Cristina, *Recreational Terror: Women and the Pleasures of Horror Film Viewing* (Albany: State University of New York Press, 1997).

Propp, Vladimir, *Morphology of the Folk Tale* (Austin: orig. 1968. repr. University of Texas Press, 1979).

Rasmussen, Randy Loren, *Children of the Night: The Six Archetypal Characters of Classic Horror Films* (North Carolina: McFarland and Co. Ltd, 1998).

Rich, Adrienne, *Of Woman Born: Motherhood as Experience and Institution* (London: Virago, 1977).

Rockoff, Adam, *Going to Pieces: The Rise and Fall of the Slasher Film, 1978–1986*, (North Carolina: McFarland and Company Inc., 2002).

Roper, Lyndal, *Witch Craze: Terror and Fantasy in Baroque Germany* (New Haven: Yale University Press, 2004).

Rowe, Kathleen, *The Unruly Woman: Gender and the Genres of Laughter* (Austin: University of Texas Press, 1995).

Schelde, Per, *Androids, Humanoids and Other Science Fiction Monsters: Science and Soul in Science Fiction Films* (New York: New York University Press, 1993).

Sconce, Jeffrey, 'Spectacles of Death: Identification, Reflexivity, and Contemporary Horror', *Film Theory Goes to the Movies*, eds Jim Collins, Hilary Radner and Ava Preacher Collins (London: Routledge, 1993).

Silver, Alain and James Ursini (eds), *The Horror Film Reader* (New York: Limelight, 2000).

Skwire, Sarah E., 'Whose Side are You on Anyway?: Children, Adults and the Use of Fairy Tales in *Buffy*' in *Fighting the Forces: What's at Stake in Buffy the Vampire Slayer?*, eds Wilcox and Lavery (Lanham, MD: Rowman & Littlefield, 2002).

South, James B. (ed.), *Buffy the Vampire Slayer and Philosophy: Fear and Trembling in Sunnydale* (Illinois: Open Court/Carus Publishing, 2003).

Stamp Lindsay, Shelley, 'Horror, Femininity, and Carrie's Monstrous Puberty', *The Dread of Difference: Gender and the Horror Film*, ed. Barry Keith Grant (Austin: University of Texas Press, 1996).

Tatar, Maria, *The Hard Facts of the Grimm's Fairy Tales*, 2nd edn (Princeton University Press, 1987, 2003).

——, *Off With Their Heads!: Fairy Tales and the Culture of Childhood* (New Jersey: Princeton University Press, 1992).

Tudor, Andrew, 'Why Horror: The Peculiar Pleasures of a Popular Genre', *Cultural Studies*, vol. 11, Part 3, 443–63 (1997).

Twitchell, James B., *Dreadful Pleasures: An Anatomy of Modern Horror* (New York: Oxford University Press, 1985).

Warner, Marina, *From the Beast to the Blonde: On Fairy Tales and Their Tellers* (London: Vintage, 1995).

——, *No Go the Bogeyman: Scaring, Lulling and Making Mock* (London: Vintage, 2000).

Wells, Paul, *The Horror Genre: From Beelzebub to Blair Witch* (London: Wallflower Press, 2000).

Wilcox, Rhonda V. and David Lavery (eds) *Fighting the Forces: What's at Stake in Buffy the Vampire Slayer?* (Lanham, MD: Rowman & Littlefield Publishers Inc., 2002).

Williams, J.P., 'Choosing Your Own Mother: Mother-Daughter Conflicts in *Buffy*', *Fighting the Forces: What's at Stake in Buffy the Vampire Slayer?*, eds Wilcox and Lavery (Lanham, MD: Rowman & Littlefield, 2002).

Williams, Linda, 'When the Woman Looks', *The Dread of Difference: Gender and the Horror Film*, ed. Barry Keith Grant (Austin: University of Texas Press, 1996).

Williams, Linda Ruth, 'Blood Sisters', *Science Fiction/Horror: A Sight and Sound Reader* (London: BFI Publishing, 2002).

Williams, Tony, 'Trying to Survive on the Darker Side: 1980s Family Horror', *The Dread of Difference: Gender and the Horror Film*, ed. Barry Keith Grant (Austin: University of Texas Press, 1996).

——, *Hearths of Darkness: The Family in the American Horror Film* (New Jersey: Associated University Press, 1996).

Wood, Robin, *Hollywood From Vietnam to Reagan* (New York: Columbia University Press, 1986).

——, *Hollywood From Vietnam to Reagan and Beyond* (New York: Columbia University Press, 2003).

Zipes, Jack, *Breaking The Magic Spell: Radical Theories of Folk and Fairy Tales* (1979; Revised edition, The University of Kentucky Press, 2002).

——, *The Brothers Grimm: From Enchanted Forests to the Modern World* (London: Routledge, 1988).

—— (ed.), *The Trials and Tribulations of Little Red Riding Hood* (London: Routledge, 2nd edn 1993).

Filmography

American Pie (Paul Weitz, 1999)
An American Werewolf in Paris (Anthony Waller, 1997)
Bell, Book and Candle (Richard Quine, 1958)
Bewitched (Nora Ephron, 2005)
The Blair Witch Project (Daniel Myrick/Eduardo Sánchez, 1999)
The Brothers Grimm (Terry Gilliam, 2005)
Buffy: The Vampire Slayer (Fran Rubel Kuzui, 1992)
Carrie (Brian De Palma, 1976)
Carrie II: The Rage (Katt Shea and Robert Mandel, 1999)
The Cat People (Jacques Tourneur, 1942)
Cherry Falls (Geoffrey Wright, 2000)
Christine (John Carpenter, 1983)
The Company of Wolves (Neil Jordan, 1984)
The Craft (Andrew Fleming, 1996)
Cry of the Werewolf (Henry Levin, 1944)
The Curse of the Cat People (Robert Wise/Gunther Von Fritsch, 1944)
Cursed (Wes Craven, 2005)
Dark Water (Hideo Nakata, 2002)
Dark Water (Walter Salles, 2005)
Dog Soldiers (Neil Marshall, 2002)
Edward Scissorhands (Tim Burton, 1991)
The Exorcist (William Friedkin, 1973)
Firestarter (Mark L. Lester, 1984)
The Fog (John Carpenter, 1980)
Friday the 13th (Sean S. Cunningham, 1980)
Friday the 13th II (Steve Miner, 1981)
Friday the 13th VII: The New Blood (John Carl Buechler, 1988)
The Fury (Brian De Palma, 1978)
The Gift (Sam Raimi, 2000)
Ginger Snaps (John Fawcett, 2000)
Ginger Snaps: Unleashed (Brett Sullivan, 2004)
Ginger Snaps Back (Grant Harvey, 2004)
Girl, Interrupted (James Mangold, 1999)
The Grudge (Takashi Shimuzu, 2004)
Halloween (John Carpenter, 1978)
Halloween H20: 20 Years Later (Steve Miner, 1998)
Halloween: Resurrection (Rick Rosenthal, 2002)
The Hole (Nick Hamm, 2001)
I Know What You Did Last Summer (Jim Gillespie, 1997)
I Married a Witch (Rene Clair, 1942)
I Was a Teenage Werewolf (Gene Fowler, 1957)

Ju-on, a.k.a. *The Grudge* (Takashi Shimuzu, 2003)
The Legend of the Wolf Woman (a.k.a. *She-Wolf*, Rino Di Silvestro, 1976)
Miss Congeniality (Donald Petrie, 2000)
My Big Fat Greek Wedding (Joel Zwick, 2002)
Never Been Kissed (Raja Gosnell, 1999)
A Nightmare on Elm Street (Wes Craven, 1984)
A Nightmare on Elm Street II: Freddy's Revenge (Jack Sholder, 1985)
A Nightmare on Elm Street III: Dream Warrior (Chuck Russell, 1987)
A Nightmare on Elm Street IV: The Dream Master (Renny Harlin, 1988)
A Nightmare on Elm Street V: The Dream Child (Stephen Hopkins, 1989)
A Nightmare on Elm Street VI: Freddy's Dead: The Final Nightmare (Rachel Talalay, 1991)
Wes Craven's New Nightmare (Wes Craven, 1994)
Poltergeist (Tobe Hooper, 1982)
Practical Magic (Griffin Dunne, 1998)
Pretty Woman (Garry Marshall, 1990)
Psycho (Alfred Hitchcock,1960)
Rain Man (Barry Levinson, 1988)
The Ring (Gore Verbinski, 2002)
The Ring Two (Hideo Nakata, 2005)
Ringu (Hideo Nakata, 1998)
Ringu 2 (Hideo Nakata, 1999)
Road Trip (Todd Phillips, 2000)
Rosemary's Baby (Roman Polanski, 1968)
Scream (Wes Craven, 1996)
Scream 2 (Wes Craven, 1997)
Scream 3 (Wes Craven, 2000)
Serial Mom (John Waters, 1994)
She-Wolf of London (Jean Yarbrough, 1946)
The Silence of the Lambs (Jonathan Demme, 1991)
Stand By Me (Rob Reiner, 1986)
Star Wars III: Revenge of the Sith (George Lucas, 2005)
Star Wars IV: A New Hope (George Lucas, 1977)
Star Wars V: The Empire Strikes Back (Irvin Kershner, 1980)
Star Wars VI: The Return of the Jedi (Richard Marquand, 1983)
The Terminator (James Cameron, 1984)
Terminator 2: Judgment Day (James Cameron, 1991)
Terminator 3: Rise of the Machines (Jonathan Mostow, 2003)
The Texas Chainsaw Massacre (Tobe Hooper, 1974)
Then and Now (Lesli Linka Glatter, 1995)
Underworld (Len Wiseman, 2003)
Van Helsing (Stephen Sommers, 2004)
The Village (M. Night Shyamalan, 2004)
The Virgin Suicides (Sofia Coppola, 1999)
What Lies Beneath (Robert Zemeckis, 2000)
The Witches of Eastwick (George Miller, 1987)
The Wolf Man (George Waggner, 1941)
Wrong Turn (Rob Schmidt, 2003)

Index

American Pie (1999), 164
An American Werewolf in Paris (1997), 94
Andersen, Hans Christian, 18, 22, 23, 24, 26, 175n6, n7
Angel (TV series), 121–4, 130
Aulnoy, Marie-Catherine Le Jumel de Barneville, Baronne d', 25

'Baba Yaga', 35
Bacchilega, Cristina, ix, 35, 148, 173n1
Barton, Sabrina, 183–4n3
Basile, Giambattista, 24
Basinger, Jeanine, 163
Bathrick, Serafina Kent, 76, 80, 86
Bavidge, Jenny, 113
Beahm, George, 174n41, 178n2
'Beauty and the Beast', 17, 36, 61–2, 64, 184n12
Bell, Book and Candle (1958), 93
Bernard, Catherine, 25
Bettelheim, Bruno, 9, 22, 28, 29, 32, 171
Bewitched (2005), 107
Birkhauser-Oeri, Sibylle, 9, 17
Black, Holly, vi
Blair Witch Project, The (1999), viii
'Bluebeard', 16, 29, 30, 37, 62, 112, 135, 154, 159, 184n4
brothers Grimm, *see* Grimm, Jacob and Wilhelm
Brothers Grimm, The (2005), 176n41
Buffy: The Vampire Slayer (1992), 114–15
Buffy: The Vampire Slayer (TV series), 4, 12–13, 17, 20, 38, 40, 110, 111–13, 158, 161, 162, 163, 166

Campbell, Joseph, 4, 24, 35, 41, 42, 43, 44, 116
Carpenter, John, 178n17
Carrie (1976), 1, 2, 4, 9, 13, 14–15, 16, 19, 31, 38, 40, 61, 68–71, 72, 73, 74–82, 83, 84, 86, 88, 89, 99, 111, 130, 144, 159, 160, 163, 164, 165, 170, 171
Carrie II: The Rage (1999), 4, 19, 38, 40, 73, 82–7, 88, 89
Carter, Angela, 100, 132, 155
Cat People, The (1942), 94, 104–5
Charmed (TV series), 40, 107, 114
Cherry, Brigid, 3, 41, 177n9
Cherry Falls (2000), 9, 185n12
Chodorow, Nancy, 73, 125
Christine (1983), 9
'Cinderella', ix, 14, 15, 16, 19, 26, 27, 29, 31, 34–5, 36, 37, 68, 69, 73, 74, 75, 78, 87, 90, 109, 112, 154, 159
Cinderella (1950), 27
Cixous, Helene, 153
Clement, Catherine, 1, 107
Clover, Carol, 2, 7, 8, 12, 13, 14, 18, 31, 32, 47–9, 50, 51, 52, 53, 56, 62, 67, 132, 149, 155, 165, 171
'Comorre', 184n9
Company of Wolves, The (1984), 25, 100
Craft, The (1996), 4, 12, 16, 19, 31, 38, 40, 89–93, 94, 95, 100, 103, 105, 106, 107, 108, 110, 111, 114, 120, 122, 157, 159, 161, 163, 164, 166
Craven, Wes, 53, 55, 62, 170
Creed, Barbara, 2, 7, 19, 37, 49, 50, 71, 72, 73, 171, 179n15
Cry of the Werewolf (1944), 94
'Cupid and Psyche', 31, 116

193

Curse of the Cat People (1944), 169
Cursed (2005), 94, 108

Dark Water (2005), 6, 13, 21, 167–70
'Demeter and Persephone', 18, 133,
    151–2, 176n36
'Il Diavolo', 184n9
Dika, Vera, 15, 58, 75, 160
Disney, Walt, 24, 28
Dog Soldiers (2002), 94
Duffy, Carol Ann, viii

Edward Scissorhands (1991), 25, 81
Edwards, Lynne, 182n11
Exorcist, The (1973), 38, 165

Firestarter (1984), 83
Fischer, Lucy, 73
'Fitcher's Bird', 30
Fog, The (1980), 177n16
Friday, Nancy, 73
Friday the 13th (1980), 47, 64, 132–3
*Friday the Thirteenth VII: The New
    Blood* (1988), 83
'Frog Prince, The', 36, 37
Fury, The (1978), 83

Gift, The (2000), 6, 13, 18, 20, 37, 38,
    40, 114, 133, 139–41, 142, 143,
    145–6, 148, 149, 150, 151,
    159, 161
Ginger Snaps (2000), 2, 4, 12, 16, 19,
    89, 94–100, 105, 106, 107, 108,
    110, 111, 159, 161, 164, 166
Ginger Snaps Back (2004), 102
Ginger Snaps: Unleashed (2004), 4,
    100–3, 157
Girl, Interrupted (1999), 93–4, 100, 101
Gledhill, Christine, 160
'Goldilocks', 171
Green, Philip, 160–1
Grimm, Jacob and Wilhelm, 18, 24,
    25, 26, 27
Grudge, The (2004), 183n25, 184n7

Halloween (1978), 18, 32, 46, 47, 51–2,
    53, 83
Halloween H20: 20 Years Later (1998),
    6, 18, 39, 59–60, 66, 149, 167

Halloween: Resurrection (2002), 60, 66
'Hansel and Gretel', viii, 36
Harries, Elizabeth Wanning, 6, 18, 25
Haskell, Molly, 60, 88, 89, 103
Hecate, 184n13
Helford, Elyce Rae, 117–118
Hibbs, Thomas, 182n15
Hitchcock, Alfred, 50–1, 177n13
Hole, The (2001), 180n18
Hollinger, Karen, 163
Humphries, Reynold, 46, 54, 77,
    132–3, 148, 178n19

I Know What You Did Last Summer
    (1997), 183n25
I Married a Witch (1942), 93
I Was a Teenage Werewolf (1957),
    106, 108

Ju-on (2003), 184n7

Kaplan, E. Ann, 17, 68
Kaveney, Roz, 182n14
Keller, Donald, 183n18
'Kind and Unkind Girls, The', 16,
    109, 111
King, Stephen, 13–14, 78, 179n8
Kristeva, Julia, 7, 71, 72, 93, 163
Krzywinska, Tanya, 70

La Force, Charlotte-Rose Caumont
    de, 25
Legend of the Wolf Woman (1976), 94
L'Heritier de Villandon,
    Marie-Jeanne, 25
'Little Mermaid, The', 26
'Little Red Cap', 30
'Little Red Riding Hood', *see* 'Red
    Riding Hood'
Lurie, Alison, 7

'Maiden with No Hands, The', 27
Marinucci, Mimi, 121, 182n15
Miss Congeniality (2000), 37
Modleski, Tania, 177n14
Money, Mary Alice, 118
Mulvey, Laura, 5, 48
My Big Fat Greek Wedding (2002), 37

Never Been Kissed (1999), 37
Newman, Kim, 47
A Nightmare on Elm Street (1984), 18, 47, 53–56, 166, 170
A Nightmare on Elm Street II: Freddy's Revenge (1985), 56
A Nightmare on Elm Street III: Dream Warrior (1987), 56, 57, 83
A Nightmare on Elm Street IV: The Dream Master (1988), 56
A Nightmare on Elm Street V: The Dream Child (1989), 56
A Nightmare on Elm Street VI: Freddy's Dead: The Final Nightmare (1991), 56, 57

One Flew Over the Cuckoo's Nest (1975), 93
Orenstein, Catherine, x

'Perceforest', 27
Perkins Gilman, Charlotte, 180n2
Perrault, Charles, 24, 30, 34
Persephone, *see* 'Demeter and Persephone'
Pinedo, Isabel Christina, 2, 3, 13, 16, 32, 177n9
Place, Janey, 162
Poltergeist (1982), 143
Practical Magic (1998), 107
Pretty Woman (1990), 37
Psycho (1960), 45, 49–51, 52, 61, 64, 71, 72

Rain Man (1988), 5
'Rapunzel', 29, 37, 142, 170
'Red Riding Hood', viii, ix, x, 25, 26, 30, 31–2, 35, 52, 94, 95, 102, 109, 112, 159
'Red Shoes, The', 175n6
'Rescue by the Sister', 148
Ring, The (2002), 6, 13, 18, 20, 38, 40, 114, 133, 141–4, 150, 167, 168
Ring Two (2005), 6, 13, 20, 38, 40, 133, 144–7, 148–9, 150, 151, 167, 168
Ringu (1998), 133, 142
Ringu 2 (1999), 142
Road Trip (2000), 164
Rockoff, Adam, 45, 46, 47

Roper, Lyndal, 37–8
Rosemary's Baby (1968), 73, 74
Rowe, Kathleen, 162, 163
'Rumpelstiltskin', 37, 160

Sabrina the Teenage Witch (TV series), 107, 114
Schelde, Per, 41
Sconce, Jeffrey, 58
Scream (1996), 4, 9, 12, 16, 18, 37, 39, 45, 47, 62–4, 83, 93, 152, 153, 159, 166
Scream 2 (1997), 4, 12, 18, 39, 64, 159, 166
Scream 3 (2000), 4, 12, 18, 39, 64–6, 159, 166
Serial Mom (1994), 99
Sharret, Christopher, 175n2
She-Wolf of London (1946), 94
Silence of the Lambs, The (1991), 134
'Silver Nose, The', 30
Skwire, Sarah E., 181n1
'Sleeping Beauty', 26, 27, 29, 36, 37
Sleeping Beauty (1959), 27
'Snow Queen, The', 22, 23, 26
'Snow White', 26, 29, 31, 36, 37, 70, 73, 142, 144, 159, 181n2
Snow White (1937), 27, 28, 163
Stamp Lindsay, Shelley, 76–7
Stand By Me (1986), 5
Star Wars III: Revenge of the Sith (2005), 166–7
Star Wars IV: A New Hope (1977), 4, 166
Star Wars V: The Empire Strikes Back (1980), 5
Star Wars VI: The Return of the Jedi (1983), 5, 166
'Struwelpeter', 25
'Subtle Princes, The', 30
'Sun, Moon and Talia', 27

Tatar, Maria, 10, 17, 18, 26, 27, 29, 30, 31, 33, 154, 155, 156, 157
Terminator 2 (1991), 84
Terminator 3 (2003), 61, 167
Texas Chainsaw Massacre, The (1974), 32, 52
Then and Now (1995), 173n7

Tru Calling (TV series), 130
Twitchell, James, 7–8, 9, 22, 23, 24, 54, 105

Underworld (2003), 114

Van Helsing (2004), 114
Village, The (2004), viii
Virgin Suicides, The (1999), 179n16, 180n18

Warner, Marina, 10–11, 15, 16, 18, 23, 25, 28, 29–30, 34, 37, 42, 62, 108, 154, 158, 163, 171
Wells, Paul, 43, 108, 150, 165
Wes Craven's New Nightmare (1994), 6, 18, 39, 149, 167

What Lies Beneath (2000), 6, 13, 16, 20, 37, 38, 39, 40, 114, 135–9, 142, 143, 145, 146, 147–8, 149, 150, 151, 153, 161
Williams J.P., 125, 126–7, 128
Williams, Linda, 3, 134–5
Williams, Linda Ruth, 95
Williams, Tony, 80, 82, 104, 174–5n2, 178n19
Witches of Eastwick, The (1987), 81, 107
Wolf Man, The (1941), 56, 100
Wood, Robin, 7, 8, 11, 39, 61, 80, 164
Wrong Turn (2003), 183n25

Zipes, Jack, 18, 25, 26, 27, 30, 31, 34, 41–2, 105, 159